P9-BYL-458

the Unofficial Guide™ to eBay® and Online Auctions

Dawn and Bobby Reno

Hungry Minds™

Best-Selling Books • Digital Downloads • e-Books • Answer Networks • e-Newsletters •
Branded Web Sites • e-Learning

New York, NY • Cleveland, OH • Indianapolis, IN

Hungry Minds, Inc.
909 Third Avenue
New York, NY 10022

This publication contains the opinions and ideas of its author[s] and is designed to provide useful advice to the reader on the subject matter covered. Any references to any products or services do not constitute or imply an endorsement or recommendation. The publisher and the author[s] specifically disclaim any responsibility for any liability, loss, or risk (financial, personal, or otherwise) that may be claimed or incurred as a consequence, directly or indirectly, of the use and/or application of any of the contents of this publication.

Certain terms mentioned in this book that are known or claimed to be trademarks or service marks have been capitalized.

Hungry Minds, Inc. does not attest to the validity, accuracy, or completeness of this information. Use of a term in this book should not be regarded as affecting the validity of any trademark or service mark.
Unofficial Guides are a trademark of Hungry Minds, Inc.

For general information on Hungry Minds' books in the U.S., please call our Consumer Customer Service department at 800-762-2974. For reseller information, including discounts and previous sales, please call our Reseller Customer Service department at 800-434-3422.

ISBN: 0-02-863866-2

Manufactured in the United States of America

10 9 8 7 6 5 4 3 2

First edition

For our loving and supportive parents: Peg and Ed Reno, and Don and Elaine Brander III

Acknowledgments

The online auction business is huge, but thankfully, so are people's hearts. We had a lot of help with the research for this book, but there are several people who went out of their way to supply information. But before we thank the auctioneers, collectors, and dealers, we'd like to extend our gratitude to our agent, Karen Solem, and our editors: Al McDermid, Karen Doran, Jessica Faust, Brice Gosnell, and Kevin Thornton. Without their guidance along the way, we would have been lost.

If not for our contacts in this ever-growing business, we wouldn't have been able to complete this book, so our thanks go to auctioneers and family members Bill Reno, Rob Reno, Bryan Cioffi, and Steven Cioffi. Family RULES! We also have a lot of great friends from our many years in the business, both collectors and dealers, and their help with this book was invaluable. Here's to Fred Elwell, Kristin Duval, Currie Pritchard, and Gail Radley.

The auction sites themselves lent us their time to answer specific questions (there truly are people behind those e-mail addresses!) and guided us through the more difficult stages in a graceful and patient manner.

In addition, we are grateful to the many buyers and sellers we met through our own dealings, as well as because of the research for this book. There are too many to thank personally, but each and every one is valued. We wish you the very best in sales and hope you find all the treasures you desire.

Finally, our thanks to our families and coworkers for lending their support and understanding.

Contents

The *Unofficial Guide* Reader's Bill of Rights xv

The *Unofficial Guide* Panel of Experts xxi

Introduction xxiii

I   An Overview of Online Auctions 1

1 Consider Your Own Needs 3

The New Auction 4

Personal Considerations 8

The Excitement of an Auction 9
  The Difference Between Online Auctions
    and "Live and in Person" 11
  The Danger of Auction Fever 15

What Do You Have to Sell? 17

Are You Ready to Part with the Family
Heirlooms? 24

How Much Do You Know About Your Items? ... 25

The Facts and How to Get Them 25

Just the Facts 26

2 The Many Different Auctions and
Their Quirks 27

eBay: The Big Kahuna 28
  What You'll Find on the Site 28
  The Basics of Using eBay 29
  The Pros and Cons of eBay 31
  eBay Versus the Other Auction Sites 32

Amazon 33
  What You'll Find on the Site 33
  The Basics of Using Amazon 34
  The Pros and Cons of Amazon 35
  Amazon Versus the Other Auction Sites 36

Yahoo!...38
    What You'll Find on the Site 38
    The Basics of Using Yahoo!......................39
    The Pros and Cons of Yahoo!....................40
    Yahoo! Versus the Other Auction Sites 41
DealDeal 42
    What You'll Find on the Site 42
    The Basics of Using DealDeal 42
    The Pros and Cons of DealDeal.................43
    DealDeal Versus the Other Auction Sites.....43
uBid..44
    What You'll Find on the Site 44
    The Basics of Using uBid..........................44
    The Pros and Cons of uBid......................45
    uBid Versus the Other Auction Sites 45
Other Sites 46
    What You'll Find on the Lesser-Known
      Sites...47
    Is Bigger Really Better? 47
Established Auction Sites Versus New Sites ...48
Just the Facts..49

II   Registering and Setting Up...............51

  3 The Business of Auctioning 53
  Remember, This Is a Business! 54
  What Types of Items Are You Selling/Buying? ..55
    Know Your Categories 57
    Watching the Skies Before You "Fly" 60
  Which Auction Should You Choose? 62
  Test the Waters in More Than One Place........67
  Doing Initial Research...............................68
    Become a "Lurker".................................69
    Online Magazines That Rate the Various
      Auction Sites 70
    Talk to Fellow Surfers 71
  Just the Facts..72

  4 Setting Up an Account—or Two 73
  How to Register and What Kind of Online
  Name to Use..74
  Handling Payment of Your Account 76

Do You Need a Credit Card?..........................77
  Using Your Credit Card 78
  What About Online Escrow Accounts? 79
  Should You Pay as You Go?......................81
What Are the Rules? 84
Being Clear About the Guidelines.................86
  Using Chatrooms....................................88
Know Your Rights 91
  Responding at the End of an Auction 93
  When the Buyer Doesn't Buy or the Seller
    Doesn't Sell 93
The Auction Insurance Plan 95
The Privacy and Safety of Trading Online 96
Just the Facts..97

**5 The Importance of Making Yourself
  Known 99**
Spread the Word 100
The ABCs of Public Relations 101
  Is Advertising Necessary?......................106
  The Best Ways to Reach
    Customers/Sellers 107
Setting Up a Personal Web Page.................113
  Online Auction Web Pages Versus
    Creating Your Own 113
  What Kind of Info Should You Include?....116
  What About Pictures? 117
  But I Can't Write!................................118
Just the Facts 119

III Buying at Auction 121

**6 The Right Way to Bid—or How Not
  to Get Auction Fever 123**
Buyer Beware!...124
  You Only Have Yourself to Blame............125
  Educate Yourself 129
  Rush—and Lose!..................................130
Watch and Learn......................................130
Save Time by Putting in Your Highest
Bid First..131

Doing Your Own Research About
an Item's Worth.....................................132
   Antiques...132
   Art 133
   Automotive 133
   Books..134
   Clothing 136
   Coins 137
   Collectibles..137
   Comics 139
   Computers/Electronics, Hardware/
      Software......................................140
   Dolls..141
   Home and Garden..............................143
   Jewelry...145
   Movies 146
   Music...148
   Photographs and Photographic
      Equipment 150
   Pottery, Glass, Porcelain 151
   Sports/Recreation...............................153
   Stamps...155
   Toys...156
Just the Facts 157

IV Selling at Auction 159

7 The Right Way to Sell............................161
Are We Making Money Yet?........................162
How Do You Get Your Items Up for Sale?.....164
How Do You Price the Items You're
Going to Sell? 166
   Setting an Opening Bid 168
   Figure in Your Costs.............................170
   Reserve Pricing 171
   Should You Bring in an Appraiser? 173
   Knowing How Much a Piece Is Worth 177
   Are You Willing to Take a Gamble? 178
Which Category Do I Put It In?...................178
   The Benefits of the Gallery
      and "Gift" Icons 179
How Long an Auction? 180
   Seven Days? Five? Three? 181
   The Pros and Cons of a Quickie Auction....182
   It's All in the Timing! 183

Scheduling Your Auctions to End
at "High Time" 183

The Value of Selling on Weekends 184

Just the Facts 185

**8 What's Important to List
in the Description? 187**

Why the Right Words Are Important 188

Use Key Words in the Title 189
   Omit All Punctuation 190
   Consider the Category 191
   Determine Other Important Factors..........192
   Be Specific..193
   *Tell the Seller What Makes Your Item
      Different or Unusual* 195
   *Try to Include the Exact Size
      of Your Item* 196
   Tell About Its Condition 196
   Reveal the Item's Age 197
   Include the Company Name 199
   Check for Marks..................................199
   Report Color or Style, if Important 199
   Point Out the Origin of the Piece 200

Be Explicit! 200

Be Honest About Condition and Age..........202

Spelling Counts! 203

Attractive Item Descriptions—The Value
of a Thesaurus 205

Honesty in Authentication and Grading
an Item—Don't Guesstimate! 206

Shipment and Address Info 207

Know Your Products—Research! 208
   How Do You Find Out? 209
   Can You Trust Your Sources?...................209
   Sites and Books for Instant Info.............211

Just the Facts 212

9 Should I Use Photos? 213

People Like to See What They're Getting 214

A Professional's Tips for Taking Great Photos ...217

Cameras: Regular or Digital? Or Video?........219
   Regular Cameras 220
   Digital Cameras...................................221

Is It Time for a Scanner? 225

Make Sure You Have Room on Your
Hard Drive! 227

Uploading Documents and Photos 229
   Load Those Pics Fast..............................230

Just the Facts 231

10 Auction Management Programs 233

Should You Make the Investment?..............234

Which Auction Management Programs
Are the Best?..235
   Andalé (www.andale.com) 236
   Auction Aid/Auction Ad Pro
      (www.firstdesign.com) 236
   AuctionAssistant or AuctionAssistant Pro
      (www.blackthornesw.com)...................237
   Auction Helper (http://members.xoom.
      com/jsamuels/) 238
   AuctionManager
      (www.AuctionRover.com/sell/)............238
   AuctionMate (www.myauctionmate.com)...239
   Auction Wizard
      (www.standingwavesoftware.com/aw/)...240
   ePoster2000 (www.auctionposter.com).....240
   Lorena 240

Tracking Your Auctions 241
   AuctionTamer (www.envsoftware.com/
      auction/) 242
   Auction Ticker (www.blackthornesw.com) ...242
   Auction Trakker
      (www.AuctionTrakker.com) 242
   OnScan (www.onscan.com/)...................243
   The Oracle (www.the-oracle.com/
      main.html) 243

Automated Bidding Programs....................244
   Auction Express (www.auctiontools.com)...244
   BidSniper Pro (www.datavector.net/
      products/bidsniper/index.htm) 245

End-User Auction Management Programs 245

Problems with the Programs 246
   Read the Directions 246
   How Much Time Does It Take
      to Learn This? 247

Make Sure You Get Customer Service........248
Does It Have a Spell Check?....................249
Loading Time Is Important 250
What About Counters?..............................250
The Benefits of Using Ads on Your Auctions...251
Just the Facts 252

11 And How Will You Be Paying for This?.....253
What Are Your Payment Options? 254
Should You Offer Credit Card Service? 255
The Pros and Cons of the Cost..................259
Will You Gain Customers?.......................260
What About the Paperwork?....................261
Getting Payment from International
Customers..264
The Value of Online Escrow Accounts 264
Getting Auction Insurance 265
Holding the Check 'til It Clears 266
Clear Explanations to Customers Are a Must!...268
If the Check Bounces... 269
Don't Spend the Money Yet 270
Just the Facts 271

V During the Auction.........................273

12 Keeping Track of the Auction.................275
And They're Off! 276
Automatic Updates 278
E-Mail Etiquette 281
Answer Promptly and Courteously—
Time Is Money!....................................283
Honesty Is the Best Policy 284
Keep Your Eye on the Action 285
Checking on the Bidders 286
Read the Feedback 288
How to Make Contact............................289
Did You Forget Something Important? 290
The Last Minutes—Going, Going, Gone! 291
Just the Facts 292

VI After the Auction............................293

13 What If the Item Doesn't Sell? 295

The Pros and Cons of Re-listing 296

Should You Lower the Price? 297

Think About Re-listing It Elsewhere............298

The Benefits of Specialized Online Auctions...299

What About Changing the Category?...........301

Negotiating with the Last Bidder
When the Reserve Isn't Met.......................302

Better Picture? More Complete
Description? 303

Maybe It's Not the Right Time 304

Just the Facts 305

14 Dealing with Problem Buyers and Sellers ...307

Hints from Other Sellers/Buyers.................308

Finding a Buyer's E-Mail Address
and Location..310

How Long Should You Wait for an Answer?...312

International Sales Problems 312
  Language and Misunderstandings............313

When You're Still Not Satisfied...................314

What If You Get Burned? 316

Bounced Checks and Refused Credit Cards ...316

Fakes, Reproductions, and Counterfeits 318
  How to Tell and What to Do 319

Damaged Items 320

The Importance of Feedback......................321
  How to Give Feedback and When.............322
  How to Read Feedback 323
  Keeping Track of Your Own Feedback........324
  Beware of Those Sunglasses 325
  An "Interesting" Experience? 325

Other Recourses 326

Just the Facts 327

15 Packaging for a Safe Journey..................329

Weigh Items *Before* the Seller
Sends the Check 330

The Right and Wrong Way to Pack a Box 332

The Right Packing Supplies and Where
to Get Them 334
    Building Shipping Costs into the Price......340
    Don't Skimp on Packing!........................341

Shipping Large or Extremely Fragile Items ...342
    The Benefits of a Packing Service............343

Insuring Your Packages..............................344

What If the Item's Damaged En Route?.......345
    Contacting the Shipper..........................346

Just the Facts 347

VII Taking Care of Business 349

16 You Mean I Need to Keep Records? 351

Accumulating a List of Clientele.................352
    An Address Book...................................353

What About Reporting Earnings?................354
    Accounting for Everything......................356
    Sales Tax?..357

Keeping Track of Expenses 359

Hello, IRS? 361

Just the Facts 362

A Online Listings.......................................363

B Glossary...367

C Resource Directory..................................373

Index...391

The *Unofficial Guide* Reader's Bill of Rights

We Give You More Than the Official Line

Welcome to the *Unofficial Guide* series of Business titles—books that deliver critical, unbiased information that other books can't or won't reveal—*the inside scoop*. Our goal is to provide you with the *most accessible, useful* information and advice possible. The recommendations we offer in these pages are not influenced by the corporate line of any organization or industry; we give you the hard facts, whether those institutions like them or not. If something is ill advised or will cause a loss of time and/or money, we'll give you ample warning. And if it is a worthwhile option, we'll let you know that, too.

Armed and Ready

Our handpicked authors confidently and critically report on a wide range of topics that matter to smart readers like you. Our authors are passionate about their subjects, but have distanced themselves enough from them to help you be armed and protected, and help you make educated decisions as you go through the process. It is our intent that, from having read this book, you will avoid the pitfalls everyone else falls into and get it right the first time.

Don't be fooled by cheap imitations; this is the genuine article *Unofficial Guide* series from IDG Books Worldwide, Inc. You may be familiar with our proven track record of the travel *Unofficial Guides,* which have more than three million copies in print. Each year thousands of travelers—new and old—are armed with a brand-new, fully updated edition of the flagship *Unofficial Guide to Walt Disney World,* by Bob Sehlinger. It is our intention here to provide you with the same level of objective authority that Mr. Sehlinger does in his brainchild.

The Unofficial Panel of Experts

Every work in the Business *Unofficial Guides* is intensively inspected by a team of three top professionals in their fields. These experts review the manuscript for factual accuracy, comprehensiveness, and an insider's determination as to whether the manuscript fulfills the credo in this Reader's Bill of Rights. In other words, our panel ensures that you are, in fact, getting "the inside scoop."

Our Pledge

The authors, the editorial staff, and the Unofficial Panel of Experts assembled for *Unofficial Guides* are determined to lay out the most valuable alternatives available for our readers. This dictum means that our writers must be explicit, prescriptive, and above all, direct. We strive to be thorough and complete, but our goal is not necessarily to have the "most" or "all" of the information on a topic; this is not, after all, an encyclopedia. Our objective is to help you narrow down your options to the best of what is available, unbiased by affiliation with any industry or organization.

Each *Unofficial Guide* Will Give You:

- Comprehensive coverage of necessary and vital information
- Authoritative, rigidly fact-checked data
- The most up-to-date insights into trends
- Savvy, sophisticated writing that's also readable
- Sensible, applicable facts and secrets that only an insider knows

Special Features

Every book in our series offers the following six special sidebars in the margins that are devised to help you get things done cheaply, efficiently, and smartly.

1. **Timesaver**—Tips and shortcuts that save you time.

2. **Moneysaver**—Tips and shortcuts that save you money.

3. **Watch Out!**—More serious cautions and warnings.

4. **Bright Idea**—General tips and shortcuts to help you find an easier or smarter way to do something.

5. **Quote**—Statements from real people that are intended to be prescriptive and valuable to you.

6. **Unofficially...**—An insider's fact or anecdote.

We also recognize your need to have quick information at your fingertips, and have thus provided the following comprehensive sections at the back of the book:

1. **Online Listings**—Web sites for various auctions, as well as other helpful resources.

2. **Glossary**—Definitions of complicated terminology and jargon.

3. **Resource Directory**—Lists of relevant agencies, associations, institutions, and Web sites.

Letters, Comments, and Questions from Readers

We strive to continually improve the *Unofficial Guide* series, and input from our readers is a valuable way for us to do that.

Many of those who have used the *Unofficial Guide* travel books write to the authors to ask questions, make comments, or share their own discoveries and lessons. For Business *Unofficial Guides,* we would also appreciate all such correspondence—both positive and critical—and we will make our best efforts to incorporate appropriate readers' feedback and comments in revised editions of this work.

How to write to us:

Unofficial Guides
Business Guides
IDG Books Worldwide, Inc.
645 N. Michigan Ave.
Suite 800
Chicago, IL 60611

Attention: Reader's Comments

About the Authors

Dawn Reno, author of many books about antiques, art, and collectibles, as well as novels and children's books, has been part of the antiques and auction business for more than 20 years. Currently, she teaches English and Creative Writing at Lake City Community College and assists her husband, Bobby, in their online auction and appraisal business. For up-to-date information on her books, as well as tips on time management and online auctions, visit her Web site: www.dawnreno.com.

Bobby Reno, eBay auctioneer and professional photographer, started selling antiques and collectibles at shows and shops in 1976. Since that time, he has traveled throughout the United States meeting other dealers. After having a triple bypass in 1996, he joined the eBay community because he found that he could feed his need to connect with other antiques dealers and collectors without the stress of being "on the road."

About the Authors

The *Unofficial Guide* Panel of Experts

The *Unofficial Guide* editorial team recognizes that you've purchased this book with the expectation of getting the most authoritative, carefully inspected information currently available. Toward that end, on each and every title in this series, we have selected a minimum of two "official" experts comprising the Unofficial Panel who painstakingly review the manuscripts to ensure the following: factual accuracy of all data; inclusion of the most up-to-date and relevant information; and that, from an insider's perspective, the authors have armed you with all the necessary facts you need—but that the institutions don't want you to know.

For *The Unofficial Guide to eBay and Online Auctions,* we are proud to introduce the following panel of experts:

Derick M. Buckley   Founder and CEO of TheSeriousCollector.com, Derick is a collector and trader of construction and mechanical toys, especially Legos. He has conducted Internet auctions and traded toys on Usenet

Groups since 1996. Derick recognized the value of creating specialized commerce sites geared to the serious dealer and collector market, and in 1998 founded The Serious Collector to bring that vision to the public. Previously, he was a strategic management consultant for Renaissance Worldwide, and a Senior Planning Analyst for Alta Bates Health Systems. He holds a BA in Economics from the University of California, Davis, and an MBA from the University of Virginia.

John Perry   An avid auction buff, John is the founder/editor of *The Auction Tribune* (www.AuctionTribune.com). He created the Internet's only all-auction news resource.

Introduction

Y ou don't have to be part of the auction world to be aware of eBay. You don't even have to be online. The first and largest of the online auction sites has been in the news from the very first moment it burst onto the scene in 1995, and it continues to reign as king of the auction world, breaking all kinds of records and garnering the interest of millions worldwide.

Celebrities have gotten into the business in a big way. Rosie O'Donnell runs regular auctions on eBay. Oprah conducts charity auctions through her Angels Network. Kevin Spacey, Kathy Ireland, Jonathan Winters, and many other celebrities have hosted or offered items for auction. Sports stars sponsor special auctions to raise money for children's charities or offer autographed gloves, bats, photos, and such to the highest bidder. Is it good public relations for these people? Yes, but they have also been known to get in on the action themselves! Olympic skater Scott Hamilton loves collecting pinball machines and has bought some on eBay. Rosie O'Donnell has been known to buy McDonald's figures and collectible toys. Michael J. Fox loves sports cards.

Why are auctions so fascinating to both the celebrity and the average person on the street? Perhaps it's the idea that one might find a treasure or get a bargain. Maybe it's the excitement of not knowing whether you're going to win that painting or comic book or computer, or whether someone else is going to come along at the last moment to raise the bid and steal what you've been lusting for. Perhaps it's that competitive edge that most of us harbor deep within. Whatever the case, online auctions are big business, and if you've bought this book, you want to know how to make that business work for you.

Are there tricks to becoming a successful online auction bidder/seller? Yes, there are. But you can also pop in to an auction, buy one item, and never go back again. Auctioneering is as simple or as involved as you want to make it—yet it's always fun!

The Unofficial Guide to eBay® and Online Auctions teaches you how to be a lurker, learning on the sidelines while not spending any money (Chapter 3). It'll also give you the lowdown on where to find information about the auctions you're interested in.

You can learn about the differences between the heavy hitter auctions like eBay, Amazon, and Yahoo! and the smaller specialty auctions (Chapter 2). There are pros and cons to dealing with both the big and the small auctions, and we're here to lend our expertise to help you get off on the right foot. Although eBay is the biggest game in town, you might have better luck getting into an auction community that specializes in the items you're interested in, such as Beanie Babies, sports cards, or even thoroughbred horses.

And what about once you get into an auction? How do you find your way around? What if you don't have a clue how to surf or search or create a Web site? Though HTML might still be a foreign language to you, relax. It's getting easier and easier to navigate online, and auctions are making it simple for the average personal computer user to have fun (or make a living) online.

We offer hints for selling items on several different auctions at once, for searching for the items you want to buy, and for uploading your images quickly and easily. You learn about auction management programs that help you account for all your sales and purchases. We show you the best cameras to use so you can show the buyers what your products look like, and we talk about scanners and give you the skinny on which auctions allow for instant uploads of your images, making it easier than ever before.

You discover the best ways to take photos of your items (Chapter 9) and the type of language that makes for a good online auction listing (Chapter 8). Did you know that the words you use in titling your auction are often the clues that buyers and sellers use to search for the items they want? If you use empty words in your title, you're not taking full advantage of that title line. And the photos you include with your listing are the tools of your trade. If your photos are too dark or don't reveal an important mark, the person surfing through your listing might surf right out again without leaving a bid. Learn how to take effective photographs and write catchy listings in the chapters on how to sell.

And if you don't know which category your item belongs in, we show you the most common and discuss what to do if you put your item in the wrong place.

We tell you what happens before, during, and after an auction, and why it's illegal to sell something fraudulent, even as a joke. (Perhaps you remember the human kidney that was offered on eBay? Or the time someone listed an incredible amount of marijuana for sale?)

When it comes time to pay for your item, we define the differences between paying by check, credit card, online checking, or escrow, and tell you which auctions offer protection and which don't. Auction insurance and customer service are important, and you find out how each auction handles those details.

Nervous about giving someone your credit card online? You should know about encryption and how to protect your privacy. You also find out about the new programs that offer buyers/sellers the convenience of having the price of their item or listing fees deducted immediately from their checking account. And if you're worried about that customer's check bouncing or the credit card being turned down, we give you a couple of options you can use to protect yourself.

What about packing and shipping those items you've decided to sell? Is the United States Postal Service the only option? Nope. Even though the USPS has happily accepted online auction shipments for the past couple of years, they're not always the best bet, nor are they the least expensive way to package your valuables for the long trek from one side of the United States to the other (or across the world). Check out Chapter 15 for information on sending those large items and obtaining insurance that will cover problems such as breakage, missing shipments, and returns. Learn why we've become extraordinarily careful in packing even "unbreakable" items.

Confused about where to go for shipping materials? There are a number of services online, and new ones are opening their cyber doors every day. We direct you to the most trustworthy, commonly used, and inexpensive sources for bubble wrap, envelopes, boxes, tape, and other shipping materials (Chapter 15). And we also tell you how you can deduct all those business costs as expenses when income tax time comes around.

If you're going to make the online auction business something that will bring more money into your household, we tell you how to get your name out to customers (Chapter 5). Using public relations on the Net is an art in itself, but creating Web sites and personal pages is getting easier every day. Most auction sites offer their customers some space to create a personal page, such as eBay's "About Me" section. Offering your fellow auction-goers some information about yourself creates good relationships, and since you probably will never see your customers face-to-face, it's a good idea to use personal Web pages to show them your other wares and to give them the opportunity to learn more about you.

When it comes to communication, the proper way of contacting dealers and buyers is vitally important in the auction business. Prompt answers to e-mails and payment are imperative. In a world of instant gratification, people expect answers to questions and comments as quickly as possible. And a lag time in communication or payment or shipment can mean negative feedback for an online auctioneer. We talk about what that feedback means in the long run and how to maintain a good level of positive feedback so you can continue in this business.

Last, but not least, you learn about the business end of auctions: how to keep good records and what you'll need to know when it comes time to file your income tax statement (Chapter 16).

With hundreds of online auctions doing business as we write this and more opening their sites every day, there are plenty of places for you to buy and sell those books, shells, collector plates, computers, whale figurines, *Sesame Street* dolls, or angel pictures. You name it, you can sell it at online auctions. So, what are you waiting for? Let's start talking auctions!

An Overview of
Online Auctions

PART I

GET THE SCOOP ON...
The different types of auctions ▪ How to avoid
"auction fever" ▪ What types of items can you
sell in auctions? ▪ What you need to know
about the items you offer

Consider Your Own Needs

Auctions have been around for many thousands of years. The early Greeks coined the term "bid" in about 550 B.C., and Romans auctioned off the loot won on the battlefield even before the cries of the wounded and dying stopped. Early settlers often gathered to auction off crops and used the auction as a social get-together. When the United States was young, piles of tobacco went to the highest bidder. Acres of land sold to people who wanted a new place to live. Crops of potatoes, corn, cotton, wheat, and barley brought enough money for a family to live on for the rest of the year. The practice of auctioning off livestock, horses, and farm goods continues to this day, though the venues have changed and today's auctioneers no longer have to rely on the ability to yell louder than the crowd gathered around them.

Auctions were held on the docks of major seaports when slave ships came in, and the social aspect

3

took on a dark undertone when people began buying other people. The dramatic shouts of the auctioneer's call for a raised bid and the moment when the gavel was brought down with those famous words "going, going, gone" became fearful seconds for those who often didn't understand the language well enough to realize they soon would be separated from their families and friends.

Today, auctions are the forum in which antiques dealers and collectors can find items to satisfy their business needs or collecting habits. Farmers still sell their prize hogs or crops, and people still gather to share news and spend time with their friends. Thankfully, the slave trade is no longer a reason for planning an auction.

The new auction

Today there are changes to the old auction format. Millions of people are participating in online auctions since the folks at eBay Auction Web opened their site in September 1995. They have experienced the thrill of selling both the common and unusual through over 400 online auction sites. Though the terminology is the same as it was when those first two phrases (bid and auction) were created, and the excitement still makes the heart pound, the auction scene has changed dramatically. But the reason most people choose to auction is basically the same: Auctions are the way to get the best price for items you have to sell.

Auctions have been held throughout time in order to offer goods to a public that hadn't quite determined the worth of the items being offered for sale. Sometimes auctions are held so that people won't have to take responsibility for the prices of the items they sell. Sometimes auctions are held because it's the best way to sell items to a captive marketplace. Sometimes auctions are held because owners of items simply can't agree on a fair price. By holding an auction, the buyer is the only one who needs to take responsibility for setting the price. The seller pretty much gives up putting a price tag on the item and doesn't need to worry about whether or not people will agree with what he or she believes is the item's value.

There are several different types of auctions, whether they are traditional or online. Some of the terminology is the same, so here's a peek into some of the lingo you'll hear:

- Dutch auctions
- Yankee auctions
- English auctions
- Reserve price auctions
- Other types: silent auctions, phone auctions, mail auctions, and sealed-bid auctions

Let's take a closer look at each.

Often used by people who have more than one copy of an item, a *Dutch auction* simply means that bidders are bidding on one or more of the item. Say, for example, you have 10 copies of a Superman comic book. They're all the same and you just want one, so you put the rest up for auction. Now one person can bid on all nine copies, or nine different people can have one Superman comic book each. The person who bids the highest amount wins the bid. That person then gets the quantity he wants, but he pays the lowest winning bid. He then wins the item (i.e., one Superman comic book at $5), or at some traditional auctions, all nine comic books at $5 per comic book. The rest of the bidders then get the option of buying the items, if any remain. If the first bidder takes the whole pile, then no one else gets a crack at the items. If not, the seller works his way down the list, offering the item to each of the high bidders until the pile of items is gone. This type of auction is useful when you have a quantity of items you want to sell simultaneously.

Because bidding in a Dutch auction can be confusing the first time, here are the steps in an easy-to-remember list:

1. When you bid, you specify the amount you want to pay and how many of the items you want to buy.

2. As the highest bidder, you win at least one of the items and you choose which of them you want. For example, if an auction offers 12 items and some are in better shape than others, you get to choose the best ones.

3. You pay the *lowest* winning bid.

4. If your bid is the same as someone else's, the person who bid first is the winner.

5. The next bidders each get an item (at the same lowest winning bid) until the items are gone.

The bottom line: Bid during a Dutch auction only when you're comfortable with how it's run, and use the Dutch auction to quickly sell multiple copies of an item.

When we were kids, our parents used to take us to auctions held right before Christmas. The auctioneer usually had crates of items, often 20 or 30 of the same type of toy, and the bidders usually went home happy because they all got at least one of the toys. The sellers were also happy because the crates

Moneysaver
If you have a regular need for an item, such as computer supplies, paper goods, books, or film, you might want to bid in a Dutch auction for those items. Usually you can get multiples of the item for less than you'd pay in a retail outlet.

of toys they were auctioning were often left over from the previous year.

A *Yankee auction* is the same as a Dutch auction, with one difference: All the bidders are required to pay their high bid for the price on the block.

For example, if you have ten sets of McDonald's toys (all the same) and want to sell them all, you put the items up for auction and let people bid. All the bidders have the option of going home with something, as long as they pay the highest bid.

When a piece is bid up (an ascending price) until one final bidder wins the item, it's an *English auction*. This is the type of auction with which we are most familiar, with auctioneers who stand in a hall and call, "I have 40, who'll give me 41, now? There's 41, and now I've got to have 42. Who'll go 42? Forty-two, 42, 42? I've got 42. Now will you give me 43, ma'am? I've got 43. Now, 44? Who'll give me 44? Forty-four once, twice. I'm going to sell at 44 ... going, going, gone for 44 to the lady in the blue jacket!" This type of selling is typical of online auctions, though the buyer doesn't actually hear the auctioneer calling out for bids.

When the auction is over, the person who has bid the highest usually wins the item. The only time the highest bidder won't win the goods he is bidding on is when the price hasn't reached the reserve. For more information on that type of auction, read on.

When a seller wants to make sure an item doesn't sell beneath what she paid for it, she might conduct a *reserve price auction*. This simply means that the buyer must bid over a certain price before the item will sell. In other words, if you have a diamond ring that you know is worth $1,500, you might

Timesaver
Do your homework before heading into an online auction to bid. Even though you might know the terminology, each auction may differ in their exact rules. Know the rules first!

put a reserve of $1,000 on it because you simply don't want to take less than that amount. Reserve price auctions protect the seller from losing her shirt on valuable items.

A lot of online auctions use reserve pricing (especially eBay). It protects sellers by enabling them to get a fair asking price for their goods. However, it is often confusing to the buyer, who might not have a clue what the reserve price is for the piece. For more information on this type of auction, see Chapter 4, "Setting Up an Account—or Two."

Silent auctions, phone auctions, mail auctions, and *sealed-bid auctions* are usually held by traditional auction houses. Sometimes a charity or organization will attempt to raise money by holding a silent, mail, or sealed-bid auction. Though bidding online is different in that all bids are instantly put up and available for the bidding public, there are several ways of holding other types of auctions. See Parts III and IV for more details.

Personal considerations

If you are considering buying or selling at online auctions, there are some things to think about before you take your first foray into that new world. Since you'll be entering into a business venture or doing some shopping for any number of items, here are a few basics to think about:

- Have you ever bartered for goods before?
- Do you love the items you might find at flea markets and yard sales?
- Are you willing to learn the basics about the world of auctions?
- Do you have access to a computer?

- Are you familiar with how to move around on the Internet?

- Have you bought anything online before?

- Do you have the time and energy to do some research before you take the plunge into one of the auction sites?

- Do you have the interest to follow an auction all the way through?

- Have you considered what you might sell?

- Are you trying to collect pieces you are having trouble finding?

- Have you ever been to an auction?

- Do you like the idea that you can control how much you spend on a particular item?

- Are you willing to gamble on whether the goods are worth what you'll pay?

- Do you know any of the auction lingo?

- Do you want to make a business of auction buying and selling, or are you just interested in pursuing a hobby?

Once you consider all these initial questions, you're probably ready to start learning the basics of auctioneering. Though buying at auction is fun and many describe it as recreation, there are certain pieces of information with which you should arm yourself before you enter into the world of buying and selling online.

The excitement of an auction

There's a lot to be said for the freedom of buying at auction. You are the one who is determining exactly how much you'll pay for an item. Sometimes you'll be lucky and wind up with an incredible buy. But you

Bright Idea
Learn the lingo of the auction world before you go online and start bidding, so you'll understand the basics.

must also take into consideration that you could end up paying much more for an item than it's worth, largely because you've gotten caught up in the frenzy of bidding for that item.

Many people think of auctions as being like carnivals. The auctioneers are actors, aware that their audience can be swayed into buying an item (or at least bidding on it) largely because of how it's presented. When you attend a live auction, you are part of an audience who is being entertained by a fast-talking, seemingly knowledgeable auctioneer who determines which bids are taken from the members of the audience and when the piece will be sold. The act of being caught up in bidding for an item often confuses people. It's also quite thrilling to sit in an auction and watch items that are rare and valuable get "knocked-down" or sold for incredibly low prices.

All dealers and collectors have stories about certain auctions they've attended and the fabulous or funny items they've seen sold. I'll never forget one of my first "big" auctions, held at a fabulous estate in Beverly, Massachusetts. By the time a few hours had passed, over a million dollars' worth of items had been sold, and I hadn't bid on anything since the prices were way over my budget. But I'd had a day of entertainment and it was all for free! I'd seen Tiffany lamps, Chippendale furniture, Oriental rugs, and fabulous paintings—items I couldn't afford to have in my own house, yet all had been part of the "cottage" on this particular piece of property. I was hooked, but the auctions I attended after that sold items at more affordable prices. Soon, I was buying prints and books for my own collection and over a short period of time, I had enough items to sell some of them at flea markets and antique shows.

Those early auctions fed my interest and began a love affair that has extended to online auctions I can find on my computer without ever leaving my home.

The heart-pounding excitement of bidding on a wonderful doll for Christmas for your child and winning the item is unexplainable. When an auctioneer is pointing at you, choosing you out of the crowd, and accepting your barely perceptible nod or recognizing that your upheld bid card means you'll offer $5 more than the other bidder, you are likely to feel a rush of adrenaline akin to the moment you win a race.

Online auctions provide the same rush of adrenaline, especially when the auction is ending and you are the last bidder with only five seconds left on the clock. If you're lucky enough to get an item at less than what you would have paid for it retail, you'll probably have an ear-to-ear grin on your face as you imagine that item in your home, collection, or as a gift for someone else.

It's fast, furious, and fun to be involved in auctions! Whether you're bidding on a new Beanie Baby for your cousin Sue or a new car for yourself, you'll most likely be swept away. So, what's the next step? Knowing the difference between buying something in person and online, and then learning the lingo and the steps to protect yourself against the impulse to overspend or buy something you didn't want, or to purchase an item that isn't exactly what the seller says it is.

The difference between online auctions and "live and in person"

Naturally, the main difference between being in the audience at an auction barn or estate and bidding

Unofficially...
Conversation overheard at local flea market: "Have you tried putting it up on eBay yet?" "Nope, but that's the next step. My girlfriend has a computer that she's willing to let me borrow. Everyone seems to be going that route..."

online is that you are able to see, smell, and touch the pieces you are bidding on when you're there in person. Bidding online means that you have to rely on photos and the information provided by the seller of the item rather than on your own knowledge and common sense. You can't turn on that computer you're considering buying, or rotate that piece of porcelain to see the line that the online seller is telling you is an age crack. You can't smell that Oriental rug to see whether it's musty from age or pet droppings. You also won't have the auctioneer telling you what the piece you're bidding on might sell for in the local antiques shop or retail outlet. You probably won't know the person selling the items you want to buy, so getting in touch to ask questions might be hard to do.

Watch Out!
If you're unclear about an item's description, ask questions. A quick message to the seller might help you make intelligent decisions about what is worthwhile to buy.

Both online and in-person auctions have their own vocabulary. For instance, a *shill* is someone who raises the price on an item so that an auctioneer or seller can get more money than what is being currently bid. Know how to recognize shills and stay away from auctions that have the reputation for using them. This type of up-bidding is very common in traditional auctions (even though it's against the law), and it's even more difficult to trace in online auctions. If you think you might be up against the same bidders on various pieces, check out the list of bidders to see whether there are any names you recognize. (There's more on this in Chapter 3, "The Business of Auctioning.")

On the other hand, you'll be privy to items from all over the world: collections of antique newspapers, those collector's plates you've been searching everywhere for and haven't been able to find, a selection of prints that rival any photo gallery within a hundred miles of your home, more dolls than you could possibly add to your collection, tickets for your next dream vacation, that 1942 Pontiac you've been dying to park in your garage, those window treatments your local decorating shop can no longer order for you, even thousands of weird items like ostrich eggs and used toothbrushes.

The pros of buying/selling at online auctions include:

- **Saves time and money.** You no longer have to drive hundreds of miles or paw through a vast array of items in order to find that treasure.

- **Variety.** Online auctions offer something for everyone. Some are very specialized, while others have categories ranging from the normal to the extraordinary and bizarre.

- **Ease of buying.** You can buy a valuable guitar from a seller in Iowa while you sit in your home in Hawaii.

- **Ease of selling.** As soon as you're ready to sell, you can upload a picture and description and have your item ready for buyers within a short period of time.

- **Feedback.** One of the ways to discover whether a buyer/seller is honest is to check his or her "feedback." If a buyer/seller has not paid someone or has offered shoddy merchandise in the past, other sellers/buyers have a chance to comment on that person's business technique.

- **Price.** You determine the price you'll pay for an item or the bottom dollar you want for the item you're selling.

- **Longer bidding time.** Traditional auctions are held at a specific time and if you're not there, most of the time you can't bid. Online auctions are held over several days, so you can bid even at two o'clock in the morning.

- **Payment.** You, the seller, decide when and how you will accept payment for your item. Auction houses often don't pay their consignees until long after the auction is over, and auction houses also charge commissions (sometimes to both the buyer and the seller).

Some of the cons of buying/selling at online auctions include:

- **Advertising.** You must create your own advertising for your product, decide how much information to give to the buyer, and ultimately, you don't have the knowledge of an auction house who might provide information and value on the items it is selling.

- **Appraisals.** Since you are the one pricing your item, you must research appraisals to find out its market value.

- **Item descriptions.** Auction houses write descriptions of items and often actively market items to particular buyers. During an online auction, the sellers must write their own descriptions, and buyers must rely on those details when determining whether to bid on an item.

- **Payment.** Though most online auctions provide insurance for both the buyer and seller, the seller must wait for the money to come through. Likewise, the buyer also takes the chance that the seller is honest. (Insurance plans will be discussed in Chapter 15, "Packaging for a Safe Journey.") Sometimes sellers need to chase bidders to get paid.

Unofficially...
The wildly successful auction site eBay.com began by selling Pez dispensers to collectors. Now millions of items are sold every week—ranging from the sublime to the ridiculous.

■ **Returns.** If a buyer is not satisfied, the auction house will deal with the problem. During an online auction, the seller must deal with returns and dissatisfied customers personally. In turn, buyers must also deal one-on-one with sellers.

■ **Shipping.** Auction houses deal with deliveries and shipping to customers. Buyers/sellers online must deal with packaging their own items and making sure they arrive safely.

What it all boils down to is whether you prefer the face-to-face action of the traditional auction and the thrill of the hunt for the type of items you want to buy, or the convenience of shopping at home at any time of the night or day, from thousands of sellers, taking the chance that the item you buy might not be exactly what you want or need. With traditional auctions, you can take your won items home with you that very day; when bidding online, you must wait for the pieces you've won to be shipped to you.

One thing is for sure: When you win a bid (whether you're in the audience at Sotheby's or at home in your robe in front of the computer), you'll feel that undeniable thrill of victory.

The danger of auction fever
What is auction fever? It's that moment when you can't stop bidding on an item, when logic is no longer your friend, when your hands begin to shake, your face flushes, and you cannot stop bidding. Unfortunately, it happens at most inopportune moments and you might end up with a lamp that looks better on Aunt Bessie's nightstand than in your modern living room, as a result.

Auction fever causes us to lose control over our normally well-functioning modes of reason and causes even the most intelligent people to go into the "I've got to have it" mode. It's the bidder's response to that intense need to act upon that impulse that brings trouble. At that moment when you find yourself waiting for the last couple of moments of an auction in order to bid, ask yourself whether you truly want the piece for whatever the cost or whether you're bidding just to keep up with the flurry of action typical of the final seconds of any auction, whether online or traditional.

The ways to curb auction fever include:

Bright Idea
Repeat this mantra to yourself when you believe you might be getting auction fever: Do I need this? Do I want this? Will it fit in the house/my collection/the room? Can I live without it?

- Check out the item's condition thoroughly before beginning to bid.

- Research the piece you want to buy to find out its estimated worth, whether there are collectors' organizations, etc.

- Determine what you will pay *before* you start bidding. Write that figure down!

- Question whether you really need the item.

- Be suspicious of an item that appears too good to be true. It usually is.

- Listen carefully to the auctioneer or read the item's description closely—one more time.

- Think before sending in that last bid, especially if it's over the amount you told yourself you would pay.

- Take a deep breath if your heart starts to pound.

- Remind yourself how much money you have in your checking account (or on your credit card) and walk away if you are over your limit.

- Congratulate yourself if you win the bid and enjoy the piece before starting the process all over again.

Everyone is susceptible to auction fever. Even the most jaded auction-goers fall prey to the impulse to buy something they really don't want or need, simply because the item appears too enticing, reasonably priced, collectible, useful, attractive, or appealing. Whatever the reason the buyer believes he absolutely, positively must have that whatizit-fromwherever, the rationality all humans are born with can fly out the nearest window. The buyer realizes, often too late, that he has bid too much for an item he really doesn't want, or simply has bought a fairly useless item.

Usually buyers only need to have this experience a few times before it dawns on them that they have gotten caught up in the heat of the moment, had a slight bout of auction fever, and will feel better once they stop beating themselves over the head for being such a dunce. Everyone who has ever bid during an auction has experienced the undeniable effects of auction fever—and lived to tell about it!

Consider the lessons auction fever can teach you and learn from them. However, a word to the wise: If you see that you're bidding just for the thrill of it and not for the items themselves, take a moment and do a quickie psychological check-up on yourself. Auctions are as addicting as gambling, alcohol, or drugs, and one needs to be aware of that possibility before beginning the bid.

What do you have to sell?

During the past couple of years, just about everything has shown up on an online auction. Though most auction houses have general rules about what they won't sell or what is prohibitive, the types of items that sell at online auctions is endless. Chances are good that you have at least a dozen items in your house at this very moment that someone would bid on during an online auction.

Consider the following list of items that recently sold online and think about whether you might have similar things you could sell (or whether there are items on this list you'd dearly love to own!):

- Set of *Star Trek* trading cards
- Used Frank Sinatra CD
- Collection of used Paul Revereware pots and pans
- Signed copy of a Nora Roberts paperback
- Lenox 5" × 7" creamware frame
- Mercedes 500SL Roadster
- Small collection of Matchbox cars
- Holiday Barbie doll
- "Indy" the Indy 500 Beanie Baby
- Ken Griffey, Jr. baseball card
- Several Hopi Kachina figurines
- Vintage Scrabble game
- Wooden rocking horse
- Limited edition plate featuring dolphin drawing by the artist Wyland
- Three hand-decorated greeting cards done by an autistic child
- Hummingbird Lily Flower pettipoint eyecase
- *The Flight of the Phoenix* VHS tape with James Stewart
- Dangling rhinestone grapes bracelet

- 1929 original Studebaker color ad
- 1929 Mercury dime
- Statue of Liberty snow globe
- Santa Claus Pez dispenser
- Set of Harlequin SuperRomance paperback novels
- Dozen Memorex computer floppy disks
- Personalized pencils
- Marilyn Monroe calendar from 1995
- Webster's New World Dictionary
- Porcelain hanging angel figurine
- Anheuser Busch 1994 beer stein
- Two one-way tickets from Orlando, Florida, to London, England
- Week in a cabin on the river in Arkansas
- Castle in Germany
- Japanese Pokémon cards
- Elvis Presley gold record
- Personally created calligraphy version of your family name
- Royal Haeger vase
- Black and Decker power tools
- Vintage wooden canoe
- Audio and video tapes of loons
- Pikachu 35mm camera
- 27 skeins of Aunt Lydia's heavy rug yarn

Well, you get the point. Everyone has something in his home, garage, or junk pile that someone else will buy online. Of the hundreds of categories included in general online auctions and highlighted in specialty auctions, you can find something for everyone, from the baby in the family to the oldest member. You can decorate the house for Christmas, buy a new computer, make sure you have film to take pictures of your latest vacation, purchase a car to take you back and forth to work, and even find personal letters written by someone famous—all by bidding online. And if you don't want to buy anything, you can make a few dollars selling those items that are stored carefully away in the burgeoning closets in your home.

Though some items will bring more in today's market than others, the chances are good that you either have something someone else will want or will want something that is currently being sold. Once you do a little more research, you can begin to understand the dynamics of how you handle the actual buying and selling of auction items.

If you don't think you have anything you want to sell, consider checking out the places where you can buy treasures in order to resell them online. Some of those items won't cost you a dime, if you use your imagination. Some will be items you can create yourself. And some of you might even end up going into business by buying various items and then selling them piecemeal during online auctions.

Here are some places where you might look for items to auction online:

- **Local garage sales.** Check the weekly or daily newspaper in your area for listings. Most newspapers list garage sales toward the middle of the week. If you get the newspaper the night before, you can map out a route for yourself, visiting as many sales as possible during the early hours of the morning. Make sure you read the ads carefully. If you get to a sale too early, the sellers might tell you to come back later. Missing a sale by half an hour or more

Unofficially...
Just for giggles, check out some of the strange stuff being sold at online auctions by surfing through http://clubs. yahoo.com/clubs/ ebayweirdness-collectorclub.

can mean the difference between snagging a bargain and wasting time.

- **Flea markets.** Most areas have weekly flea markets that are held during the summer. Here in Florida, we're lucky to have them all year round. Prices range from the very cheap to the absolutely ridiculous. I recommend going to flea markets on a regular basis and picking up anything that appeals to you and your pocketbook. Eventually, you'll get to the point where you might specialize by buying only particular items, such as baseball cards or certain types of pottery, but at first, just have fun.

- **Church sales.** The people who usually contribute to church sales are doing so out of the goodness of their hearts or to help their churches raise money for a particular event. If you show up early, you might be able to help some of the contributors unload their cars or set up, and by doing so, you'll be the first to see some of their items.

- **Estate sales.** Usually organized by professionals, these sales might not yield too many great bargains, since the person who prices the items is usually hired because he knows what they're worth. If you're in the market for antiques or collectibles that are highly popular, you might be able to find something of value, but remember that items that are cracked or otherwise damaged will only be worth half their original estimate. Though you might be able to get into an estate sale early, the most effective use of your time will be to scan the items quickly, grab what you want before someone else does, and negotiate with the estate sale manager for a discount.

▪ **Craft sales.** Handmade and signed items are often one of a kind, which makes them a little more valuable in a collector's eye. Craft sales are the place to find the unusual, unique, and artistic type of item that might be peculiar to your region and difficult to find elsewhere in the world. Until you get a handle on what kinds of items will sell on the auctions you've chosen to participate in, stick to buying useful crafty or arty items.

▪ **Thrift stores.** Sometimes run by charitable groups or organizations, thrift stores are another place to find the items you can turn over easily in an online auction. Stores must sell their items quickly because they're taking up floor space. Some thrift stores offer discounts on items that have been in the shop for a certain period of time. You might leave your name and phone number with the owner of the shop so that she can call you when the items you are seeking come in. Most thrift and consignment shops are happy to know they have an immediate sale by calling people looking for particular things.

▪ **Antique shops/malls.** Though these shops might be more high priced than flea markets or garage sales, sometimes you can get lucky. Antiques dealers often have to clean out a whole houseload of goods in order to get five or six pieces they really want to add to their inventory. They may not want the rest of what they've bought and would be happy to deal with someone who will take it off their hands. Depending on what you want, you might get a regular offering of items from antique dealers. And you might hit a bargain occasionally if you haunt the shops and let the owners know what you're looking for.

- **Used bookstores.** Often used book and music stores simply mark an item half of what it originally sold for, not taking into consideration other key factors, such as whether the book is a first edition or the record or CD might fit into a particular collection. People who sell books online have told of buying paperback first editions for $1 or less and then turning around to sell them online for at least 10 times that amount.

- **Attics and basements.** Many enterprising folks make their living offering themselves out to clean attics and basements. Whatever the house/apartment owner agrees should be thrown away is up for grabs. Sometimes the cleaning folks simply get dirty and come up empty-handed, but there are plenty of other stories of being told to "take everything" and finding the rare valuables that earn the cleaners thousands of dollars.

- **Freebies.** Some of the more interesting items in online auctions are those that didn't cost the sellers a dime. Crafty people take found items, like seashells, bird feathers, interesting branches, and pinecones, and turn them into decorations or works of art which are eagerly bought at auction. Savvy online traders have also learned the value of those items we naturally throw away: bottles, cans, cereal boxes, newspapers, magazines, and advertising items.

With some thought and imagination, you can easily find objects that will interest others, perhaps catapulting yourself into a profitable online auction business!

Are you ready to part with the family heirlooms?

There are some tough questions to answer before you start pulling out Grandma's pearls and Uncle Ed's favorite flyfishing lures. Although you might be excited about the thought of earning thousands by selling the gaudy costume jewelry you inherited from Aunt Mildred, you need to examine the reasons why you want to sell these items in the first place.

Ask yourself the following questions:

1. Am I sentimentally connected to this item?
2. Will I feel guilty if I sell it?
3. Is there anyone else in the family who might want this piece?
4. Is the item legally mine to sell?
5. Do I want to sell this piece strictly because of the money it could bring?
6. Is this something I'll ever need in the future?
7. Have I had this piece for a long time, promising myself to find a place for it (or to frame it, put it under glass, clean it, or fix it) and I haven't?
8. Would it be wiser to keep the piece since it might increase in value in the future?
9. Would clearing the attic/basement/trunk of the junk I've kept help me get a life?
10. Will I make others happy if I sell the items Uncle Henry willed to me from his overflowing farmhouse?

Money isn't the only reason you should clean out your closets, drawers, and storage units. You should also clean them out simply because you need the space for more important things or because it's time to move on with your life. The fact that you can make money selling those items should be secondary.

How much do you know about your items?

When you're about to sell something, it's best to know everything you can possibly find out about the item. If you're dealing with an everyday product, there's not much you need to know other than standard information that the buyer must have in order to recognize it. For example, if you're selling a box of cereal, the buyer must know the type of cereal, the size of the box, and how much you want for it. But if you're selling a string of pearls, the buyer will want to know much more, such as how old they are, whether they're cultivated, and what type of pearls they are.

If you're selling family heirlooms or anything that's vintage or antique, you'll want to know the history of the item. The simple fact that your Grandma Agnes had the item stored in her hope chest and that the item must be old because she owned it isn't enough.

The facts and how to get them

Whether you're unsure of the maker or origin of an item or you simply have no clue what the item might be, you need to have enough information about the piece to answer a buyer's questions. This is especially important since you'll be selling online, and other than a few photos, the buyer can't physically inspect the piece for clues about what it might be worth or how it might fit into a collection.

Inspect all items for tags or "signatures." Clothes have labels in the collar or the maker's name sewn

Bright Idea
Before selling anything, you might want to get the item appraised. Check out eAppraisals.com, Auctionwatch. com, or contact your local expert (i.e., antiques dealer, jewelry appraiser, computer salesperson) for the fair market value before putting your goods up for auction.

somewhere on the garment. Pottery, glass, silver, and gold usually have a maker's mark. Sometimes the mark is a simple name or set of initials. Other times, it's a hallmark that gives some indication, symbolically, of the company. Perhaps you'll find a company logo (i.e., crossed swords, a crown, a crescent moon), but you won't be able to tell what company that logo belongs to without some help.

Appraisers deal with identifying items all the time. Check your local Yellow Pages for appraisers in the area, ask people who sell the same types of items for information, or go online to eAppraisals.com for more information. Whatever the case, be armed with those simple facts before you go online.

Now let's march on with the reason for this book: to learn how to buy and sell these valuable trinkets in one of the liveliest marketplaces on Earth!

Just the facts

- The traditional auction lingo is also used by the online auctions, so you need to familiarize yourself with the commonly used terms.

- Auction fever is a common malady among auction-goers and can be remedied with a little self-control. But some bidders can become overwhelmed by auction fever and let it control their lives, buying items they don't need and eventually getting into debt as a result of overspending.

- Items you can sell on online auctions are as varied as the people who sell them.

- Before you decide to sell the family heirlooms, you must determine fair prices for them and be honest with yourself about whether you really want to let go of them.

The Many Different Auctions and Their Quirks

Though online auctions are a fairly new phenomena, there are hundreds of them now active. eBay, however, is still the king, leading the pack with millions of active buyers and sellers on the site and millions of items available. Because there are so many auction sites, in this chapter we give you an overview of the best ones and what others you should watch or visit for more specialized items.

One thing should be comforting to those of you who find this whole business daunting: It gets easier and easier every time you log on to any of the sites. When eBay first started putting items up for bid, we had to learn not only how to list, but later on, how to add images to our listings. Then the auction management programs started coming out, and business got easier. Today we have programs to help with shipping (we even get our postage online!), accounting, graphics, and all the other details. And some auctions let you list items directly from your own computer without using an additional program.

The choices are varied, the benefits are great, and the excitement is enough to keep anyone interested for the next decade. By the time you read this, there will be even more choices, and the field will have grown much larger. So, hold on to your hats as we introduce you to the world of auctions! For more specific information, check the chapters on your subject of interest. For now, we'll just offer a general snapshot of the major players.

eBay: The big kahuna

Founded on Labor Day, 1995, by Pierre Omidyar, eBay is the number one person-to-person auction site on the Web. Omidyar began the business to share his wife's enthusiasm for collecting Pez dispensers with other collectors. Thinking that it might be neat to begin a trading community with collectors of Pez dispensers and other unique items, Omidyar developed the idea to share both information and sales with others on the Internet. It turned into the world's largest online auction site and, ultimately, made millions for Omidyar.

eBay has since offered more than 12 million items in the five years they've been in business and have pretty much established the auction scene that everyone else has imitated.

Unofficially...
eBay published its first issue of *eBay Magazine* in 1999, bringing the then world-famous auction site even closer to the collectors.

What you'll find on the site

You'll discover that just about anything that is saleable or collectible is available on eBay. In fact, when one of your authors, Dawn, and her co-editor for her college's literary magazine wanted to create a unique cover for the magazine, they got some of their ideas from visiting eBay—a truly different way to do research for a literary magazine, but it proves what we've said all along: If someone wants it, eBay has it.

More than 4,320 categories are available on the site, including furniture, cars, vacations, Beanie Babies, dolls, porcelain, computers, comic books, real estate, sports memorabilia, and much, much more.

The basics of using eBay

If you're new to eBay, simply visit the home page and click on "New to eBay" for a tour. You can browse the site as much as you want, familiarizing yourself with listings and procedures, but before you can do any business as a buyer or seller, you must register. Have your credit card ready or be willing to put some money into an escrow account because eBay protects both its buyers and sellers by knowing their identities. Bidders/sellers must be at least 18 years old in order to register, which we think makes a lot of parents a bit more comfortable. (See Chapter 4, "Setting Up an Account—or Two," for more information on registering at different auction sites.)

Once you're registered, you can either bid on items or sell; all the steps for how to do either are easy to follow. eBay has anticipated all questions and provided answers for them right up front. There are separate instructions for both buyers and sellers (you can click on them from the "New to eBay" section), as well as information about fees, how to add photos to your listings, and how to protect yourself. If you can't immediately find the answers to your questions, try using eBay's search engine.

eBay requires that you have an e-mail address, and that you give them credit card information, as well as a mailing address, phone number, and user ID. The ID is something you can choose at registration, and it doesn't have to be your real name. In addition, eBay asks that both buyers and sellers provide feedback about their transactions with other eBay users. The feedback forum was instituted in order to provide a way for customers to determine whether the buyer/seller with whom they are dealing has been honest in dealings with other customers.

Watch Out!
If you're buying or selling in several auctions, it's a wise idea to divide your incoming e-mail into several folders so that your mail doesn't get out of control.

When you bid on an item, you'll instantly know whether you're the current high bidder, and if you win that item, eBay will notify you via e-mail. You can also check your account (items you're selling or bidding on) at any time by clicking "My eBay" (at the top right-hand corner of the screen). Once you've won an item, you're responsible for contacting the seller in order to arrange shipment—and you're also responsible for making prompt payment and for following through if there are any problems.

If you have problems, eBay provides several ways of dealing with them: feedback, insurance, the SafeHarbor program (used to settle disputes), i-Escrow (a way to pay for your items only after you're satisfied), and SquareTrade (a new program for settling disputes about items valued at over $100).

In addition, eBay has built a community of buyers and sellers by offering space on their site where you can chat with other eBay users. The "Community" section of the site offers discussion, chatrooms, news about the site, a library, information about charity auctions, details about the eBay Foundation, the *eBay Insider* newsletter, a store with eBay-specific items, and even information about jobs at the site.

The pros and cons of eBay

The pros of joining eBay are many. The company is the largest and most influential auction site on the Net and became that way through a lot of trial and error. You can find just about anything you want on eBay, so that's a definite plus for buyers. You can also sell just about anything, and there are plenty of buyers willing to bid on items as diverse and unusual as the types of people who click on the site from all over the world. eBay also offers all kinds of practical advice and links to programs that will help with uploading images, managing auctions, and protecting yourself from making costly mistakes.

The cons? Sometimes eBay is just *too* big. Your listing might not get the attention it would at more "collectible-specific" auctions. For example, we had a piece of wonderful Southern pottery up on eBay, and every time we put it up, it wouldn't sell. We tried everything: We put it in different categories, tried new headings, did further research on the artist, and still nothing. Finally, we put it up on PotteryAuction.com and found people who were looking for exactly the type of item we had.

Another negative aspect of eBay is that you pay a fee every time you list a piece, whether it sells or not. Though this fee is part and parcel of getting the excellent protection eBay provides, it can add up. There are quite a few other auctions that don't charge fees, and the chances of getting burned are fairly slim. The people who deal on auctions are just like you and me, for the most part. So, if you don't want to pay the fees, you might be better off taking your chances on another auction.

Timesaver
Remember to efficiently list your pieces, making use of every word in the listing (i.e. no "empty" words like "LQQK"). Chances are, you'll have less to re-list if you do it correctly the first time—saving yourself both time and money.

The third drawback is that eBay has become almost megolithic in its command of the marketplace, and being an American-based company, it bothers some people that they've pretty much cornered the market. Yet the Internet has become the place where just about anyone can rule, as long as they have the gumption and know-how. eBay has made themselves known and backs up what they promote with solid action. No empty promises here.

By and large, the positives far outweigh the negatives with eBay. There's a reason why they've been so successful!

eBay versus the other auction sites

The fact that eBay is absolutely huge and commands the Web through the sheer force of their ads (just about every site you click on, even another auction site, features an ad or direct link to eBay) determines their standing in the marketplace.

Their customer service is finely tuned to the needs of their buyers/sellers. Whenever there's a problem, eBay does its best to take care of it. In addition, they not only offer community support to their members—for example, Q&A boards on how to upload images—but encourage free communication between buyers and sellers.

Most buyers/sellers on eBay have also taken advantage of building a Web page of their own on the site. The "About Me" pages are a great way to get additional information about other eBay users. Click on "About Me" to search the site for any buyers/sellers with whom you're thinking of doing business. Or you can see their page (if they have one), by clicking on the link next to their name when you view one of their listings. Some eBay users use this page to show off what they have for sale or what they've found.

In short, eBay offers not only exceptional customer support but also the most well-developed and easy-to-navigate Web site of all the auctions we've visited.

Amazon

Originally a Web site for buying books and still the largest of that ilk, Amazon started in 1995, giving the virtual community a chance to explore the world of books by offering literally millions of titles online. (Dawn was pleasantly surprised to find copies of her children's books, which had been unavailable for a long time, for sale online with Amazon.) This company entered the auction market in March 1999, and since then has given eBay a surprising run for its money. In November 1999, Amazon and the well-known auction house Sotheby's joined forces to produce Sothebys.Amazon.com. During that same time period, Amazon began offering live auctions on its site. Since early 1999, Amazon's auction listings have grown substantially, and they have quickly become the second most active and well-advertised auction site on the Net.

What you'll find on the site

One of the main differences between Amazon and other sites is that there's more than just auctions. When you reach the main page, you'll have to click on the "Auctions" tab in order to enter the auctions. (You can also do business through the zShops, which provide a way for a small business to send retail through a large shop—without the stress and charges of setting up its own Web site.)

Once you get into the auction, you'll discover that Amazon makes things as easy as possible for both buyers and sellers by allowing for instant

Timesaver
Bookmark the auction site for Amazon so you won't have to always go to the home page of their massive site and waste time clicking to the auction part of their company.

uploads right from your computer (images can be immediately loaded onto the site without the benefit of an auction management program). Amazon also provides several payment options not available elsewhere.

You'll discover 19 main categories and hundreds of subcategories, including such items as books, electronics, toys, antiques, watches, home and garden items, timeshares, motorcycles, boats, teddy bears, and prints. The prices range from less than a dollar to millions, with most items falling in the $1 to $100 range.

The basics of using Amazon

Like most other sites, Amazon requires you to register before you can either sell or bid. They require an e-mail address and a credit card number to confirm your identity, and they make it a point to state "None of our more than 17 million customers has ever been a victim of credit card fraud while shopping at Amazon.com."

Once you're registered, entering a bid or listing an item is fairly easy. To enter a bid, you browse through the categories to find what you want. You can enter a specific search for an item of your choice, or by time the auctions are ending, or even by the amount of money you want to spend. Browsing is made even easier on Amazon because thumbnails of the items are included with some of the short descriptions. (A thumbnail is a small version of a picture—if you click on the thumbnail, you'll get the full screen version.) You enter your bid in the top right-hand side of the page. The item-listing page also offers you the option of finding other items like the one you're bidding on.

When you're a regular customer, the main auction page will instantly give you information about whatever you're bidding on and the items in which you might be interested. In addition, featured sales and notices are available for you to check out (or not!).

If you're in the market to sell, Amazon lets you upload your images directly from your computer's hard drive to their site. Like eBay, Amazon offers bidders and sellers the option of creating a home page that helps develop the auction community. You can also monitor your account by simply clicking on the tab marked "My Account" at the top of any page as you travel through the site.

Amazon deducts charges for listing the items directly from the seller's account and offers the buyer several options for payment, including escrow, Amazon.com payment, and payment by credit card.

Customer service protects both bidder and seller in several different ways. The Amazon Bid Click raises a buyer's bid incrementally so that you don't have to keep coming back to bid, and their Amazon A-to-Z Guarantee pretty much covers the buyer against fraud and any kind of misrepresented or unsent items. The seller is protected via escrow services, which make sure the seller gets paid. They'll also attempt to settle any disputes if the buyer backs out, as well as refund any amounts the seller has paid for listing the item.

The pros and cons of Amazon

There are plenty of items available on Amazon, but it appears that some sell better than others. Collectibles, movies, books, and like products are hot, and Amazon's connection with Sotheby's offers

Bright Idea
If you're dealing on more than one auction, it's a good idea to manage all of them through a site like AuctionWatch. com.

art and antiques collectors some fabulous options. Though they also have plenty of electronics and software on the site, experts tell us that some of the more specialized auction sites for those items are better supplied with a variety, and that the prices are often more consistent on those sites, as well.

The best part about Amazon is that you can upload your listing immediately to the site. They also offer a more efficient way of bidding and collecting money through their patented 1-Click plan, which we'll tell you more about in the next section. In addition to payment options, you can automatically convert currency when you're on the listing for the item you want to bid upon.

Like eBay, you can find out about buyers/sellers through feedback and personally created Web pages, but it's not as easy to tell whether someone has changed their identity recently (eBay shows you a new identity by placing a "sunglasses" logo next to the bidder's ID name).

Another plus is that if you include a photo with your listing, it automatically comes up with the listings, whether you search the category or for a specific item. This allows the bidder to see the item before clicking on a more detailed listing and saves lots of time.

The drawbacks of dealing on Amazon are few. The seller is not as well protected as the buyer is on this site. Customer service is fairly well developed, but not as extensively as eBay's. In addition, because they're newer than eBay, they don't offer as many items, but that's changing on a daily basis.

Amazon versus the other auction sites

The major difference between Amazon and the others is that Amazon is not just an auction site. They still continue to sell books, CDs, DVDs, electronics, software, toys, and so on, while they are conducting auctions. Is this a good idea? Well, Amazon has been making the most of their varied business ventures by promoting each one on the others' pages. What does that mean? If you put an item up for auction, you can have it linked to other pages, meaning you get free advertising. For example, if you're trying to sell a Pokémon character, you can link your auction listing to a Pokémon book or to one of the toys offered in the toy department, or to a video, or to a CD or DVD. You get more bang for your buck that way.

Another thing that makes Amazon different is their patented 1-Click service. Customers who have signed up for this service just click on the item they want and it's automatically added to their shopping basket; their shipping/payment information is already entered. This makes it a lot easier to shop. Amazon has had problems with this service, though, because other companies want to offer that convenience to their customers. Amazon's legal staff has, thus far, protected the company and kept this feature Amazon-specific.

If you make a purchase, Amazon will remember it and automatically list recommendations in those categories, specially chosen for you, as soon as you log on to the site. In addition, Amazon provides a "wish list" service for all its customers, encouraging them to create a list of items they would like to purchase and making that list available to customers who might like to buy a gift.

In addition, Amazon has promoted its First Bidder discount policy (if the first bidder ultimately buys the item, that person gets 10 percent off the purchase price), and Amazon.com Payments (which

Unofficially...
In 1999 Amazon sued Barnes & Noble for trying to imitate their 1-Click technology. Amazon won a temporary injunction.

enables anyone who puts an item up for sale to accept credit cards).

Yahoo!

Yahoo!, the first navigational guide on the Web, went public in 1996, offering 2,600,000 shares at $13.00 per share. One of the best known search engines, this company offers both local sites (for cities) and international sites (in different countries, as well as languages). In addition, they "provide targeted Internet resources and communications services for a broad range of audiences, based on demographic, key-subject, and geographic interests. Yahoo! is headquartered in Santa Clara, Calif." (Yahoo! company site).

Moneysaver
Pound for pound, Yahoo! beats the others hands down regarding expenses paid up front for listing your items: zero!

Yahoo! Auctions officially opened on September 14, 1998, teaming up with ONSALE, Inc. to create an auction that began directly competing with eBay. A person-to-person auction site, it started with more than 2,000 categories and has expanded rapidly since then.

Recently it's been rumored that eBay and Yahoo! are going to pair up, but as of this writing there have been no official announcements (although, in this world of e-commerce, things change every second, so who knows what's going to happen next?).

What you'll find on the site

You get to the site either by going to the Yahoo! home page and clicking on "Auctions" or by entering the site address (auctions.yahoo.com) in your location box. Once there, you can navigate to Selected Auctions, Charity Auctions, or any of the more than 2,000 categories. The 12 major categories are listed on the home page, and by clicking on each, you can browse through them. In addition, you can scroll to the bottom of the page and click on "Auction Sites" for other countries, if you're in the mood for something international.

Items range from the mundane to the sublime. You can search through baby items, baseball cards, flowers, automotive tools, video cameras, or record albums, or you can find unusual items in the charity auctions. For example, the day we wrote this section, you could bid on Allen Iverson memorabilia to benefit Sixers Charities (the basketball team) or you could bid on items in seven other charity auctions, as well as on items sold by charitable organizations such as Breast Cancer Angels and Cure for Cancer.

The basics of using Yahoo!

If you're new to the site, take the Auction Tour, which takes you through the process step by step, including an overview that offers auction terminology and definitions. In addition, Yahoo! offers an Auction Diary that takes you through a day-by-day simulated auction so that even the first-timer can understand what happens in the bidding/selling process.

In addition to the Auction Tour, Yahoo! offers detailed information (including examples of what the auction pages look like, with definitions) about how to bid or sell. Simply click on "How to Bid" or "How to Sell" for the complete lowdown.

Like the other auctions, you must be registered to buy or sell. However, Yahoo! doesn't offer any customer service, so it's truly a matter of buyer beware when you're bidding on this site.

In addition to being able to view the listings by title, you can view them by photo by simply clicking "Show Photos" at the top or bottom of any page of listings. This makes it a lot simpler to find what you want—or to just browse until something interests you.

Listing items is easy for the seller because you simply upload your images with a click of your mouse. Listings aren't fancy, but they do the trick. You can fine-tune the listing to your satisfaction, description-wise, but the frames are all pretty generic.

Monitoring your account is easy, clicking through steps. We've learned on Yahoo! that we click a lot more to go places, but once you know Yahoo!'s terminology, it's not hard to navigate.

Like the others, Yahoo!'s "yahooligans" are identified by their rating and by clicking on the number. You can read the seller's profile, including how many positive, negative, and neutral comments the seller has, and how many have happened in the past six months.

The pros and cons of Yahoo!

Yahoo! is a free service and most buyers/sellers with whom we've spoken really like the idea of being able to easily list items and not have to pay for them. They also report great sales and a wide variety of items from which to choose. The fact that Yahoo! offers its customers all of the same things the other major sites do, as well as e-mail addresses, and the ability to be online to deal with questions at any time during the auction, are all pluses.

On the negative side, the transaction is between the buyer and the seller. There is no support offered by the company, and they make it quite clear up front that if there are any problems, you're on your own.

There's a notice on the bottom of the Yahoo! site that they collect personal information. If you click on the "Privacy Policy," it tells how they use it. Some

> 66
> Yahoo! provides a method for us to supplement our incomes, so that my husband who is the "packer" and picture taker could retire early … I also do the "flea market" scene, and have certain items I purchase when I have a customer looking for them—I can purchase it and make some profit on the item when I resale. Thank you Yahoo!, you are an important part of our lives.
> —Carol Ann Eichelmann (a Yahoo! customer)
> 99

people are not comfortable with this type of info being seen by others and you do have the option of deleting it, but Yahoo! makes it very clear that they're evaluating traffic patterns, as well as other demographics. Be aware of that (and realize that most sites do this kind of evaluation but might not reveal their policy as clearly as Yahoo! does). Also, be warned that you might receive offers from some merchants as a result of Yahoo!'s collecting information about you.

Yahoo! is also not the easiest auction site to navigate. They don't offer a site map, so finding answers to questions is often difficult, and in order to get a history of the site, we had to go out to Yahoo!'s main page and do some searching through press releases.

Yahoo! versus the other auction sites

The biggest difference between Yahoo! and the other major auctions is that Yahoo! doesn't charge for their services. The second biggest difference is that Yahoo! doesn't offer any kind of insurance or negotiation program to help settle disputes between buyers and sellers.

There are a couple of options on this site that are less important than the first two, but interesting nonetheless. For example, you can create customized winning e-mails in the "Sellers' Options" section, as well as design a customized "auction booth" to showcase your wares. We also like the option to talk to a dealer in real time if that seller is online. You can find out immediately upon entering the listing whether the person is available or choose to leave a question for the dealer to answer at his or her leisure.

Timesaver
It often saves at least 10 or 15 minutes of browsing when you go to an auction site that specializes in the items you want. For example, it can take half the time to search for a cell phone on DealDeal than on eBay.

DealDeal

Rated the "number one electronics site" by auction-ranking site AuctionInsider.com, DealDeal has a great selection of electronics equipment at good prices. Most everything on this site is surplus, close-out, or refurbished. If you don't mind getting your electronics products that way, this is the place for you. This is a consignment online auction for manufacturers, liquidators, and wholesalers.

DealDeal's "About" section tells us that the company auctions off "surplus, closeout, and refurbished products ... by leading manufacturers, like SONY, JVC, Dell, Krups, and Wilson."

What you'll find on the site

DealDeal specializes in electronics, and you'll be able to find computers and accessories, scanners, software, video cards, home audio equipment, cameras, and much more.

There are five main categories on this site, and they're heavily weighted on the computers and electronics end of the spectrum. However, DealDeal does offer some home and garden items, as well as a special category called "Skis and Snowboards."

The basics of using DealDeal

Naturally, you need to register in order to bid, and DealDeal requires your credit card information to register your name to bid.

Once you're registered, you can bid on the items by clicking on the "Bid Button" link (if you do a search on this site, your list comes up as clickable titles). Every bid earns an "extra" called "DealBucks," which basically means you get $5 off any item you win. You can earn this special bonus in other ways, as well. For example, every new customer you refer to DealDeal who signs up earns some DealBucks for him- or herself as well as for you, the recruiter.

You bid on items the same way as on other auctions, but selling is a bit different. The auction is set up to handle small and medium-sized businesses, so it's best if you are able to handle your own credit cards and drop-shipping (taking orders for items stored by someone else, who will then ship them directly from a warehouse). They will also ask if you have your own reseller's license, usually obtainable from your state tax office.

The pros and cons of DealDeal

The "Customer Service" section of this site is very helpful. Questions that none of the other sites seem to answer are answered on DealDeal. In addition, you can get all your problems solved in one place rather than deal with both buyer's and seller's issues. On DealDeal, you are the customer, and they are there to help you, whether it's with credit card problems, packing problems, or installation problems.

One drawback of this site is that it doesn't get the advertising attention it deserves; the site owners should be getting the name out there in a more pervasive way. And you have to be at least fairly well established to sell on this site. This site does not foster the personal connection between the buyer and seller that eBay does.

DealDeal versus the other auction sites

DealDeal has an extremely easy-to-navigate site that's visually stimulating, as well as customer-friendly. Their "Customer Service" section gives you specific places to go for certain problems. For example, if you're having problems navigating the site or finding anything, you can go straight to the "Site Design or Navigation" button to get your answer (or write to someone who specializes in that type of problem).

uBid

Frank Khulusi, President and Chief Executive Officer of Creative, announced the launch of uBid in November 1997. Determined to "sell computers, computer-related products and consumer electronics, from a variety of leading manufacturers, through an auction format," the company has built steadily on its reputation.

Based in Chicago, uBid is considered the number one site for computer-related products. They have a plethora of models and different types of computers, plus all the related supplies. The site states that they have a constantly revolving inventory of over 3,000 items during any given auction, have over 1,030,000 registered users, and host an average of 100,000 customers daily.

What you'll find on the site

uBid offers thousands of computers, computer products and supplies, electronics, and more. They are definitely better stocked with computers and electronics than any other site we've seen, so if you're interested in upgrading your computer or in buying that new digital camera, this is the place for you. It's also the place for the professional computer operator to buy parts, as well as cutting-edge equipment.

The basics of using uBid

Like Amazon's home page, the uBid home page is tabbed at the top, so navigation on this site is a piece of cake. If you're a newcomer, click on the "New User" line at the top of the inside frame for a tour of the site.

Placing your credit card number with them when you register is optional, leaving you to decide whether you'll use it in the future or choose another payment method.

The pros and cons of uBid

If you need to sell something, this isn't the place for it. When you get to the bottom of any item listing, you will see this note: "Y2K disclaimer! All products sold by uBid are third party products and are subject to the warranties and representations of the applicable manufacturers, including but not limited to Y2K compliance. Accordingly, uBid makes no representation or warranty with respect to the Y2K compliance of product sold." Basically, what this means is that there are no person-to-person sellers on this site. That may be good news for those of you who want to make sure the item you purchase is guaranteed, but for those of you interested in the action of dealing with another individual, it won't happen here. Everything is handled by uBid's personnel. (This can be either a positive or a negative, depending on your perspective.)

uBid versus the other auction sites

uBid asks you to choose the categories in which you'd like to bid when you're filling out their registration form. After you've registered, you can browse through any category. If you choose to look at an item's listing, your customer ID is automatically entered into a box, making it easy for you to bid quickly and efficiently.

All items are owned by uBid or its vendors. It appears that this is a business-to-person Web site, rather than a person-to-person site. In other words, you have to be a valid business with a company

“
February 10, 2000—CMGI, Inc. (Nasdaq: CMGI), the world's largest and most diversified network of Internet companies, announced today that it has signed a definitive merger agreement to acquire uBid.com (NASDAQ: UBID), a leading e-commerce auction site, in a stock-for-stock merger transaction valued at approximately $407 million.
—CMGI Public Relations/ General Press Release
”

name, Federal Employer ID Number, and financial reference information in order to sell on uBid, though anyone can buy items here. Vendors contract directly with uBid to send products on the site. So, if you're thinking of selling your kids' baby furniture, this isn't the place for you.

Other sites

Because there are so many other auctions out there, we give an overview here, then give bits and pieces of specific details about certain ones throughout the book. The best place to research auctions that either specialize in your type of item or are a certain type of auction (i.e., person-to-person, business-to-business, collectibles-oriented, connected to a search engine) is AuctionInsider.com. This site can save you time by searching multiple auctions simultaneously for the type of item you'd like to buy.

Another site that is very helpful when searching for the other options is AuctionWatch.com. They not only list the auctions, but offer ratings of each. Naturally, this list changes fairly frequently, with new auctions starting up and others going out of business, but you can easily check on whether there's an auction out there specifically for you.

As we've said, there are many other choices of auctions available. Because so many of them have nowhere near the exposure of the top half-dozen or so already mentioned, we won't waste your time going into the details of each site. All sites usually have a good orientation system that you can easily navigate once you've familiarized yourself with the terminology used by the big shots.

Quite a few of the major newspapers, including the *Orlando Sentinel*, sponsor their own auctions. Check your local newspaper's Web site to see if yours

"
The Silver Dolphin Antiques and Collectibles has its heart in eBay, but its fingers in some of the rest of the pies.
—President, The Silver Dolphin Antiques and Collectibles
"

is one of them. Additionally, certain areas of the country host sites specific to them, such as University of Michigan Auction Bot, the Ohio Auction & Classifieds, and Central Missouri Internet Auction. You can also find auctions that specialize in automobiles, such as Insurance Auto Auctions, or in historical documents, like the Gallery of History Simple & Direct. Collectibles are sold at sites like Hobby Markets Online, USCollector.com, Stein Auction, and My Beanie.com.

What you'll find on the lesser-known sites

The lesser-known sites often refer to their bigger and older brothers and sisters (eBay and the others), seemingly realizing that they are smaller and are dealing to an audience that will be shopping elsewhere, as well as on their sites.

Though some of the smaller sites are well done, some are rather amateurish, difficult to maneuver, and generally not worth a visit. Because we believe they'll die a natural death, we don't see any reason to name them here. It goes without saying that if you can't see any bids on the "going, going, gone" page of an auction, there's usually not much action going on and you should place your bid (or sell your piece) elsewhere. On the other hand, you can often get a bargain at these sites because there isn't much bidding competition.

Is bigger really better?

Going to a more specialized site will often give you the feeling of truly belonging to a small family community. There is more likelihood of getting a relationship going with their customer services staff (because the site is usually run by a small staff rather than a group of thousands), but there is also more likelihood of mistakes being made.

Watch Out!
Whenever you visit a lesser-known site, take the tour first and see if you can read any of its press releases. If the site hasn't advertised itself, it probably doesn't have much of a following.

Another thought is that the more specialized the site, the more likely you are to find what you want to buy or people interested in your particular product. Sometimes people and their items tend to get a tad "lost" on the bigger sites. If you're selling vintage Superman comics, you'll do well on eBay and Yahoo!, but you might want to find another auction if you're selling computers or have a huge inventory of widgets. It's just not efficient to deal with the larger auctions when the smaller ones attract just the right kind of clientele for your needs. There's a definite benefit to not having to wade through thousands of items to find the ones you want. When an auction specializes in comic books, for example, they'll be the only thing you'll buy—and everyone will probably be knowledgeable about what they're selling/buying. It makes things a lot more interesting!

Established auction sites versus new sites

Bright Idea
Sell your items in one of the big auctions first. If they don't sell or you don't get the price you want, try your luck at a smaller, more specific auction.

Our suggestion is to maintain a perfect mix of active registrations with one or two of the big kahunas and the occasional dip into more specialized sites when you need to sell those Beanie Babies (www.beaniebabiesauction.com) or an antique set of golf clubs (www.livetoplay.com).

The biggest advantage of the big shots is that they are established with large customer bases. They pay a fortune in advertising and it pays off. There are certain pluses to being well-heeled, and one of the most important is that they are able to get the word out to new customers. That can only mean a better chance for you to find a buyer for your item— and if you're a buyer, someone who is selling an item you want or need.

The larger auctions all offer the benefit of their expertise, as well. There, you'll have an established auction community filled with people who have had varied experiences and can offer advice on everything from the best camera to buy to how many days it takes to deliver a package from New Zealand to the United States.

eBay has the best reputation, and understandably so, but they've also had occasional problems. Any visit to the chatrooms and bulletin boards reveals people who are dissatisfied with various things. For the most part, people are satisfied with their eBay experience, but the people who aren't are the ones we most often hear from.

Whatever your choice, we can assure you that you'll have an interesting experience and meet lots of people you would never see or hear from if you sold at a flea market, yard sale, or store.

Just the facts

- eBay is the biggest and most powerful auction site on the Net, making it a good place to learn how auctions work.

- Yahoo! auctions doesn't charge a fee for buying and selling on their site, but they also don't offer a way for disputes to be settled.

- Amazon's auctions are only part of their site, but they do a great job of linking your item to other items on the site, increasing your item's exposure.

- Some of the smaller auctions were created to fill a specific need, such as people who only wanted to buy or sell vintage automobiles.

- Larger online auctions provide a wider customer base and a higher certainty of selling items.

Registering and
Setting Up

PART II

GET THE SCOOP ON...

How to determine what you'll be buying/selling
- How to research the right auctions for you
- The types of auctions and their quirks - The various ways to rate auctions

The Business of Auctioning

How do you know when you're ready to actually join an auction and officially register? Do you need to join every auction you check out or just the ones that look profitable? What are your chances in a small, specialized auction versus one of the giants like eBay? Should you know all the rules ahead of time or can you learn as you go in the auction business?

Questions like these pop up in conversations we have with people new to the online auction business. They are always amazed at how much fun we have and fascinated by the changes in this ever-growing business. Some have gone on to become online auctioneers themselves and are now enjoying the tumultuous excitement of creating ads for auctions, surfing the online sites to see where to sell their goods, uploading the information to the auction of choice and then watching the bids steadily go upward. When those buyers/sellers speak to us, it's with a gleam in their eye about one particularly important piece or a new contact they've made in Prague. Many people who didn't know the first thing about computers a couple of years ago are now not only sitting down at the keyboard on a regular basis, but handling a business and all the details that come with it.

Are you ready to join the crowd? Or are you new to the excitement and willing to spread your wings just a little? Do you want to drop in on one auction and see what's happening or would you like to visit several? Let's take the next step and put your name on the dotted line.

Remember, this is a business!

Though you'll meet interesting people, have a great time buying and selling, learn a lot of fascinating trivia, and find some really great stuff, the truth of the matter is that the auction business is big time e-commerce. If you're willing to put in the time and energy, you could make a very good living buying and selling at auction.

Even if you're just online once a week and never spend more than 10 dollars, one of the most important things to remember is that auctions are a business—and no two people run their auction businesses the same way. Sometimes it can get confusing, especially if you're used to dealing strictly with traditional retail businesses. Yet with all the attention that's been focused on the auction community in the past couple of years, both buyers and sellers have become more savvy. People are keeping records of their transactions in a much more organized way, using specially made programs, and learning new methods of uploading their auction items or more efficient ways of sending e-mail and attachments.

The more auctions that open up, the more comfortable the whole business becomes. Cottage industries have sprung up with companies designing everything from programs to help you create more attractive Web pages to accounting programs specifically designed to include all the information necessary to keep auction records. Some companies are making a decent living selling the packaging materials so necessary in this business, while others are earning a living from offering online auction insurance.

The point is, whether you're a participant or an onlooker, you're peering into one of the biggest online businesses to come along since the Internet's debut. Even though it's a new and different venue, the online auction generally upholds the same standards as a real-time auction; you have every right to expect you'll be treated fairly when you buy something. On the other hand, you are also responsible for maintaining upright business practices.

One of the ironies of the fabulous success of online auction businesses is that more and more people are subject to fraud or getting ripped off. That gives you all the more reason to know as much as possible before making your first bid or selling your first item. So, come along with us and watch the action from behind the starting line.

What types of items are you selling/buying?

One of the first things you need to do is decide what you're interested in selling or buying. Walking into the sea of auctions without a goal is a little like entering a bullfight with no clue what you need to do to evade the bull. Sooner or later, you're going to have to face his angry snorts—just like sooner or later you'll have to deal with the details of what happens during an auction.

Timesaver
Make a list of your interests, wants, and needs before heading online. Then check out the categories where you think you might find those items. Preparing ahead of time will save the time usually wasted by surfing.

If you're like most people, you have several interests, and you might be surprised at how easily those interests can be satisfied with the vast array of items available at auction. Just during the time we've been writing this book, a number of unusual items have passed through auctions, as well as millions of what we'd call "normal" pieces. For example, we always find good deals on packing materials online, so that's fairly "normal," but how often would you go shopping for a prosthetic arm with a stainless hook? Both items were available for sale at an auction within the past month.

You don't have to be a collector to haunt the auctions. You might just need a new garage door opener, or maybe your computer needs to be upgraded, or you're having trouble finding that carburetor for the 1965 Dodge Dart your aunt left you in her will. You might want the latest Barbie for your daughter's birthday next week, or perhaps you can't find Alfredo's of New York Spaghetti Sauce since you moved to Timbuktu.

Chances are, you'll find all of these things on one of the major auction sites—and perhaps the prices will be better than what you'd pay at a store or through a private seller. Whatever the case, you're better off knowing what you're looking for before entering an online auction.

One of the most important reasons to know what you are going to look for is that it will determine which online auctions you want to explore. For instance, if you are looking for the perfect vacation, you probably won't go shopping at

Auction-Warehouse.com. (However, you'd be at just the right auction if what you wanted was computer hardware or software, because that's what Auction-Warehouse specializes in.) But you *might* shop at TravelBids.com, where you enter your desired destination, and travel agents bid on *your* business. Hmmm … an interesting twist in the auction game!

As we've discussed in the previous chapter, there are many different kinds of auctions. If you focus on the ones that will best fit your needs, you'll save yourself time and energy, and possibly some money. We have yet to meet an auction lover who's able to resist a good bargain—even if it's something she wasn't necessarily looking for!

Know your categories

If you're not quite sure what you're looking for, it's best to hit the big auction sites first and browse through their categories. If you're new to the business, it's best to familiarize yourself with the major auction houses such as eBay, Yahoo! Auctions, AuctionAddict, Amazon, uAuction.com, Auction, Inc., and Auction Universe. These auctions offer everything possible and all use basically the same type of subject breakdown.

The general categories include:

- Antiques (defined as items that are at least 50 years old)

- Automotive (often meant to include anything with wheels, including motorcycles and trucks)

- Books (eBay adds Movies and Music to this category, but some of the other auctions separate these three collectible subject headings)

- Coins and stamps (some major auctions list these items as collectibles)

- Collectibles (anything a person might think of accumulating)

- Computers and accessories (some auctions call this category "electronics")

Bright Idea
If you find an item that you like and the seller has a Web site, bookmark the Web site so you can check in periodically to see whether the seller has anything else you might be interested in.

- Dolls and toys (often these categories are separate)

- Jewelry (eBay includes gemstones in this listing)

- Photo (some auctions include electronics in this category)

- Pottery and glass (though eBay lists this as a separate category, you can find other related items in additional categories such as antiques or collectibles)

- Real estate (most auctions differentiate between vacation real estate, such as condos, and timeshares and actual residences)

- Sports memorabilia (you can also find sports-related items in the collectibles categories of most auctions)

- Travel (this category often houses travel real estate as well as tickets and destination packages)

Now that you have a general idea of where you're going, you can start surfing, and learn some more.

Where are you likely to be lucky selling a copy of the original sheet music from *Showboat?* What might be the best auction for finding a pair of tickets from the original Woodstock Music Festival? How about for getting Billy a copy of a Willie Mays rookie baseball card? Or where might you find the telephoto lens you need for the camera you want to take with you on your canoeing trip next week? Do you need a general auction or are you more likely to find what you need in a specialized auction? Might it be easier to surf through an auction search engine to see what's available?

We can give you the answers to all of these questions, but first, we must add a caveat: After you've decided where to shop and what to shop for, remember to always check out the current listings just in case what you want isn't showing up where you *think* you should be looking for it! One of the aspects of auction-buying that keeps customers coming back for more is the possibility that someday, somewhere, you're going to find an unexpected bargain that everyone else has missed.

Some of the questions to ask yourself about the items you are buying or selling are:

- Is there more than one term used to describe my item? For example, a magazine that features Elvis Presley might be listed under Elvis Presley memorabilia, movie collectibles, magazines, or even ephemera (anything short-lived or transitory).

- Would a bidder be more interested in the age of my item or its country of origin? (What's more important: the fact that the vase is 300 years old or that it's from Egypt?)

- Is the item one that a buyer might purchase impetuously (for example, a folk art windmill) or is it something people are specifically looking to buy (such as print cartridges for a Canon color printer)?

- Can I trade my version of this item for something someone else has? If so, maybe the specialty auctions are going to better suit my needs for buying and selling. (When involved with that type of auction community, your

Watch Out!
Remember, the easier an item is to find, the more people will see it and bid on it.

chances of finding the missing piece to your *Star Wars* collection or the ultimate Beanie Baby are much better in a collector's auction rather than surfing the millions of extraneous items in a large general auction site.)

- Would it be better if I conducted a specific search for my items with one of the auction-related search engines? (For example, you're looking for the last copy of a particular piece of art and don't have time to search each and every auction site. By using a search engine, you're saving time and checking many different types of auctions simultaneously.)

Watching the skies before you "fly"

Take the time to do a little surfing to familiarize yourself with the terminology, get a feel of the lay of the land, and understand the pros and cons of the various auctions.

One of the easiest ways to "watch the skies before you fly" is to pick out a common item and see whether you can find it on several of the major auction sites. For example, we have collected Marilyn Monroe items in the past and know they're plentiful on auction sites. If we searched eBay, Amazon, Yahoo! Auctions, and AuctionAddict for Marilyn items, chances are we'd come up with similar ones on each site. If we watched the hammer fall on several Marilyn dolls, for instance, we'd have a pretty good idea of what kind of bidding each site gets. And we could surmise a lot more from a couple of days' worth of snooping around.

How? Follow these easy steps:

1. Choose three or four auction houses you'd like to explore. (If you're not sure, look at the list

in the previous chapter or check appendix A at the back of this book.)

2. Conduct a search for a particular item (e.g., Marilyn Monroe postcards) either through the auction house's search engine or through an auction-related search engine such as www.bidfind.com. It's easier to conduct a search through an engine, but certain auction houses (like eBay) are not included in the findings, so it might be wiser (though slower) to go to each auction house separately.

3. Bookmark one version of the item in each auction house. (For example, although each of the postcards I bookmark might be different, they are all in the same category. If I get one representative item from each auction house, I'll be able to compare.)

4. Check in on the items at least once a day. Find out how many bidders are hoping to win the items. In what increments are they bidding?

5. When the auctions end, compare the number of bidders for each item, whether the piece met its reserve, whether you can tell how many times the ad was viewed (the more people who look at your items, the more you'll sell), and also notice important details about the bidders and sellers themselves. How high is their feedback rating? How many other auctions are the sellers running? Is there any way of communicating with the other buyers/sellers?

6. By watching a specific item in an auction, you'll literally have a sideline seat to the action. Though you're not participating, you are an active entity watching the process of the

Moneysaver
Know the retail values of as many of the items you're looking for as possible. You won't know if you're getting a deal if you don't know what the item would sell for in a retail market!

sale. If you keep your eyes open and watch the differences—both subtle and obvious—in each auction, you'll be a lot more comfortable when you enter the fray.

Which auction should you choose?

Now that you've nosed around a couple of auctions, you should have a fairly good idea which ones are the most powerful. Naturally, eBay is near the top of the list, as is Yahoo! Auctions. Depending on what kinds of things you like to buy, there are several other big names up there at the top of the batting order. Some buyers like Amazon, while others like the fact that Keybuy.com is one of the few auction sites that's completely free. The average buyer finds that AuctionAddict has a pretty good selection but no guarantees, while AuctionUniverse.com is easy to navigate.

All of these sites are what we call "general auctions," meaning that they have a little bit of everything. There are many other auctions, just as powerful though not as well visited, that specialize in certain categories. Here are some of the specialists (and you can find lots more, since they change every day, at Internet Auction List.com):

- **Art:** Art auction sites include everything from Sothebys.com, a traditional auction house linked with a Web site for the wealthy and knowledgeable art collector, to Artnet.com, which not only gives information about auctions of art, but also includes biographical info about artists, as well as recent news throughout the art world.

- **Autos:** You can buy a car at a federal government car auction (eqmoney.com/cars.htm) or a classic

British sports car (www.classic-car-auction.com).
Many local car auctioneers have Web sites, but
you still have to travel to the physical site to pick
up the vehicles.

- **Clothing:** Visit Clothingbids.com for wholesale
  clothing to the industry, and www.cowboy.net
  or VintageUSA.com for interesting vintage
  clothing. FirstAuction.com also offers women's
  apparel.

- **Coins and stamps:** Conducting a search for
  "coin and stamp auctions" brings up so many
  hits that you could spend the rest of the year
  just exploring the many auctions. Try
  Apfelbauminc.com, Sandafayre.com, www.
  stampauctions.com, and www.coinauctions.com.

- **General collectibles:** These are the items most
  collectible because of their price range and availability. You can find Beanie Babies, autographs,
  comic books, sports cards, movie memorabilia,
  political collectibles, and many other types of
  collectibles. General collectibles sites are great
  for the collector who's looking to build a reasonably priced collection. Some of the better sites
  include Popula.com, a slightly funky site where
  you can get cool Hollywood memorabilia, and
  BoxLots.com, which had a smattering of collectibles of all kinds when we visited. Collectors
  Auction (www.collectorsauction.com) not only
  has auctions of such collectibles as coins and
  cards, but also offers articles about the business,
  as well as an appraisal service.

- **Computers and equipment:** Many of the general
  auction sites have a large category devoted to
  computers and accessories, as well as quite a few

> **"**
> Consider the
> Source. High-
> rated seller feed-
> back (anyone
> with more than
> 50 responses and
> few or no nega-
> tives) is a good
> sign that a
> person-to-person
> transaction will
> work smoothly.
> —BiddersEdge.
> com
> **"**

computer auctions. Like other Web sites, these businesses tend to come and go, but here are a few of the ones that appear most stable: Bid.com (though not exclusively computer products, they have a strong selection and are reliable); Egghead.com (linked with SurplusAuction.com and OnSale.Com, this major computer sales site offers electronic products as well); and Haggle.com (mostly computers, both new and used, with a few other items).

- **Dolls and toys:** Doll Nation (http://mall.sitesolutions.com/ dollsbeanienationcomdollsshtml/index.html) has all dolls on its auction site, but appears young and unsteady on its feet. Theriault's, long known as one of the major auction houses to specialize in dolls, is entering the online market and should be up and running with online auctions by the time you read this. CollectingNation.com has a large Beanie Baby auction online, while PeddleIt.com specializes in—you guessed it—peddle-driven toys. It also has established categories for a lot of other items. Most of the toy collectors we know do their business in the big general auctions such as eBay, Yahoo!, and Amazon.

- **Jewelry:** Though most people in the know say that the best jewelry and antiques are found on eBay, there are many other sites that focus on just jewelry, such as Dicker and Dicker (www.dickeranddicker.com), which offers catalogs online for their auctions and accepts bids online, but holds the actual auction onsite in the traditional manner. Some interesting New Age jewelry is available at New Age Auction (www.newageauction.com), while traditional jewelry is sold at auction at Jewelnet (www.jewelnetauctions.com). You can search by designer (e.g., Tiffany), but the auctions don't seem to be very active. Gemtraders.com (www.gemtraders.com/auction/) is a fun site for both participating in auctions of gems and for getting information about gems and jewelry.

■ **Photo and electronics:** Photographicauction.com (www.photographicauction.com) offers not only photographs, but all of the photographic equipment a professional would need. When doing our search for photographic auctions, we discovered that there were quite a few "temporary" auctions being held at galleries and museums, so you might want to do a search for those. They change constantly, so listing any of them would be fruitless here. Auction-Warehouse (www.auction-warehouse.com) offers auctions on consumer electronics (as well as a lot of computer products). Cyber-Swap offers computers and electronics and some downloadable software (http://mall.sitesolutions.com/wwwcyberswapcom/index.html).

■ **Pottery and glass:** Pottery Auction.com (www.potteryauction.com) is the place where all types of pottery, porcelain, and ceramics are auctioned. Treadway Gallery (www.treadwaygallery.com) offers online catalogs of their auctions of pottery and links with Amazon's LiveBid auctions. Heckler's (www.hecklerauction.com/) sells antique glass and bottles, but their auctions are not online—they are traditional. Another traditional glass auction with an online site is

Bright Idea
Since there are new auction sites coming online all the time, it's wise to occasionally conduct a Web-wide search for the items you are interested in. You might find a new site and be able to enter the auction with little or no competition.

Pacific Glass (www.pacglass.com), with catalogs available for online customers. Just Glass.com (www.justglass.com) is just that: all kinds of glass objects at auction. Biddington's (www.biddingtons.com) has a good selection of art and antique pottery, porcelain, and glass.

- **Real estate:** A quick trip to InternetAuction.com brought up 80 traditional real estate auctions on the day we wrote this chapter. Most real estate companies have been auctioning property since the day they opened their doors, but the online auction community has started offering their own selections. The major online auctions have real estate selections, and Auction Advantage.net (www.realtycentral.com/auction/) is one of the best places to find real estate auctions on the Net. Bid4Assets (www.bid4assets.com) is an unusual auction since all of its goods come from foreclosures, government seizures, and bankruptcies—and its real estate offerings can be quite interesting.

- **Sports memorabilia:** Sports Auction.com (www.sportsauction.com) is one of the most active bidding sites, with the emphasis on baseball cards. Boekhout's Collectibles Mall (http://azww2.com/mall/) offers links to many different sports auctions, while Sports Trade (www.sportstrade.com/RwQS4apd/) lists featured auctions of more one-of-a-kind items, such as autographed memorabilia.

- **Travel:** Vacation Harbor (www.vharbor.com/) offers vacation real estate rentals all over the world, while BidTripper (www.bidtripper.com/) auctions everything from whole packages to just transportation. GoingGoingGone (www. goinggoinggone.com/going/homego.htm) auctions off cruises, complete vacations, and other interesting travel packages.

There are many, many more auctions available on the Net, but we have discovered that some of the smaller ones are here today, gone tomorrow, and we hesitate to recommend any that don't seem to have any action. You can always count on the big general auction sites to have a varied selection of goods available. The specialty sites are better for those collectors who are very savvy about their items and are looking for specifics. That type of collector usually gets quite frustrated wading through all the "other" items before finally spotting one he wants.

The charity auctions are good places to shop around for something interesting. They also offer you the opportunity to do something positive while you're having fun.

Test the waters in more than one place

Although most buyers/sellers would be perfectly happy staying in one of the large, general auctions, there are lots of reasons why you should test the waters at several different auctions. Having bidding/selling names in at least two of the large auctions and several of the smaller ones gives you distinct advantages. For example, if you're selling and the items you've got on the block at eBay or Yahoo! don't sell, you can always turn to one of the smaller specialists where there are fewer items competing with yours.

By registering in more than one auction, you're also allowing yourself the opportunity to see

Watch Out!
Many of the online auction sites that were active a year ago no longer are. Be sure to keep up with the ones in which you become involved. If they close, you lose any recourse in dealing with sticky situations.

whether the bidding is different, whether certain objects garner better prices, whether buyers and sellers are more likely to form tight communities, and whether you might be able to get a bargain. You can also check out the costs of listing items, the variety of items listed over an extended period of time, and the likelihood that you'll find items you'd like to buy or sell.

With the hundreds of auctions available online, there is no reason why half a dozen should be monopolizing the market (with one as its kingpin). Give the others a chance, test the waters, and see whether you might find treasures and sell them in various places rather than just one or two.

Moneysaver
Join the auctions that don't charge a registration fee, and you'll be able to both lurk and buy/sell without spending extra money.

Doing initial research

The first few times you explore an auction site can be very educational, if you know what you're looking for. When we were checking out sites for inclusion in this book, we watched specific control factors to decide whether the online auction was, in effect, active.

On your initial trip surfing through a site, check the following:

- Number of items up for sale.
- Number of average bids on a sampling of items.
- Average bid increment.
- Sampling of ending prices for an easily recognized item. (If you are familiar with computer items, check out the price of one that has already sold. Is the price higher than retail or did the bidder get a deal?)
- Number of bidders/sellers with high feedback ratings.

Checking out these variables will give you an idea of what kind of auction community you've entered, how many people participate, and the average number of items available. Naturally, these variables fluctuate, depending on the day of the week, the sellers involved in the auction, and even the time of year (at Christmas, auctions see a lot of traffic). For now, all you want to know is that there's someone else in the auction besides you, and that you're in an auction you can afford! (We checked out UltimateBid.com recently, and although we love the fact that you can bid on playing golf with Arnold Palmer, there wasn't anything being auctioned that was within our price range.)

Become a "lurker"

In the language of the Net, a lurker is someone who watches the action from the sidelines for a while, only rarely coming "out" to participate in a chatroom (or via personal e-mail) when they choose to say something. There are always lurkers in online chatrooms and one must not forget they are there. What people believe are private conversations are *never* private online.

So, what's the advantage to lurking? You get to see what's going on without spending any money, for one. You can also participate vicariously in an auction, pretending what you'd bid and seeing how close your guess comes to the actual closing price for the item. This way, you are testing yourself to see how comfortable you are with pricing (and you should be fairly comfortable with what you're going to spend or make before you put that first finger on the keyboard to make a bid). You will also be learning about the categories in which you lurk. Reading the descriptions of various items, surfing through

Unofficially...
Since 1994, the number of people online has more than quadrupled. Millions of buyers and sellers participate in the large online auctions, but millions more are happy to simply watch the action vicariously.

what's available, and searching for specific versions of your item allows you to ask questions of the buyers/sellers, if you want to. Lurking will also lead you into other sites, perhaps the home pages of a seller who specializes in exactly the type of item you are interesting in buying. By shopping a linked Web page, you'll step out of the auction action momentarily, but use that moment to learn more about the items that seller offers—and bookmark that page! You might want to go back to "visit" again sometime soon.

Though the word "lurker" has a negative connotation, lurking is a valuable way of educating yourself in the online auction business and everyone should practice it on occasion.

Online magazines that rate the various auction sites

There are several ways to get a handle on the news about each auction site:

- Two of the Web sites to watch regularly are AuctionPatrol.com (www.auctionpatrol.com) and Auction Watch (www.auctionwatch.com). These sites offer information about what's happening in the online auction world and sometimes provide ratings of the various sites.

- Newspapers like *USAToday* (www.usatoday.com/marketpl/auctions.htm) often offer articles or devote sections of their papers to online auctions, providing readers with information about the newest offerings in each of the major auctions.

- Newspapers and magazines that deal with collectibles, such as the *Maine Antique Digest* (www.maineantiquedigest.com/Welcome.html), are now online and offering up-to-date reports about the online auction industry, as well as the traditional auctions.

- eBay has its own magazine (www.eBay.com) that subscribers can now receive at home. It relates the latest news, including updates about services and articles about some of the interesting items offered during auction.

Talk to fellow surfers

Whenever possible, drop in to the chatrooms, message boards, or bulletin boards that are open to registered auction participants. Not only can you post want ads about the items you are searching for, you can also talk to fellow collectors/sellers about any help you might need to figure out where to place an item or where to look for one.

The relationships made in chatrooms and the deals struck by simply reaching out and asking whether anyone has answers to some of your questions are well worth the fee you sometimes need to pay to be part of the community of auction-goers.

Remember to follow the rules of Netiquette when entering any new chatroom. Be courteous, and don't forget to add your new friends to your e-mail address book. You never know when you might want to drop them a line about the new auction you're running—or perhaps give them some information about an item they might like to buy. Keeping an active address book is one of the smartest things a buyer/seller can do. When you get to the point of having a Web page, you can see that keeping the addresses of your customers, friends, connections, and family on hand will give you an instant "audience" to view your latest creation.

Timesaver
When reading a magazine, if you come across an ad for a Web site you'd like to check out later, jot it down in a little notebook devoted to "interesting Web sites." If you have one place where you store this info, it'll be a lot easier to find it when you have the time to "surf."

Just the facts

- Have a list of items you want to search for in hand before you enter the first auction. You'll save time and energy.

- The time spent researching various online auctions may seem like wasted time at first, but it will pay off when you decide it's time to buy or sell.

- It's often better for the collector to enter smaller, specialized auctions where there is less competition.

- Requesting newsletters and updates from auction sites keeps you up-to-date on what's being offered.

- If you enter a chatroom, you are likely to find people with your interests, as well as professional auction-goers who can answer your questions.

GET THE SCOOP ON...
How to check out the auctions ▪ The different
ways of registering ▪ How to set up online
escrow accounts ▪ Which auctions offer
protection and insurance

Setting Up an Account—or Two

Chapter 4

Most successful auction-goers report that they are registered in at least three auctions and are active in all. Some have stated that they register at every auction that they come across (as long as registration is free) because you can easily find the items you want to buy, or, conversely, sell something you might not have sold on another site.

Are there disadvantages to belonging to more than one auction? Yes, if you consider that you might spend a little too much money, or that you'll lose track of what you're buying or selling. However, those are issues that you need to personally consider. The benefits to belonging to more than one auction far outweigh the negatives.

In this chapter, we'll tell you how to deal with registering in different types of auctions, how to gauge the variances in auction rules, and, most importantly, the safest way to trade online.

How to register and what kind of online name to use

Each of the auctions currently online has a slightly different registration procedure, but each requires the following before you go online to register:

- Name, address, telephone number
- E-mail address
- The name you'll use while bidding/selling
- A password you'll remember

When registering on eBay and many of the other auctions, you'll be asked some personal questions, but you don't have to answer them if you would rather not. Generally, the auctions use these questions to determine the kinds of people who are joining the action (i.e., age, sex, hobbies, income, personal interests) in order to market their auction to people who might not be registered.

If you're an adult who might want access to the erotica or adults-only sections of any auctions, you will be asked to present a credit card number so that the auction can verify your age. This information is usually encrypted, so it's fairly safe. However, be aware that *any* information you give out on the Net can be found, should someone desire to badly enough (there's more about credit cards later in this chapter). There are professional hackers out there who make a living attempting to break codes, sometimes even bringing down whole Web site enterprises.

Recently a group of hackers disrupted service on Yahoo! for several hours, proving that even one of the best search engines has weak spots. In *Harper's* magazine last year, an interview with several Internet business owners, as well as a former FBI agent, revealed that even though they promise customers'

Bright Idea
Before registering with auctions, surf the sites that evaluate online auctions (such as AuctionInsider. com or Auction. Watch.com) to find which auctions might interest you.

information won't be shared, nothing they can do can completely prevent any hackers from breaking codes and stealing credit card numbers. However, the point was made over and over again that the chances of your card number being stolen is minimal. (The point was also made that the government doesn't "spy" on computer users, even though every step you've ever taken and every site you've ever looked at is easily accessed.)

Okay, now that we've warned you that Big Brother is watching, let's talk about the rest of the registration process.

Once you've entered the general information asked of you, you get to the fun part: picking out an online name. It's important that your name is something memorable since you'll need to enter it without a second thought upon entering an auction (and there's nothing more frustrating than forgetting your name or password when there's only three minutes left on the auction!). It's also important that you maintain some sense of anonymity. Using your real name as your user identification is not usually a good idea since you are broadcasting literally to the world. Though the online auction will have your personal information (your real name, address, telephone number, and e-mail address), you can maintain your privacy by using an online name that indicates something about your interests or what you might collect/sell without revealing your identity (for example, BarbieDollQueen or IM4Barbies). If it's a nickname that you give yourself, you'll be more likely to remember it.

Most computer users will tell you that to maintain online security and privacy, you should choose a password that isn't easily decipherable. Here are some

> **❝**
> I have a simple rule when I shop online: no lock, no deal . . . If I am not in secure mode when I am asked to supply my credit card, I log off.
> —Al Gordon, Boston-based consultant and contributing editor for the online newsletter "The Naked PC"
> **❞**

Watch Out!
If your kids or spouse know your password, it's almost as good as having your credit card in their hot little hands!

of the things you should remember about passwords:

- Don't use the same password at all the auction sites where you register.

- Use at least six characters/numbers or more. The more characters, the harder it is for a code-cracker to break.

- Stay away from any word that can be found in a dictionary. A garbled word or number/word combo is much tougher to break.

- Don't use something obvious (such as your name and birth date, your telephone number, or your child's birth date).

- Change your password every so often.

- Keep your various passwords easily accessible, but don't put them on a PostIt note that you stick to the computer!

Handling payment of your account

We've registered in at least a dozen auctions and checked out the registration procedures in lots of others. Depending on the auction, you can pay for your account in a number of ways, the most common of which is to enter a credit card when you register. However, some auctions don't ask for a registration fee and listings are free, so you don't have to worry about payment at all. And others have options that not only help sales but also make it easier for you to accept payment. For example, Amazon offers its sellers the option of having payment made with Amazon 1-Click, which gives the buyer the option of paying in whatever manner they want— and Amazon will forward the money right into your checking account. Nothing could be easier!

How many ways can you take care of your account? Here are the most common options:

- Credit card
- Online escrow
- Check
- Money order

The choice is up to you, but naturally, the safest way is to use online escrow since you'll be able to budget exactly what you're going to spend. (See more about this type of service later in the chapter.) With the other options, you don't really have control over how much you're spending because your expenditures are largely determined by how much your auctions cost (and you can't figure that out until the auction is over). For more information, check out Chapter 11 regarding how to pay for purchases or sales.

Do you need a credit card?

It's a lot simpler to have a credit card for those times when nothing else will do, but you don't need one to participate in auctions. If you're buying items, the deal is most often between you and the seller. If the seller accepts different types of payment, you can pay in whatever way you feel comfortable. However, there will be times when a seller insists on holding a personal check, so if that's your preferred method of payment, be prepared to wait a week to 10 days for your item, since that is how long it takes most checks to clear.

A credit card makes it easier to do impulse buying, so most people have and use them. However, if you would prefer not to use one, there are other options open to you, such as online escrow accounts, payment by check or money order, or shipment of your item COD.

There are many pros and cons to using a credit card online. Many people are nervous about giving private information like credit card numbers to sellers they don't know or who don't have high enough feedback levels to make the buyer feel safe making the transaction. That's understandable, yet it's also true that you often need a credit card to prove your age or identity when entering different sites (i.e., eBay requires you to register with a credit card if you're using a free e-mail service).

Whether you decide to use one or not, educate yourself about when it's safe and when it's not. Read on!

Using your credit card

Most people who have bought and sold at auction report that their credit card transactions went smoothly. Though we have a personal experience of getting charged for something that we didn't want by a Web site we'd never visited, our experience is not a common one. Millions of people have used their credit cards to purchase something online and the practice is relatively safe. However, there are certain precautions that you should take. Education is truly the key here.

When information is encrypted online, it means that the credit card number you are punching out on the keyboard is transformed into a series of algorithms, complex mathematical formulas that are essentially unreadable unless someone has a key (and that is the reason you look for the big yellow padlock before giving that information).

Up to this point, we've dealt with entering your credit card number when you're dealing with the Web site itself. If you're dealing directly with a seller,

Timesaver
When you are asked for any kind of personal information, such as a credit card number, look for the large yellow padlock. It indicates that your transaction is encrypted or encoded, which means it's safe. Some sites will tell you that they have a "secure server." A box will open on your screen and you should click on it so that you can access that security system.

you should never just write your credit card number in an e-mail. If a dealer is reputable, they will have the ability to accept your credit card information on their site, through a secure connection. Again, look for the yellow lock!

What about online escrow accounts?

With an escrow account, neither the buyer nor the seller can lose. What happens is that a third party acts as the go-between, assuring that the seller gets paid and that the buyer receives the goods. Both parties win here, because the seller doesn't have to wait to ship out a package. Confident that the escrow service will send the payment for the item as soon as the buyer notifies him that it is satisfactory, the seller can send an item as soon as the auction is over.

On the other hand, the buyer using an escrow service has the option of paying any way she wants, even if the seller doesn't have a merchant account (doesn't offer the option of paying by credit card). The buyer is also assured that the seller won't take off with the money before sending the goods.

If both parties in the transaction agree to use an escrow service, they usually split the fees (some of the services and what they charge are shown in the following table). Then the buyer sends the payment to the escrow service. Some will take all kinds of payment, while others are more particular. Once payment goes through, the service tells the seller to ship the item. The buyer inspects the item, makes sure everything is as expected and then notifies the escrow service. Immediately upon hearing from the buyer, the escrow service pays the seller, and everyone is happy.

There are a number of auctions that offer escrow services as part of their registration package, but there are also independent escrow services available that often work hand-in-hand with the auction houses.

TABLE 4.1: ACCEPTED FORMS OF PAYMENT FOR THE MAJOR AUCTIONS

Auction	Accepted Forms of Payment	Fees
Safe2Trade.com (Canadian company, offers choice of American or Canadian fund transactions)	Cashier's Check, Money Orders, Personal Checks and Business Checks. No Credit Cards.	Orders up to $5,000: Fee is 5% ($5 minimum); Orders over $5,000: Fee is $250, plus 1% of amount over $5,000.
Internet Clearing Corporation (www.internetclearing.com)	Discover, MasterCard, VISA, Wire transfer, Cashier's or Certified Check.	Buyer and Seller each pay 2.5%.
iEscrow (www.iescrow.com)	Electronically with VISA, Mastercard, American Express, Novus/Discover, Diners Club and Carte Blanche credit cards; through Wire Transfer by faxing credit card information to iEscrow; by mailing Cashier's Checks, Personal or Business Checks, and Money Orders to iEscrow.	Rates vary depending on transaction amount and the payment option the buyer chooses. Check the Web site for latest rate information.
D&M Internet Escrow Services (www.ibuyescrow.com)	Money Order, VISA, MasterCard.	Minimum and maximum transaction amounts are determined by form of payment. Fees range from 1–5%, depending on type of payment.

Moneysaver
If you choose to use an escrow service, make sure you split the fees with the buyer/seller.

Though we have offered information on a variety of online escrow services, you should be aware that there are others and that they all have different rates and accept different types of payments. Shop around until you find the one that will best suit your needs.

Should you pay as you go?

When you begin selling, you will incur fees at most of the auction sites (some notable exceptions are auctions.Yahoo.com, ReverseAuction.com, 4AuctionDeals.com, MakeBid OnSite Auctions 2000, Barter-n-Trade.com, Bidfarm.com, Polar Auctions (Canadian), SellAndTrade.com, and several others that allow buyers and sellers to participate in free auctions). The way you pay these fees is, again, your decision.

There are several different types of fees you can be charged as a seller, but most sites do not charge the buyer for bidding or browsing. The seller, on other hand, needs to consider whether the auction charges insertion fees, a charge paid by the seller to list the item (i.e., eBay charges 25¢ to $2.00, depending on the opening bid), commissions (on the final sales price), or any additional charges for such services as changing the typeface of your listing or specially placing your item in feature auctions or special categories. (For example, eBay charges $2.00 to put your item listing in bold, and $99.95 if you want your auction to be featured.)

If you've registered with your credit card, you can activate an automatic billing feature used by most online auctions. Your fees are deducted automatically, usually once a month. You can check your account at any time during the month to see where your fees stand, so you won't be shocked when you see your credit card bill.

The following table shows a dozen different auctions, all sizes and specialties, and the goods on whether they charge fees and commissions.

TABLE 4.2: AUCTION FEES AND SALES COMMISSIONS

Auction	Fees (Type and Amount)	Final Sales Price Commissions
eBay.com	Bold $2; Category Featured Auction $14.95; Featured Auction $99.95; Gift Icon $1; Gallery $0.25; Featured Gallery $19.95	1. Take the first $25 of your final value and calculate 5% of that. If your item sold for $25 or less, this is your Final Value Fee. 2. If your final value value was more than $25, take the additional amount (from $25.01 to $1,000) and calculate 2.5% of it. 3. If your final value was more than $1,000, take that additional amount and calculate 1.25% of it. 4. Add these amounts together, and you have your Final Value Fee!
auctions. Yahoo.com	None	Free
Amazon.com	Listing fee $0.10; Bold Listings $2; Category Features $14.95; Auctions Home Page Featured Listings $99.95	5% of $25 or less; $1.25 + 2.5% of any amount over $25 up to $1,000; $25.63 + 1.25% of any amount over $1,000
AuctionAddict. com	Free listing	Charges a commission on the final price. The commission is dependent upon which "membership level" the seller chooses when registering.
Auction First	Free listing	Charges a commission only if the piece actually sells. Sales Commission is 3% of the total sale up to $100; 2.5% over $100

continues

continued

Auction	Fees (Type and Amount)	Final Sales Price Commissions
		and up to $1,000; and 2% over $1,000 in the auctions and online stores.
Biddington's	Free listing	10% Seller's commission with a $10 minimum ($3.50 minimum on books). This commission structure may be changed with 30 days' prior notice. Commissions are deducted from payment due the Seller. (The Seller receives payment of 90% of the auction price + shipping and insurance.)
Keybuy Auction House	Free	Free
Auction Universe	Free	2.5% of the final selling price
Auctions. Excite.com	Free listing; Featured on Home Page $49.95; Featured on Category $9.95; Bold $2	5% from $0.01 to $25; 2.5% from $25.01 to $1,000; 1.25% over $1,000
Lycos Auctions	Free listing; Special Merchandising Listing Options: Home Page Listing $50; Bold Listing $2; Category Featured Listing $10	5% from $0.01 to $25; 2.5% from $25.01 to $1,000; 1.25% over $1,000
www. CoinAuctions. com	Free listings	5% of the final selling price up to $50, and 2.5% for any amount above $50
www. sportsauction. com	Charges a buyer's fee and shipping	3% of final bid (requires credit card number on file for sellers)

We've already talked about your choices for how to pay for the expenses you incur while selling,

Watch Out!
Remember that some of the fees you paid are going to be due whether or not you sell the item—or whether the buyer comes through with payment.

but some auctions offer other options (such as Amazon's 1-Click feature). Check with the auction you've decided to participate in and see whether you need to pay by credit card or whether you can use online escrow, payment by check, money order, certified bank draft, or another form of payment.

What are the rules?

Some of the rules are pretty basic, common-sense kind of things, like if you buy something, you stick with the deal and pay for it, and if you're selling something, you are honest about the item's condition, age, size, and so on. But there are other rules, as well.

Different auctions have vary slightly in what they expect from buyers and sellers, though most agree that certain items are simply not acceptable (such as the human kidney that was up for bids on eBay last year!). And certain actions are also not acceptable. If you are not selling anything illegal, you are pretty safe, but that doesn't mean you can sell anything you like. You must, first of all, own the piece (no stolen items, please!), and it must be as you represent it. And if you bid on an item and win it, you must come through with the money. Those are rules common to most auctions.

Now for the particulars of some of the auctions we've researched:

- On eBay, one of the basic rules for buyers is that they must e-mail the seller within three days of the end of the auction to claim the item. Sellers are also responsible for making that contact within three days. One of the ways eBay protects both buyers and bidders is by offering insurance, as well as feedback ratings, and their newest assurance, the SafeHarbor program, which deals with fraud, trading offenses, and illegally listed items.

- Yahoo! auctions doesn't give buyers a specific time frame in which to respond to the seller. They also do not tell the seller how quickly to respond. Yahoo! takes no responsibility whatsoever for their auctions; thus the transaction is left in the hands of the buyer and seller. Items that are not acceptable are illegal items, tobacco, firearms, alcohol, live animals, stolen goods, and items that "infringe or violate" another's rights (it's unclear what kind of items that refers to).

- Auctions.com's Rules of the Road state right up front that users must be 18 years of age or older. They also remind bidders and sellers that placing an item on the market constitutes a promise to sell and that bidding on the item constitutes a promise to buy, and that if anyone breaks any promises, they might be denied continued membership. Though Auctions.com states they are not responsible for the legality of the items sold on their site, they do reserve the right to take questionable items off the market. They also strongly warn against bid manipulation (bidding on your own items to drive up the selling price) and warn against soliciting bids.

- Because Bid.Com (a Canadian company) is the seller for all their items, their guidelines only cover bidding. Bidders must be 18 years or older and have a valid credit card. Bid.Com has very strict rules on the process of bidding and warns bidders not to place fictitious bids, as well as to remember that if a bid is made that is ultimately the winning bid, the buyer is responsible for making payment. The bidder's credit card is charged with the amount of the sale, as well as any applicable taxes and shipping fees. (U.S. bidders must bid on the American side of the site, while Canadian bidders bid on the Canadian side.)

- Biddington's (www.biddingtons.com) acts as the intermediary for buyers and sellers, holding the seller's payment until the buyer has received and inspected the goods. They ask that bidders be of "legal age and legally competent," warn against shill bidding and bid manipulation, and state that they are not responsible for inaccuracies in any seller's descriptions. Biddington's reserves the right to end any auction or fixed-price offering early, and to ban any user from its network at any time, at its sole discretion, without liability.

As you can see, each auction has its idiosyncrasies and its rules can change, so even though some rules are basic (such as age requirements), you should still review the rules set up by the auction in which you are participating. Not all of them are alike!

Being clear about the guidelines

Though most of the auctions employ guidelines, you must be aware that the reason there are so many auctions is because people have different needs. Someone who's quite happy with eBay may be surprised to discover that some of the independent specialized auctions might offer more for them. Bidders might also be surprised to see that some

Unofficially...
When stocks for some online auction sites went public recently, their initial prices shot up over $100 in mere seconds.

auction houses require them to register using a credit card. The reason for the credit card, in some instances, is to verify age; in other instances, it's so that payment is guaranteed. Make sure you understand why you are being asked for your credit card—and that the transaction is secure.

Most auctions are person-to-person auctions, while others are business-to-person or business-to-business, which means they deal with the transactions a little differently. How?

- In a *person-to-person auction,* you are dealing directly with the seller, who is probably a regular Joe/Joanne, just like you.

- In a *business-to-person auction,* you are bidding for an item made and sold by a company (no personal contact there, even though questions might be answered by a human being).

- In a *business-to-business auction,* businesses bid on items sold by other businesses (sort of like a wholesale market, where a business, such as a flower vendor, might go to a warehouse, buy a number of flowers from the larger company, and then return to the corner where the vendor sets up and sells small bouquets all day).

If you are a Barbie doll collector and you happen upon an auction that is a business-to-business auction, chances are good that you won't find any Barbie dolls. What you will find are companies who have excess inventory they want to sell—to other companies. Sometimes the sellers only want to sell to parties they know or with whom they've done business in the past. It's a waste of the collector's time to spend more than a couple of minutes in this site. Any more than that will cause a great deal of frustration.

Watch Out!
If you're unsure
about anything
in an online
auction's guide-
lines, ask! Send
an e-mail to the
site's customer
service depart-
ment or the
Webmaster.

By reading the guidelines carefully before plung-
ing in, you can tell whether the auction is for you,
whether the items are the type you want to buy, and
whether you can abide with any specialized "rules
and regulations" the auction states its customers
must follow.

You should also set your own guidelines before
you get any deeper into this business. What is it you
want out of an auction? What do you expect to give?
Are you going to be a buyer, seller, or both? By determining your own requirements, you can read any
auction's list of rules with an eye for how this particular auction might work for you. With so many of
them out there and new ones popping up every day
(and many going out of business, as well), you have
the reins in your hands. You have a choice. Make an
informed one!

Using chatrooms

Chatrooms, or the areas where collectors and dealers can talk to each other about the site—what's hot
and what's not, how to best use the tools of an
auctioneer, where to get supplies—and find questions to answers or solutions to problems, are the
places where auction-goers hang out. It's also the
place where you can "lurk" (read posts or discussions but not participate) and get the skinny on how
the site works, what kind of people are members,
and whether there's a buyer out there for a 1970s
Phyllis Diller album. You can learn the shortcuts to
using the site, find out what kinds of items are
garnering the most attention from the auction community, and be one of the first to hear about the
latest innovations in e-commerce by simply scrolling
through messages left by other members. And if you
really want to get into the thick of things, you can

leave a few messages yourself—either on a general bulletin board or by e-mailing other auction-goers directly.

Some chatrooms and online auction bulletin boards are open only to registered members of the site, while others are open to anyone who wants to surf in and lurk for a while. Since the terminology used and the access is different on each site, you should make it a part of your research to check out this feature of the site before you decide whether you want to stay. There's lots to be learned in chatrooms!

Here's how some of the major auction sites' chatrooms work and what kind of terminology the auction uses to define them:

- The term eBay uses on its home page is "Community." Click on this button to find the latest articles on eBay, get questions answered about HTML code or uploading images, read the newsletter created strictly for eBay users, find support for new users, and participate in discussions.

- The eBay Support Q&A board is open to anyone, member or not, and provides valuable answers to questions like, "How do I get information about what I've sold on eBay so I can file my taxes?" or "How do I find the item I bid on last night? I've forgotten the number." or "Can I get an eBay gift certificate for a friend?"

- The Community Help Board is broken down into many categories, so you can easily find the answers to your questions. (You can even do a search so that you don't have to wade through hundreds of other messages to find the answers.) And you don't need to be registered to check out this section.

- You *do* have to be a registered eBay participant to enter any questions or comments in the eBay Cafe. Although you can scroll through messages (and there are thousands), you can't answer any without entering your User ID and Password.

- Yahoo! Auctions' home page does not indicate a chatroom or bulletin board; however, if you click on "Help," you'll see a screen where there are many different places you can go to chat or find answers to your questions. The chatroom is not directly linked to the auction, however, but to Yahoo! in general. So, you might find answers to your questions or other auction-goers in that chatroom, but it's not limited to the discussion of auction items. If you click on the "Auction" button while on the Help screen, you'll get a search option that allows you to search for items you want, but the only answers to questions are those in the "FAQ" section of the site. The Chat Room calendar on the Yahoo! site is set up for special events, most of which involve celebrities or experts. None appear to be auction-goers talking to other auction-goers.

- Amazon.com has a "Community Guidelines" section that states their rules and regulations, but there are no open chatrooms or bulletin boards.

- AuctionAddict.com makes it easy to find their Community Center by using cartoon-like characters (whispering into each other's ears) to show you the way. Once you click on to the Center, you'll find a number of different chatrooms and bulletin boards, such as a General

Discussion Area, an Appraisal Area, a Fraud Watch, Newcomers Area, and a Wanted Board where you can post the items you're searching for—and hope someone out there has one they are willing to sell. Though you can go into these chatrooms and lurk for a while, you can't enter a conversation unless you're a registered AuctionAddict user.

Bright Idea
If you meet helpful auction-goers in chatrooms, ask for their e-mail addresses so you can keep in touch later. Add those addresses immediately to your address book.

- GavelNet.Com, an auction devoted to premium collectibles and decorative and fine arts, offers an extensive help section, but since they don't allow outside sellers to list things on their site, they don't see the need for a community bulletin board or chatroom.

- Times Auctions (www.auctions.nytoday.com) is the auction site for The New York Times newspaper. A fairly new site, it doesn't offer any chatrooms, bulletin boards, or community information—just auctions.

What else can you do in chatrooms? You can find out about the auction's rules, the success other buyers/sellers have had, and the best ways to use the auction's services. You can also "listen" to complaints and get a feel for the positives and negatives of the auction site. And you can learn about what's hot and what's not—and what's more valuable than that?

Know your rights

A few years ago, physicians started posting a patient's bill of rights on the walls of their offices. Before that point, patients often looked up to doctors as a type of god who could do no wrong, a person who held the patient's life and general welfare in their capable hands. Now more and more people are realizing that they *hire* the doctor and that the patient has rights.

So, too, do auction-goers. As a seller, you have a right to:

- Expect prompt payment from customers who are honest, forthright, and communicative.
- Be sure that checks from buyers will not bounce.
- Know that problems will be solved quickly (if the auction promises to act as intermediary).
- Expect that your well-wrapped packages arrive safely.
- Expect that any questions you have about the auction process will be answered by one of the auction staff.
- Rest assured that your personal information will not be released to the rest of the world by the auction house.

As a buyer, you have a right to:

- Feel confident that the items you are bidding for are exactly as the seller has represented.
- Expect that the goods you win at auction will be packed safely and shipped promptly.
- Rest assured that all of your questions to the seller will be answered promptly and courteously.
- Count on the seller to deal with any problems that might arise.
- Anticipate that the auction will protect you (if that is part of their contract with you when you register), but their protection and liability are fairly limited. Read the "fine print" to see exactly how much and what kind of protection the auction will offer.

Responding at the end of an auction

Each auction has a different spin on how quickly they expect buyers and sellers to connect once an auction is over. While Yahoo! lets the person-to-person contact be the responsibility of the buyer and seller, most others expect the buyer and seller to connect within a couple of days to a week. eBay gives buyers three days to contact sellers, but we have had some buyers contact us within hours of the end of the auction while others wait a week or more. Your right as a seller is to expect the buyer to abide by the rules of the auction; as a buyer, you are also expected to abide by the rules. However, there are times when people are ill, have personal problems, are on vacation, or are having problems with their computer, so make sure you build in a little bit of a cushion for those circumstances. What you *don't* want to do is to give a buyer/seller negative feedback *before* checking with her to see what the reason is for her non-responsiveness.

Most auctions now immediately send e-mails to both the buyer and seller as soon as the auction ends, so there is very little excuse for either to hesitate in making the contact to complete the sale.

When the buyer doesn't buy or the seller doesn't sell

Though we deal with this subject in detail in Chapter 15, "Packaging for a Safe Journey," let us state here that if you are in this business for a while, you are likely to have situations occasionally where a buyer doesn't come through with payment on time—or the payment isn't good.

eBay paved the way for other auctions to provide protective services for both buyers and sellers, but even with those services in place, there are times

Moneysaver
As a seller, you can save a lot of money by adding information about where to send the check to the e-mail you send to buyers at the end of an auction.

and circumstances where the online auction house is going to hand responsibility for dealing with the problem back to you.

If the buyer doesn't come through, first try to contact him or her. The second step depends on whether or not your online auction provides any recourse.

Here is an overview of what some auctions (other than eBay) offer for buyer/seller protection:

- Yahoo! offers no protection for either the buyer or seller. Transactions are in your hands once you sign on with them, and their guidelines specifically state that they are not liable in any way for problems. To be fair, they do offer suggestions for what to do in case bidders back out (wait three days and contact the next highest bidder).

- Amazon.com helps buyers and sellers solve problems by first attempting to contact either to see if there is a communication problem. If Amazon's Sentinel staff can't take care of it, they will assess a completion fee on the sale and sellers can request a credit. Buyers also have recourse and can count on Amazon's A-to-Z Guarantee (we'll tell you more about it in the next section).

- AuctionFirst.com is another online auction that expects the buyers and sellers to resolve their complaints on their own and takes no responsibility for any problems. However, they do make it clear that they won't tolerate any selling of illegal items or any fraudulent actions.

- AuctionUniverse.com protects both buyers and sellers through their BidSafe program, which guarantees transactions. For more on that, see the following section on insurance.

- Auctionscape.com offers the simple plan that sellers can sell to other bidders if the winning bidder doesn't contact them within three days.

■ Excite's Classifieds 2000 (www.auctions.excite. com) suggests that if you have problems with the sale, you first contact the bidder/seller, then resort to placing negative feedback, and finally, file a complaint with www.fraud.com. They note in their guidelines that they do not file complaints on behalf of customers.

As you can see, each auction deals with this situation differently. We again urge you to read the guidelines for both buying and selling when you are considering registering with any of the hundreds of online auctions.

The auction insurance plan

As we've already stated, most auctions have very clear policies about whether or not they'll provide support for buyers and sellers when the auction is over and something has gone wrong. Either they are there for you with a written insurance plan, or they are not there for you at all. It's as simple as that.

One of the reasons so many people stay with eBay is because of their insurance plan. The SafeHarbor plan instituted at eBay states that "Purchases will be covered for up to $200, less a $25 deductible. This will be provided to our users at no cost." Lloyd's offers this plan specifically for the eBay community, and users have reported it works quite well.

Amazon's A-to-Z Guarantee provides a refund to the buyer if the seller does not deliver or if the item is drastically different from the way the seller described it. Amazon requires that you wait 30 days after the close of the auction to submit a claim, at which time you have another 30 days to file a claim.

Timesaver
Once you've read the rules about what happens after a transaction, print them out so you'll have them readily available should you need them in the future. It's quicker to pull out your notes than to search for them online.

In other words, to use this guarantee, you must file within 60 days of the problem. Buyers can only use this service three times.

iCollector.com announced in November 1999 that they were about to launch the "highest insurance for e-commerce transactions on the Internet, designed specifically to protect customers of the icollector site." The insurance is called iGuarantee and covers items up to $50,000.

In addition to the insurance provided by some auctions, there are companies beginning to pop up who offer insurance for all Internet transactions. For example, TradeSafe.com acts as an intermediary between buyers and sellers during online transactions. The funds are escrowed while the seller ships the goods and the buyer inspects them. If the buyer is pleased, TradeSafe will release the funds to the seller. Although termed "auction insurance," this is basically an escrow fund corporation.

Unofficially...
During a program called "Summit in Silicon Valley" hosted by Tom Brokaw recently on MSNBC, one of the computer experts participating said, "You've lost your privacy. Live with it."

The privacy and safety of trading online

After all is said and done and all the warnings are posted, let us say that the security standards under which most auction companies operate are high. You are just as safe bidding online as you are when you give your credit card to someone over the phone. Yes, you are taking a risk, but the chances of your losing something you've bid on or of having a buyer back out on you are fairly slim. And you do have recourse, so you should use it.

In the near future, there may be a program instituted that will recognize your voice, thus making privacy issues less of a worry to those of us who do business online.

Though there are risks in using your credit card online, there are precautions being taken every day by all the auction sites and other e-commerce businesses as well. Security has been tightened and pretty soon, we will realize that the odds are in our favor that we will have safe transactions with others online.

Just the facts

- You should have a credit card and be prepared to use it in order to register as a seller.

- Though most auctions offer online escrow accounts, some deal with them differently.

- Be sure to read each auction's guidelines— not all of them have the same rules.

- You have several options if your transaction isn't concluded to your satisfaction.

- Online transaction insurance is available from other sources if your auction doesn't provide it.

GET THE SCOOP ON...
Reaching your target audience ▪ Setting up a
personal Web page ▪ Using online auction Web
pages ▪ Sending newsletters and auction
notices to former customers

The Importance of Making Yourself Known

Whenever you are in the market to buy or sell something, the hardest part of the whole process is getting the word out to the people you need to reach. Advertisers have been dealing with this conundrum for years, and you've probably realized by now that even the online sites have to reach out to the public in other ways, such as by placing ads in magazines or spreading the word via television commercials.

Even movies and television programs are reaching out to customers via the Internet. You'll notice that most TV ads now include the company's e-mail address or Web site. Check your local newspapers and magazines. The local grocery store may have a Web site or e-mail address, as do many doctors, lawyers, local craftspeople, nurseries, hospitals, plumbers, homebuilders, artists, writers, musicians, computer sellers, and just about any other type of businessperson.

People who buy and sell items have always known that it's important to spread the word about their products, and not just by placing an ad in the local newspaper or creating a commercial. Public relations means that the company or person is reaching out to the market—to the people—making their product known. Sometimes that means literally talking to people face to face, connecting a name with their product. Sometimes it means that the CEO of that company goes to parties or functions, subtly spreading the news that his company is in town or his product is on the market. And it doesn't have to be a product like a new gadget that opens everything in sight. The "product" can be the services a doctor has to offer or a new book written by the romance author who just moved into town. Or it can be the decorating services offered for free by the antiques business down the street.

Spread the word

Like any business, one of the first things an antiques shop owner does is to make up business cards. The next thing he does is tell his friends and family he's in business and start handing out those cards. Pretty soon, that shop owner gets a phone call from Mrs. Jones, who has a collection of pretty Dresden figurines that she needs to sell. The shop owner gives her a good price and his card, telling her that if she knows of others who might have something to sell, she should tell them about him. The word spreads, the shop owner gets more business, and the public relations "net" works to garner the businessperson the type of business he needs.

But is that enough? It used to be. During the years when the local shop owner just dealt with the people in the neighborhood, the business card and

Moneysaver
Create some business cards for yourself on your computer. You can buy packets at your local office supply store and save yourself printing costs. Make sure you include your e-mail address and Web site!

word-of-mouth was good enough. That was the way many doctors and lawyers started out, and even companies who are now giants in the industry depended on simple public relations techniques like spreading business cards or getting local newspapers to write articles about them in the beginning. But with the advent of the Internet, everything changed. We are no longer dealing with just the people in a neighborhood. We are dealing with the *worldwide* neighborhood. Today's customer might be someone whose face you never see; thus public relations has taken on a whole different spin and today's businessperson must look at things differently.

But why go to that time, effort, and expense to spread the word about my little online auction business, you ask? The answer is simple: If you want to make money selling items during auctions, or if you are hunting for the next Beanie Baby to add to your collection, you need to spread the word and make yourself known.

The ABCs of public relations

Public relations is just that: relating to the public at large. The way specialists in the field have been promoting goods, items, special services, or their own talents for many years is by simply informing the public at large—every chance they get. The key word is to "relate" the products/services you have to offer, and to keep on offering that information on a regular basis.

Let's first of all distinguish publicity from advertising. Advertising is the space you pay for in a printed publication (a magazine or newspaper), on-air moments (radio or television), or online ads. Publicity is free space in news programs, magazines, newspapers, and other media. Publicity and "news" are pretty synonymous; thus we can define publicity more succinctly as press releases, photographs, news stories, news releases, and press kits that you (or an agent) generate and send to the media for you or your business. The only thing you pay for when creating publicity is a public relations' specialist fee (when you can't do the basics yourself), the mailing, duplicating, photography, and paper costs.

Professionals versed in the many positive aspects of public relations have often said that persuading people to believe a certain way or to accept a particular point of view is all determined by how effective a person or company's public relations techniques are. Are you more likely to do business with someone who knows your tastes? In today's busy world, it's highly desirable to have some personal connection with the people who you buy from or sell to. Sometimes that only means that your name will be recognizable or that a person has bought from you once before, been satisfied, and will spread the word to buy from you again.

eBay capitalized on this simple public relations ploy when they created their "About Me" sites. By giving the buyer/seller a view of the person behind the item they're interested in buying, the seller/buyer can get a sense of whether they can trust the eBay dealer. One of the reasons eBay has succeeded is because it has a distinct knowledge of the positive feelings that personal connection creates. Even though many of us are sitting behind keyboards these days, people still want to know the person behind the product. In creating "About Me," eBay has provided its customers with that information.

Bright Idea
Before creating your own Web page, check out 20 to 30 personal pages (such as eBay's "About Me"). Then use the best ideas from all you've seen and create a Web page that will attract attention.

One group of people outside the online auction market who have mastered the art of public relations are romance writers. Romances constitute 50 percent of the novels sold in today's publishing world. During the past couple of decades, romance writers have realized that public relations tools are not only a cheap way of advertising, but also necessary to their careers. They must fight the stereotype that the romance author is a woman in her 30s who has a glamorous life. The truth is that most romance writers work regular hours, juggle checkbooks and families, only travel when they're meeting with other writers, and spend their days doing business. They work hard to keep their mailing lists current, get their books written on time, care for their public (romance fans are insatiable for more books— the genre is quite competitive!), and maintain a certain level of public relations.

Romance writers are some of the hardest working writers in the business. They know that being friends with the local journalist is vital, and every time they have a piece of good news, they'll dash off a press release, pop it in the mail to the newspaper, and rest assured that the article will be printed (most of the time) free of charge. In this way they succeed in meeting the number one rule in public relations: keeping their name before the public.

Our point? Online auction buyers/sellers could take a lesson from romance writers. Romance authors are so organized that there are several major annual conferences held in the United States that garner incredible interest from the media. These authors know how to launch a promotion campaign. They create bookmarks to hand out with their

Unofficially...
Successful auction sellers and buyers often run contests on their Web sites so bidders will return on a regular basis.

new novels. They keep extensive mailing lists and use them to send postcards telling friends, acquaintances, colleagues, and people of note about their new novels. They shoot off regular press releases to local newspapers, newsletters, and national magazines so that the public will know what they're up to. And most of them maintain their own Web sites, where chapters from their latest books, biography information, and recent photos offer the Net surfer valuable insight into the writer's product: their work.

Repetition is the key. All good teachers (and advertising people) know that in order to rest assured that your audience will remember you/your product, you have to repeat the information at least three times. Repetition is the key. So, if you're trying to sell something or to make sure someone remembers your name, repeat it three times. Repetition is the key. (Did you get that? Don't make me repeat myself!)

"Fine," you might say. "It's great that public relations works to make a name memorable, but you're talking about businesspeople; I'm just someone who wants to sell an item online. How will public relations work for me?"

The answer to that question is simple: If you're just going to go online once or twice and sell several items, you don't need to worry about anything other than putting your item up for sale and paying attention to the keywords you're using to identify it. (If you're one of those people, you can skip this section.) But if you're interested in a lucrative business selling and buying at online auctions, keep reading.

Conversely, if you really want to expand your search for hard-to-find items for your collection, consider using the media to assist you. It's never been easier to reach out to thousands (perhaps millions) of people. An appropriately placed ad on a Web site or word in a chatroom may result in an incredible find. You just need to know where to spread that lather of public relations froth!

Getting the word out often means spending a bit of time on your presentation (of yourself and your needs or of the product you're trying to sell) and exploring the way the media and Internet can help you expand your horizons. But that time will more than pay for itself in increased sales. Savvy business people know how to capitalize on their assets, whether those assets are physical or mental. There's no reason why you can't make the most of selling yourself or your products. That positive presentation of you, your product, and your needs to the world can make the difference between a mediocre hobby and a successful investment.

The creation of a good and effective press release is one of the first skills public relations specialists will learn how to use (we include a sample press release later in this chapter). They also learn that the common business tools that every person should have are business cards, stationery, a business phone, and a business address. Today that also includes a Web page and an e-mail address. If you get nothing else for your business, you need these basics to bring the news of your business to the people you want to reach.

Some reasons you should use publicity include:

- Announce a new business
- Announce changes/additions to an old business
- Tell customers about new items/new designs

Watch Out!
Remember that every word counts, whether you're writing an ad for a piece you want to auction, creating a Web site, or writing a press release. Choose the most specific and descriptive words and forget the vague ones such as "beautiful," "wonderful," "super," and "great."

- Relate important events like promotions, mergers, acquisitions, employee honors/awards
- Respond to changes in the market
- Discuss future business plans
- Celebrate an important sale or trade
- Announce a search for a particular item
- Offer a human interest story related to you, your business, or the items you collect/manufacture
- Report interesting information about the business
- Connect with a certain facet of John Q. Public
- Spread the news about a move, new shop, new employee, new line of goods, or new item to sell
- Tell readers about a new book (or collectors about a new item or creation)
- Share your accomplishments

The key to good public relations is using your time and energy wisely. Most of the media interested in being the conduit for public relations accept press releases and news bites for free. Why not use these tools to support and expand your online auction business? When you create a Web site, let your customers know. When you decide to make changes in the business, tell everyone about them. When your staff changes or grows, give the information to the local paper so that people can spread the word.

Is advertising necessary?

How many of you have bought an item because you saw it advertised on television or in your favorite magazine? If there's one person out there who hasn't been affected by advertising, I'll eat my hat (and the pages of this book, as well).

One of the reasons you need to advertise both online and in print is because there are millions of items out there in cyberspace. For yours to get noticed, it'll take a little work on your part. Yes, you can still sell items through online auctions with little or no advertising, but if you intend to make a business of this, you need to consider other options. Competition is still tough and the more people who enter the fray, the harder it will be for you to sell your items.

At first, the online auctions were wonderful, but when the items online started numbering over a million at a time, sellers started seeing a drastic drop in the prices they were getting and the number of hits they were getting on their items. Sellers then started realizing that the way they presented their items mattered, and sales of programs like Auction Assistant rose (see Chapter 10, "Auction Management Programs," for more information).

For every article sold in the world, there are at least two or more prospective buyers. Hopefully, your goods will be of interest to many more than two people. So, the first thing you need to do is identify your audience and then go after that audience. Offer them some information about the products that you'll regularly sell. Let them know how to contact you. Tell them why your goods are better that John Q. Smith's. Give them a reason to buy from you!

The best ways to reach customers/sellers

There are so many ways to contact buyers/sellers and to stir up some public relations that we hardly know where to start. But in order to best focus your time and money, a little research is in order.

Unofficially...
If you're planning on being in the business for a while but are not sure about how much to spend on Web sites, simply reserve a domain name for your business. You can "hold" the name and construct the actual Web site later, when your business is more solvent.

Ask yourself these basic questions to identify your target audience:

1. Who will want to buy my item?

2. Are there any organizations or associations devoted to studying or collecting the types of items I have to sell (or want to buy)?

3. Do these organizations/associations have a Web site or newsletter?

4. Are my items so unusual that they are in a category by themselves?

5. Am I up against retail sellers who might offer my item at a lower price? If so, how can I attract the same customers?

6. Are any of the buyers/sellers likely to be part of my hometown?

7. What occupations might the people who'll buy my item be likely to hold?

8. What kind of disposable income would those sellers/buyers have?

9. Am I appealing to a wide range of people or a very specialized group?

10. How have other people reached these sellers/buyers?

You might not come up with all the answers to these questions, but they'll give you a jumping-off point and start the wheels moving in your mind. The trick to successfully spreading the news about your product or your needs is to identify the people you want to reach. By asking yourself some of these questions, you'll at least identify some of the particulars. As you move along in this process, more pieces of the puzzle will fall into place. And as you meet more of the people involved in online auctions, you'll be able to ask them some of these questions as well.

Naturally, everyone will answer these questions differently, so we won't attempt to identify all the organizations or groups of people to whom you might appeal. Just to give you a rough example of what you would be up against, let's talk about Native American art and collectibles for a moment. Not only do we collect Native American art, we also sell it on occasion. Currently, there are many different categories our collectibles fall into, such as paintings, Hopi Kachinas, artifacts, pottery, baskets, blankets, and jewelry.

Each of those categories is divided into subcategories, according to collectors and buyers. For example, paintings could be oil or watercolor, contemporary or antique, done by one particular tribe or one particular artist. There are several organizations/associations that represent Native American artists and many magazines/newspapers that specialize in articles on the genre. A well-placed press release, article, or ad in one of these publications could result in the sale or acquisition of some paintings. One particular artist might have a fan club we could contact, or perhaps a certain gallery represents her and that gallery sends out a newsletter to all their customers.

In addition, perhaps the artist's hometown newspaper regularly does articles on her and an ad in that newspaper might attract people who own copies of the artist's paintings. And what about checking on the Internet to see if the artist has her own Web site? Perhaps we might be able to contact her directly.

See how many options we have? By spending one weekend putting together all our options, we could decide where we could best advertise our need to buy or sell items, then do a publicity campaign to kick off our business.

Bright Idea
Utilize the "notes" option of your e-mail address book to add a little information about the customers you're adding—for example, "collects teddy bears" or "looking for Superman comic books, ca. 1969."

There are many different ways to attract attention. Besides the press release we mentioned earlier, other types of publicity might include:

- Placing a small free ad in a local classifieds newspaper.

- Sending your local newspaper a picture of you with one of your best items and a suggestion that one of their writers do an article on your interesting collection.

- Hanging colorful copies of "wanted posters" in local supermarkets, stressing the types of items you want to buy or sell.

- Taking the same "wanted posters" to shops and asking them to pass them out to interested customers.

- Speaking to museum groups, computer clubs, classes, or associations about the types of things you collect or sell.

- Offering to do a free appraisal during a charity event for the high school or college in your area.

Those are just a few ideas. If you can think of more creative ones, go for it! Nothing is lost with publicity.

Some of the places where you might create good public relations include:

- Local newspapers

- Organization newsletters or informational brochures

- Company newsletters

- Church newsletters

- TV/radio "bulletin boards" or "community calendars"

- Public broadcasting channels with streaming video components (pieces of live or pre-recorded video)
- Local school/college newspapers and TV or radio stations
- Alumni newsletters
- Family letters/holiday cards
- Senior citizen center newsletters
- Collectors' magazines
- Specialty magazines (computer information, automobile enthusiasts, sports, women's issues, etc.), depending on what kind of items you are selling
- Hobby magazines/newsletters/newspapers
- Online chatrooms
- Online sites that specialize in your business/item
- Web sites that offer free advertising in exchange for a link to your site
- Your own Web site
- Web sites of friends and businesses that will link to yours

The possibilities are endless!

When you're creating a press release, poster, or ad, keep these tips in mind:

- Include your name, address, phone number, e-mail address, and/or Web page address.
- Be specific!
- Use the minimum number of words to get your point across.
- Make sure your grammar and spelling are correct.

Bright Idea
If you're going to write a press release to advertise your foray into online auctions, think about a "hook" (something special or interesting to attract a collector/buyer). For information on how to write a press release, check out www.webpr.com/primer.htm.

- Use catchy phrases and bright graphics to grab your reader's attention.

- Include the "why, how, where, who, and what"—the details you want readers to know.

Here's a sample one-page press release you might follow to introduce yourself and your business to the community at large. Use your imagination to contact as many people as you can with simple news like this:

Timesaver
Keep the names of the editors and addresses of all newsletters, newspapers, magazines, and Web sites in one file for quick reference.

TO: Any local newspaper

FROM: Mom and Dad Smith

FOR IMMEDIATE RELEASE: The world of collecting has spread via today's online auctions to our little town. Mom and Dad Smith, owners of Mom and Dad's Collectibles and collectors of Exciting Toys, have announced today that they have opened business on eBay/Amazon/AnyWebAuction.

The popularity of this highly collectible toy has prompted interest from the media all over the world. Recently, a very rare Exciting Toy sold online for a record price of $150. The news quickly spread through the collecting business, convincing Mom and Dad to introduce their own collection to the marketplace.

Their Web site on Some Online Auction provides information on their favorite Exciting Toys, how to handle them, and how to display them. In addition, Mom and Dad will answer questions from collectors and sellers alike.

For more information, contact Mom and Dad at their phone number or address, or by directly connecting to their online auction Web site at www.MomandDadSmith.com.

Setting up a personal Web page

Some of the online auctions, like eBay, have places where you can insert information about yourself, but if the auction you want to participate in doesn't, consider creating your own Web page. Not only is it useful when uploading information to your auction site, it also gives you the opportunity to spread the word about your business.

Most ISPs (Internet Service Providers) offer their members a certain amount of space on which they can place personal Web sites. Check with your ISP to see if this is a possibility. We have accounts with two different ISPs and both offer Web space to their customers. We have an "About Me" page on eBay, plus a personal page on our ISP, and another Web page where Dawn works.

Once you brave the waters and put together your first Web page, you'll discover it's not very difficult at all. Other books about online auctions take you through the secrets of HTML (Hyper Text Markup Language), but it's actually a lot simpler than it looks. Most word processing programs will let you save whatever you write in HTML. (Since other books deal with HTML in detail, we won't do so here.)

Online auction Web pages versus creating your own

We're assuming you know the basics of going online and that you're already connected to an Internet Service Provider, but perhaps you don't know the basics of putting together a Web page or uploading information to a site. More information about the actual step-by-step process of loading pics and other graphics is included in Chapter 9, "Should I Use Photos?" For now, let's just theorize about the possibilities of either creating an online auction Web

> **"**
> One of the first things I did after hooking up my WebTV and going online with eBay was to create a Web page to store photos for online auctions.
> —Bill Reno, eBay buyer/ seller since 1997
> **"**

page (which most auctions are offering free of charge to their sellers/buyers these days) or creating a Web page that stands on its own somewhere else on the Web.

Bright Idea
Remember that photos take a long time to load. Keep your Web page simple and link directly to your auctions, where the bulk of your photos are.

If you're going to include photos with the descriptions of the articles you'll sell at auction (and we suggest strongly that you do), you'll need a Web page. In order to get photos uploaded to an auction site or to sell, you need a Web page or image hosting service. (Some of the more well-known ones are listed below.)

As long as you need to create a simple Web page (and most ISPs don't appreciate it when their customers create a page that is obviously used just for storing pictures), why not make your Web page a place where you can invite other customers or sellers to see what you have available for sale? If you also include some information about what you like to do and who you are, you're likely to build the kind of trust it takes to get someone to buy from you or sell to you on a regular basis.

Even if you decide you don't want to do anything special with your own Web page, at least use the ones the online auction site will provide for you.

There are a lot of free programs on the Net that will walk you through the whole process, teaching you about HTML and how to insert photos, create an attractive layout, use different fonts, and insert buttons. Here are a few:

- Netscape Composer
- Yahoo!
- Global Cafe
- Microsoft FrontPage
- Dreamweaver
- Homepage

If you'd rather leave the Web page design to someone else, there are thousands of professionals offering their services on the Web. Or you can call the local college's computer department and see if a student would be willing to create your page for you for a small fee. Some might even be willing to do it for free if they can manage to get class credit for the project!

Some of the Web page designers online will also host your Web page and provide maintenance of the page (connections to search engines so Net surfers can easily find your information, regular checks to see whether your links are working, etc.) for fees ranging from $150 up. Most average around $250, which includes domain registration, hosting, support, and e-mail addresses. If you want a professional-looking site where people can order goods from you, this is the way to go. Having someone else design your site will allow you to spend your time selling (or buying).

We were going to list some sample Web page designers here for you, but a search on AltaVista.com brought up 30,000 hits, so our best suggestion is that you use your favorite search engine to do a little comparison shopping.

The following are places where you can get free Web site space or register your domain (your name). You should also check with your ISP. They often charge you approximately $20 a month to have access to the Net and an e-mail address—and most also offer Web space too. In addition, they might offer a short tutorial on how to upload your graphics and text, as well as tech support.

- Freewebspace.net
- Yahoo! Geocities
- xoom.com
- Angelfire.com

- Tripod.com
- Crosswinds.com
- pBay.com
- AuctionWatch.com
- Spree.com
- Internet-club.com
- Hypermart.net
- Freeyellow.com
- AOL.com
- Prodigy.net
- Fortunecity.com

There are many others all over the world, but these are the hosts that will come up on most search engines.

What kind of info should you include?

What you include on your Web site largely depends on the focus of your information. If you want to connect with other collectors, you might include some personal information. If the site is going to be purely business, then no personal information is necessary.

Here are some of the common pieces of information included on most Web pages:

- Your name/business name
- Names of other people associated with your business
- E-mail address
- Physical address (If you have a shop or business with a storefront, add the address. Otherwise, a post office box is wise.)
- Phone number
- Information about what you sell/collect

- Information about your other hobbies, pets, etc.
- Photos of some of your items
- Links to your online auction site or other Web pages
- Links to other sites (try to also get them to link back to you)
- A list of the items you want to buy or sell
- Information about when the page was created, by whom, and when it was last updated

Bright Idea
Make sure you register your Web site with as many search engines as possible. Hosts often run specials that will list a site with hundreds of search engines for approximately $50 a year.

Naturally, what you place on your Web page is largely a matter of personal taste, but you should be clear about the intent of your page before you upload it to the Web. Remember that anyone who surfs can find your page eventually, so you should only include information or photographs that you don't mind the rest of the world knowing or seeing.

What about pictures?
Remember the sayings "Every picture tells a story" and "A picture is worth a thousand words"? Well, both are true. If you're going to auction off your grandmother's pearls or the latest bootleg version of a concert tape, you need photos to show the buyers what they'll win if they bid on your auction.

Uploading photographs to your Web page can be done several different ways. When we first began creating Web pages, the only way to get a photo on was to:

1. Take the picture.
2. Get it developed.
3. Scan the photo.
4. Adjust the photo for size and clarity.
5. Insert the photo in the page.
6. Make sure the hyperlink is created.

7. Upload the page and the photo to the host via an FTP (file transfer protocol) program.

8. Add the photos to the auction online listing.

Some of you will still have to go through all those steps, either because you are scanning photos or your computer equipment isn't up-to-date, but today there are other ways to get photos of your item online, and they're a lot easier (thankfully!). Check Chapter 9 for more information about the different ways you can enhance your Web site or online auction page with photos.

But I can't write!

You've decided that a Web page is necessary and you've gotten all the basic information, but now you're concerned about how to add the text. You can't write? Well, rest assured that most programs have a spell check included in them—and if you create your text in a word processing program before inserting it on your Web page, you will also be able to check the grammar.

Most word processing programs created in the past five years or so include spelling and grammar checks. Use them! They'll help you clean up the mistakes you might not have seen, and by doing so, will help you create a site that will be easy to read and, more importantly, easy to find. And remember: All errors are NOT caught by spelling and grammar programs. Be sure to proofread your text carefully.

Make a few notes for yourself before you write the text for your site or your online listings. Then follow these guidelines:

1. Use the minimum number of words necessary to describe your item or deliver your message.

2. Make sure all words are correctly spelled.

3. Use a clear, easy-to-read font (no special, fancy fonts—they're difficult to read and are often not accepted by other personal computers).

4. Make your text interesting, but stay away from overdoing it with exclamation points and question marks.

5. Don't use profanity.

6. Keep it simple.

Now that you have everything together, you're ready to present yourself to the world, and you've probably learned enough so that you'll feel 10 steps ahead of the game. One of the reasons we decided to discuss this step before talking about buying and selling is because we know that once you start trading, you won't want to stop the auction to learn everything else!

Just the facts

- Public relations tools such as business cards, press releases, and Web sites can be powerful tools for an online buyer or seller.

- A Web page is the best way for sellers to showcase their goods and for buyers to let sellers or other collectors know what they're looking for.

- Online auction Web pages (like eBay's "About Me" pages) are a free and easy way to advertise your goods as well as to give buyers/sellers information about you and your interests.

- ISPs often offer free hosting services for personal Web pages.

- Free tutorials for creating Web pages are available online.

- Photos are a necessity when you're selling online.

Buying at Auction

GET THE SCOOP ON...
Determining when and how to bid ▪ Protecting
yourself from overbidding ▪ Researching the
items you're bidding on ▪ Finding the items you
want to collect

The Right Way to Bid— or How Not to Get Auction Fever

Chapter 6

One of the reasons so many people love auctions is the rush of adrenaline they get when the hammer falls and they've won the item they've been bidding on. It makes you feel a little like a child at Christmas, a little magical, a little like an unexpected gift. Because that feeling, that rush of excitement, is something that is pleasurable, people seek to experience it again and again. And some get caught up in that rush and lose sight of what they really want and how much they want to spend for it.

This chapter is designed to put a bit of a damper on that overwhelming urge to bid, bid, and continue to bid. Yes, it's fun to buy at auction, and no, we don't want to ruin that pleasurable feeling you get when you've discovered you have placed the winning bid, but we do want you to be aware that bidding can become a tad dangerous—you could possibly pay too much for something you really don't need, or not pay attention to the piece's defects and, ultimately, experience a major disappointment.

Are these big problems? No, not really. As long as you educate yourself ahead of time and remind yourself that you need to keep that education ongoing, you should be able to pick yourself up and dust yourself off if you have an occasional setback. Take it from many people who have spent years running or bidding at auction: Auction fever exists and human beings make mistakes. If you are careful, you can minimize or avoid these mistakes altogether and still have a good time at auction.

Buyer beware!

The adage "buyer beware!" is especially good advice when buying at auction. What it essentially means is that you are responsible for your own actions at an auction. You are the one who needs to ask questions, touch the object, smell it (if necessary), look for all imperfections, and make a mental note of how much you would spend for the object. If you don't thoroughly check out the items on which you wish to bid, you have not followed one of the most important rules of an auction. And that rule is doubly important when you're bidding in an online auction where you *can't* touch or smell the items you're bidding on.

You might laugh when we talk about the sensory details when buying at auction, but we've seen far too many rug dealers with their noses buried in the fibers of the rugs they're considering buying. That sense of smell is important to collectors of textiles, as well as other items. That's one of the things that handicaps an online bidder. We don't have the added information supplied by our other senses to

Timesaver
Keeping the simple reminder "buyer beware" on a sticky note on your computer screen can save you hours of time and many dollars' worth of heartache!

help us determine whether we want to purchase the item.

Not only are your senses handicapped when bidding online, you are also temporarily blind about whom you're buying from. The person who's selling you the goods is pretty much faceless and nameless until the end of the auction when addresses are shared. Some online auctions offer some kind of rating system so that you are at least aware of whether anyone has had a problem with the seller in the past, but you must take additional precautions.

It's very easy to get caught up in auction action, especially during the last moments of an auction when you're not quite sure your bid made it in on time to win the treasure you've been searching for, at a price you can barely believe. You hold your breath, hoping that someone else won't surf in at the last moment and steal the bargain or the piece you need to complete your collection. For that brief moment, all your senses and sensibilities are cast by the wayside. You don't have time to e-mail the seller to ask a question, and the photo you're seeing on the screen isn't very clear. Do you take the chance? Are you willing to gamble? Think about it before you bid. Sometimes that one- or two-second pause is worth hundreds in time and money saved.

You only have yourself to blame

One of the hardest philosophies to accept is that you are responsible for your own actions. If you didn't spend enough time researching the item or got in a bid at the last moment and paid more than what you should have, you can't turn around and make the seller suffer because of your all-too-human error.

Instead of sending the seller a nasty e-mail or returning the item, think about whether you were

Watch Out!
Don't promise to pay for something by check if your credit card is maxed out. It's easy to win a bid, but it's not always easy to pay for it—especially if the rent is due!

carried away by auction fever. Here are some questions to ask yourself about the item, the seller, and yourself, and some actions you might take to prevent mistakes in the future.

Ask yourself about the item:

- Do I really need this item or am I just bidding to get in on the excitement?

- How much have I paid for similar items in the past?

- Is this piece necessary to my collection?

- Will the piece ship easily, and will it be inexpensive to ship?

- Can I tell what this item's condition is?

- What about the age of the piece?

- Are there any identifying marks I should be aware of?

- Would I buy this item for this price if there were still six days left in the auction, or am I just bidding because I'm in on the final moments?

- Can I truly afford this? Is buying this item going to change my budget for the month?

Ask yourself about your own intentions:

- Do I really need the item on which I'm bidding?

- Do I have space for this item in my house?

- Am I satisfied with the way the item is described, or is there some question in my mind?

- Am I bidding for the excitement or for the item itself?

- Do I find myself online at all hours of the day and night, searching auctions for something to bid on?

- Do I feel I've failed if I haven't bid on anything during my time surfing the auctions?

- Am I neglecting my family and friends so that I can spend my time placing bids?

- Am I monitoring how much I'm spending on items?

- Do I pause to think before bidding?

- Am I getting lax about doing research on the items I'm buying?

- Do I explore all the options of gathering information about the pieces I'm buying?

- Have I considered the financial implications of buying the item? Am I maxing out a credit card or not paying a bill in order to buy the object up for auction?

Ask yourself about the seller:

- Is this a new, inexperienced seller?

- What is the seller rated?

- Has anyone said anything negative about this seller/auctioneer?

- Is the seller located in another country (if so, are the additional shipping charges noted in the ad)?

- Does the auctioneer/seller reveal all shipping and handling charges up front in the ad?

- Has the seller offered all obvious information about the piece upon which I'm going to bid?

- Has the seller placed a reserve on the article? Has it been met?

■ What kind of payment does the seller expect?

■ How professional looking is the seller's ad? Are there any hints that the seller might not know much about the article he or she is selling?

■ Has the seller offered any kind of guarantee?

■ Is the item sold "AS IS"/"No Returns"?

Now that you've gone through a veritable library of questions about yourself, the item, and the bidder, it's time to think about how to prevent the problems that can arise from impulse buying. Here are some suggestions for the future:

1. Set a specific time each day to place your bids.

2. Check out all the information about the piece and the seller *before* placing your bid. A second spent now can save time and heartache in the future.

3. Be honest with yourself. Check out your financial situation before bidding on something that can put you in hock indefinitely.

4. If you can't control your spending, consider having a family member or friend share the auction action with you. When there are two people involved in a transaction, one of them can usually offer some logical advice to the other.

5. If you don't have all the information you need to make an educated purchase, pass on the item. There are millions of objects being sold every day in online auctions. The chances are good you'll find a similar item.

6. Don't make a bid if it's over your budget. You might be able to recover from that first expense, but later on, you could be in a heap of financial trouble. Learn to control your expenditures early in the game.

7. Do some comparison shopping. Check out what your item might be bringing in another auction. Using one of the online auction house search engines, such as AuctionInsider. com, do a search that will look for your item in a number of online auctions rather than looking in just one. If you're satisfied that the prices you find for your item are comparable to what you intend to bid, then bid on!

Educate yourself

One of the best ways to make (and save) money in the online auction business is to educate yourself about the items you're bidding on. You can build an immediate sense of confidence when you have all (or most) of the information you need about an item. Because so many bidders online are collectors, we offer some sources here that might help in the research process, but because of the enormous number of items sold at online auctions, there will be categories we can't cover. You'll see that there are innumerable sources in print and online that can help answer any questions you might have. The point is that you should always strive to make an educated decision when participating in an auction.

Buyers should know what to look for when purchasing at online auctions. Because there is so much to learn, be patient with yourself. Don't expect to know everything about the product. Even those people who sell the same items over and over are often amazed at how little they know. Later in this chapter we offer specific tools for getting started, but for now, keep in mind you should know something about the item before you place that first bid.

Unofficially...
Statisticians have noted that 90 percent of auction-goers have made a bid on an item they did not consider buying before coming to the auction.

Rush—and lose!

As we've said, you need to know exactly what you're bidding on and why. If you think you might not need the item or you might not be able to afford it, stop and reconsider before bidding on it! Take your time. Try to get into the auctions early, keep an eye out for the types of items you want, and don't get carried away by auction fever.

Watch and learn

If you're new to a particular online auction, it's a good idea to lurk for a while before throwing in your first bid. Visit the auction site whenever you have a spare moment. Watch how many items are online. Try to figure out which categories are the most popular.

Look for telltale signs regarding the sellers:

- Does the auction site rate their sellers? If so, how?

- How many average bids do the items have?

- Does the auction appear to be specialized?

- What do the ads look like? Are they professional?

- Are the sellers listed in more than one auction site? (Check the ads and see whether some of the sellers' home pages also list other auctions.)

Sometimes it'll be to your benefit that there aren't too many bidders on a site. Sometimes there won't be enough bidders simply because the auction is new or it hasn't received enough publicity. We have entered some chatrooms where we can almost hear our own voices echo. In fact, recently we were doing research for this book and went into one auction's chatroom where there was only one message, asking whether anyone was out there bidding. There was no answer. This can be good for those of you who are looking for specific items to fill out your collection. When you have a lot of competition, the prices will be driven higher. So, check out the other auctions besides the most popular ones. You might find some bargains!

Save time by putting in your highest bid first

Though auctions are getting more and more savvy about letting you know where you stand against the other bidders (even to the point of encouraging bidders to carry pocket-sized computers that beep or send messages when you've been outbid), one of the ways to make sure you get the item you want, at the price you want to pay, is to put your highest bid in first.

Think about it this way: If you are in the market for a new computer program and you know that the local computer market just had the same program on sale for $24.99, it would be safe for you to bid $20 for the program. You know you'll be getting it for less than at the computer store.

How does it work if the current bid for that program is $5 and there are six days left for the auction to play itself out? Basically, anyone who leaves a bid of more than $5 will get a message that someone else has outbid them. Unless someone bids more than $20, you are the winner. And if no one bids more than $10, you get the program for $10. Your bids go up sequentially, depending on whether someone is bidding against you—and you have already capped your own bid at $20, so you won't be tempted to bid more than that amount.

Doesn't that make a lot more sense than chasing down each item you're bidding on and making sure you're in at the end of the auction? Save yourself time. Bid your highest amount first, then wait for the e-mail message that tells you you've won the auction!

Doing your own research about an item's worth

Sometimes you need to find out a little more about the items that you're bidding on before taking the next step. If you're not quite sure what you are buying (or selling), it might be necessary to get some help.

Timesaver
Subscribing to a newspaper or newsletter that focuses on your area of interest will often serve you by offering articles and (surprise!) information about online auctions you might not have known about.

Using the main category listings in six of the major online auctions (eBay, Amazon.com, Yahoo!, UTrade.com, Auction First, and AuctionAddict.com), we have put together a list of the most common categories and various sources for researching items that fall within these categories. You also should check out the appraisal services offered by the auction sites themselves.

Antiques

- Collectibles Books (www.collectorsbooks.com). Books are separated by category. Chances are, you'll find the book you want on your specific topic (as well as many others).

- Ruby Lane (www.rubylane.com/). This site offers links to many others, a searchable database that contains millions of items, a newsletter, and a list of shops associated with this search engine. It's a great place to begin a search and acts like a labyrinth of antiques, collectibles, and auction information.

- National Association of Dealers in Antiques, Inc. (www.nadaweb.com). This association lists all the appraisers, separates them by category, and provides information about the expectations the association has of its members. NADA thoroughly examines all members and offers links to certain members' Web pages.

Art

- Artline (www.artline.com). This site features certain artists and offers an auction of art. The site connects to other sources of research material on art and artists.

- Guild.com (www.guild.com). This site offers information on artworks by discipline, as well as by artist. Has a selection of books about various topics. Sells artwork as well.

- World Wide Arts Resources (wwar.com/java/index.html). This site offers a chatroom where you can talk to others interested in art and possibly find the information you need.

- *Who Was Who in American Art* (Sound View Press). This book, and others like it, is invaluable when you are trying to identify an artist.

- *Jacobsen's* annual painting and bronze price guide. This guide is now out of print but still available from some used bookstores or online booksellers such as bibliofind.com. Its listing of auction values for certain artists gives you a general idea of what the artist's works are worth.

Automotive

- *2000 Edition Ultimate Collector Car Price Guide.* Written by *Car & Parts* magazine, this book

Timesaver
If you have a specific interest, keeping a library of books on the subject is a good idea and will save you the time of looking up the information on the Net.

gives information about the most collectible cars and their values, as well as loads of pictures you can use for researching the vehicle you are trying to buy.

- *Car Memorabilia Price Guide* (Krause Publications). The authors of this guide, Ron Kowalke and Ken Bottolph, offer 740 photos plus invaluable information about the values of all types of items pertaining to cars.

- PL8S.com (www.pl8s.com). This Web site, devoted to license plate collecting, offers an interactive way to see the license plates produced in every region of the world. It also provides links to other sites where you can further research this collectible.

- The Auto Channel.com (www.theautochannel. com). A heavenly site for anyone interested in cars or anything to do with them, Auto Channel offers a chatroom, a media room where you can pick up the latest news, information on new car prices, research materials on classic automobiles, and other valuable information, as well as connections to other sites.

- Corvette Club of America (www.corvetteclubofamerica.com). One of the many organizations devoted to collecting certain types of cars. You can find information about the vehicle(s) you're researching, as well as lots of cool collectibles you might want to add to your own collection.

Books

- The major online bookstores (Amazon.com, Barnes & Noble.com, Powell's Bookstore, BooksAMillion, Borders, FatBrain,

WordsWorth). These offer information about the authors whose books they handle. Some of them also link with other sites, where you can discover exactly what certain books are worth.

- *Old Book Value Guide 1999–2000* (Huxford). This guide lists over 25,000 titles, many commonly known.

- *Old Magazines Price Guide* (L-W Publishing). This guide covers a good portion of the magazines published in English, offering dates of publication, values, and special information.

- *Autographs (Collecting) Standard Guide* (Baker). Because books and other paper materials rise in value if they are autographed, this guide is a good tool to use when researching items that are signed.

- Society for the History of Authorship, Reading and Publishing (www.indiana.edu:80/~sharp/intro.html). This association was formed to study the history of publishing. Their site offers information about books and certain publishers. It does not offer information about what certain books are worth, but it does list many valuable links. Historically, this site offers more connections for bibliophiles interested in researching the history of their works than others we've seen.

- ABAA (Antiquarian Booksellers Association of America) (www.abaa.org). This site lists all the dealers who belong to the association. It has a feature that allows you to search for the title or author of a specific book. It also offers articles about collecting books and has a Collectors' Corner feature, where you can contact dealers

Bright Idea
Joining associations that specialize in your favorite collectibles will sometimes offer you the added benefit of newsletters, as well as provide personal connections with other people who share your interests.

or collectors for the information you need to
sell your book.

- International Book Collectors Association
  (www.rarebooks.org). This site offers anything
  necessary to the person researching how much
  a book is worth, including information about
  authors, the essentials of collecting, grading
  books, identifying first editions, and getting
  appraisals. It even gives information about
  what is *not* collectible.

Clothing

- Victorian Elegance (www.gator.net/%7edesigns/
  links.html). This Web site has over 50 links to
  many other vintage clothing and jewelry sites all
  over the world where you can buy, sell, or
  research your clothing.

- Piece Unique (www.pieceunique.com). Advertised
  as an online store that sells unique used clothing,
  this is a place where one might browse to see
  whether the clothing is anything like the piece
  you want to sell. Compare prices here before selling or buying.

- *Vintage Clothing 1880–1980: Identification and
  Value Guide* (Americana). This book, written by
  a vintage clothing dealer, is the most comprehensive of all the vintage clothing guides.
  Others specialize in certain areas, but this one
  covers the whole century.

- Costume Society of America (www.
  costumesocietyofamerica.com). This association is dedicated to educating and preserving
  ways of dress. They publish a magazine, have
  national and regional members, and offer
  symposiums about clothing.

Coins

- Professional Coin Grading Service (www.pcgs. com). This service will authenticate and appraise your coins for a fee.

- Numismatic Guaranty Corporation (www. ngccoin.com). Like the previous service, this Web site offers appraisals of coins.

- *Coin Prices* (www.coinprices.com). This periodical has long been valuable to coin dealers and collectors. The Web site offers a streaming value index (CCDN Coin Market Index) and there are articles, book suggestions, and indications for what is hot and what is not.

- Numismatists Online (www.numismatist.com). This site offers auctions, information about dealers, and the world of coins.

- *Coin Connoisseur: The International Magazine for Investors and Collectors* (www.coinmag.com). This site offers articles about rare and interesting coins, spotlights collectible coins to watch, offers links to Internet auction sites where you can find coins, and provides a resource directory that lists experts and dealers.

Collectibles

We highly suggest you search for each collectible separately, but if you're not quite sure what you have, some of these resources might help you identify it. From there, you should do a full Web search for your item, and we can pretty much guarantee you'll find a Web site out there devoted to it. If you don't, check with Harry Rinker's site or the Kovels' site (see below) for more information.

Bright Idea
If you have an interest in a certain collectible, join a group of people with the same interests and find out if they have an online newsletter. Subscribe to the newsletter and get the latest info on the collectible and its value—as well as valuable connections with others who might be able to offer more information.

- The Price Guide Store (www.priceguidestore.com). The guides are separated by general categories and go from the general to the specific, as far as what kinds of collectibles are covered. The books are sold at discounted prices.

- CollectingChannel.com (www.collectingchannel.com). This site is jam-packed with links to all kinds of information about every type of collectible. It also connects to appraisers, newspapers, and magazines for the collecting world, museums, registries, and so on.

- Harry Rinker Enterprises, Inc. (www.rinker.com). Rinker has long been a figurehead in the collectibles business. He is known for maintaining research files and a vast library of information, and has been offering publications to collectors for many years.

- Collectors.com (www.collectors.com). This site appears to have information about all types of collectibles, but we had a difficult time getting into it and navigating. Perhaps you'll have better luck.

- Ralph and Terry Kovel (www.kovels.com). The Kovels have been publishing books, newsletters, and articles about antiques and collectibles for many years, and their searchable database on this Web site is very useful. They also offer a unique five-year market trend graph so collectors can see whether their item's value has peaked or is about to.

- *Antiques and the Arts Weekly* (www.thebee.com/). This newspaper is well known for its coverage of antiques, arts, and collectibles. Its news articles often give in-depth information about collectibles of all kinds. It also offers a link to an antiques reference library that lists hundreds of books and other materials useful in research.

- The Best Antiques and Collectibles Site on the Web (www.computrends.com/antiquering/). This Web ring offers links to a number of antiques and collectibles sites. If you can't match up your item with what is offered on some of these sites, the Webmaster suggests you wait a moment.... The good thing about Web rings is that you can travel to similar sites and always find your way back to the beginning. Often we've discovered that we can research more effectively this way—especially when we haven't a clue what the item we're researching is worth.

- *Antique Trader Weekly* (www.collect.com/ antiquetrader/). The newspaper version of the *Antique Trader* has been around for 40 years. They update every Wednesday morning. The Web site is packed with useful information, searchable, and equipped with a listing of their advertisers, as well as links to their Web sites.

Comics

- Cyber Comic Store (pages.prodigy.com/source/ comics.htm). This site offers information about collectible comics and pricing, a newsletter, and links to other sites.

- CollectiblesNet (www.collectiblesnet.com/ comics.htm). This site lists wanted and for sale ads—mostly comic books and comic-related items, although there are a few other collectibles included.

- *Collectors' Showcase* (www.collectiblesnet.com/cshowcase.htm). This magazine offers articles about comic books and similar items, as well as information about the latest auctions (online and in person). The online version offers links to other sites.

- 4comics.com (www.4comics.com). This site offers a search engine with links to the publishers who create comics, some retailers who sell rare comics, and news/reviews of interest to comic collectors.

- Comic book links (www.westol.com/~informer/links/comic.html). At this site you'll find a group of links to certain comic book characters, publishers, artists, dealers, and collectors. It's certain to satisfy just about every comic book collector. There's a very thorough selection of sites.

- *Overstreet's Comic Book Price Guide* by Bob Overstreet. Well-respected in the collectible comic books world, Overstreet has been writing his price guide for many years. A new edition with updated prices, photos, and information is printed every year.

Computers/electronics, hardware/software

- The Computer Museum of America (www.computer-museum.org/). This museum, established in 1983, might offer research information to those who collect computers or computer hardware/software. They are located in La Mesa, California.

- The Computer Museum of Boston (www.mos.org/tcm/tcm.html). Located within the Museum of Science, this museum often has

Timesaver
Bookmark or save the sites you find while researching and then file them in folders so they'll be easy to find when you try to find more information about the subject.

special presentations and is putting together
an exhibit of the history of computers from
the 1940s forward, scheduled to open within
the next couple of years.

■ PriceGrabber.com (www.pricegrabber.com/
index.php3?mode=findwhat). This searchable
site lets buyers look at the best prices for
computer software and hardware, electronics,
cameras, and all types of accessories. This is a
good source for a seller who wants to find out
approximate prices before putting an item up
for auction.

■ Cyber Surfer Computer Resource Centre
(www.cyber-surfer.com). This resource lists all
types of computers, laptops, software, proces-
sors, sound cards, video cards, and other
components, claiming to have kept track of
the developments of each. It's a historical
resource with lots of information for those
interested in learning more about their
collectible computers/computer parts and
devices.

Dolls

■ Dolls.com (www.dolls.com). This loaded site is
designed for the doll collector who wants to do
everything in one place. Buyers, sellers,
appraisers, traders, and researchers are all
encouraged to share the wealth.

■ Doll collecting (http://collectdolls.about.com).
Here you'll find an ongoing discussion about
collecting dolls, with links to other sources and
a chatroom where dealers/collectors can discuss any kind of doll.

- Barbie (www.barbie.com). The official Barbie Web site offers all kinds of information for those who collect Barbie dolls. The site is searchable, offering a place where you can purchase the dolls, as well as a section on collectible Barbies, in which the history of the doll is discussed in detail. The site also offers a preview of the special edition Barbie dolls offered in the near future. There are lots of photos.

- Madame Alexander (www.madamealexander.com). Like the Barbie site, the Madame Alexander Web site offers historical information, a listing of dealers, connections to collectors, and photos. It also houses a store where collectors can buy the newest Madame Alexander dolls and get a peek at what's coming up in the future.

- Raggedy Ann and Andy (www.raggedyland.com). Devoted to the history of the raggedy dolls, this site offers information about the creator of the dolls, Johnny Gruelle, as well as prices, links to dealers, information about a newsletter, and a festival devoted to these popular dolls.

- *Blue Book of Dolls and Values* by Jan Foulke. This book is one of the best known for identifying dolls of all types. Though dealers and collectors often refer to it, some have said that other books have better information on contemporary dolls.

- *Modern Collectible Dolls Identification and Value Guide* by Patsy Moyer. This guide is loaded with photographs, listings, and values for dealers and collectors.

Moneysaver
Free e-mail newsletters are often available from collecting associations, museums, and dealers. Ask if they have one when you log on to their site.

- *200 Years of Dolls: Identification and Price Guide* by Dawn T. Herlocher. This guide to dolls is separated by category instead of by individual dolls. The sources for pricing are varied and thorough, other reference books are listed, and 200 categories are covered.

- *Dolls Magazine* (www.dollsmagazine.com). For 17 years, this magazine has helped to inform collectors of trends, showcase new dolls, provide histories of old dolls, and connect the collectors' community with the dealers. Now they also have a searchable Web site sponsored by the publisher, Collector Communications Corporation.

- United Federation of Doll Clubs, Inc. (www.ufdc.org). This association publishes a magazine called *Doll News* and offers research and archival library services (ReAL Services) for its members. They also sponsor conferences, meetings, traveling seminars and lectures, and an annual national convention. They also offer links to other doll-related sites. Basically, any research you want to do can be done from within this organization's site.

Home and garden

This is a huge category that is incredibly difficult to divide. Though we've offered some suggestions for beginning research here, we suggest you search for specifics or you'll be overwhelmed by the information offered. The best place to start is right in the auction pages themselves. See how others are listing their items before you attempt to list yours. Then find an expert for an appraisal—especially if you don't know anything about the piece you're trying to research.

If your item appears to be antique, your best bet is to go to a general antiques site (e.g., The Best Antiques and Collectibles Sites on the Web) and search from there. Or you might try one of the appraisal sites (i.e. Eppraisals.com).

■ AntiquesWorld.com (www.antiquesworld.com). This site offers a wide variety of books to help collectors identify items. This selection is devoted to country items and includes *300 Years of Kitchen Collectibles; American Colonial Architecture, Its Origin and Development; Collecting American Country: How to Select, Maintain, and Display Country Pieces; Encyclopedia of American Farm Implements;* and many other books that are devoted to the homes and gardens of yesterday.

Timesaver
Find household and garden implements at online auctions and decorate your living space with items you might have to otherwise travel hundreds of miles to find.

■ Architectural Antiques of Boston (www.archant. com/). Based in Boston, this company sells at shows and out of a shop, as well as online. They also answer questions and welcome requests.

■ Southern Accents Architectural Antiques (www.antiques-architectural.com/). This company offers appraisals for $50 per item. They sell from their shop, as well as over the Net, and are located in Alabama.

■ Doors of London (www.doorsoflondon.com/). This architectural antiques catalog from England offers "one-stop shopping for the best of British architectural antiques, gathered from locations throughout England." The site also offers links to view their architectural antiques, as well as their reproductions. Surfing through this site provides a good lesson in how reproductions differ from the real thing.

- Home & Garden/About.com (toledo.about.com/ local/midwestus/toledo/msubmenuhomegarden. htm). This site offers links to other home and garden sites for information about furnishing, decorating, collecting, and remodeling/repair.

- The Treasure Garden (www. treasuregardenantique.com/). Here you'll find a catalog of antiques sites from around the world. The site is divided into a number of categories, into which items are catalogued. It's useful for research—just match your item to the picture.

- Garden Park Antiques (www.gardenpark.com/ antiques/). Located in Nashville, Tennessee, this site provides information about the architectural and decorative antiques they offer, as well as definitions of antiques terminology. It's great for reference.

Jewelry

- Gems.com (www.gems.com). This simple site offers photos of various types of gems and jewelry, prices, and a connection where you can ask for more information.

- Jewelcollect Auction (www.playle.com/jewels/). This auction site is a good place to browse and research the jewelry or gemstones you're interested in selling or buying. It includes a message board, as well as links to other sites.

- Costume jewelry (costumejewels.about.com/ hobbies/costumejewels). About.com offers links to many sites that feature costume jewelry. This site also provides articles about specific aspects of costume jewelry, as well as information on auction procedure and the highlights of what's up for sale around the world.

■ 999fine.com (www.999fine.com). Devoted to Native American jewelry, this site also connects to the Arizona Gold Exchange. The items are accompanied by photos and prices, which helps the researcher learn the approximate value of a piece.

■ Accredited Gemologists Association (aga. polygon.net/index.html). The site is not meant to be a research tool for those interested in jewelry, but a resource where one can find appraisers of gems and jewelry.

Watch Out!
When reading ads for your item in auctions, watch the way they are worded. If the seller has said the piece of jewelry "looks to be" solid gold, it means she doesn't know.

■ American Society of Appraisers (www.appraisals. com). A quick search for gem/jewelry appraisers on this site brought up a hundreds of certified appraisers in locations all over the world.

■ *The Official Identification and Price Guide to Antique Jewelry* by Arthur Guy Kaplan. This book offers over 4,000 black-and-white photos and information on 200 years' worth of jewelry. It claims to be the only comprehensive guide of this field.

■ *Collectible Costume Jewelry: Identification and Values* by Cherri Simonds. This text offers hundreds of color photos, warnings on how to spot fakes, and other important information. This book received great reviews from Amazon.com customers.

Movies

We strongly suggest that you search by the movie or actor/actress, as well as in the general movie category (horror, science fiction, action, etc.) because collectors/dealers tend to specialize in this category.

- *The Official Price Guide to Movie/TV Soundtracks and Original Cast Albums* by Jerry Osborne. Osborne has written many movie and music-related collectibles books. Check his listings in Amazon.com or Barnes & Noble.com.

- *Hollywood and Early Cinema Posters* by Bruce Hershenson. A "must have for film lovers," the poster reproductions might help movie buffs identify their film or the actors in it.

- *Lyle Price Guide: Film and Rock 'n Roll Collectibles* by Anthony Curtis. Often difficult to find, this guide is the most recent to cover the entire movies field (as well as all of the collectibles generated), and offers prices and information. Some of the prices might be dated, but the photos and general research info are invaluable to the collector.

- Film Collectors International (www.film-collectors-intl.com). The site offers a search feature, as well as items currently on sale. The collectibles include posters, lobby cards, inserts, and photos from all over the world.

- ScoreLogue.com (www.scorelogue.com/main.html). Designed to focus on the music written for movies, this site also maintains archives of interviews, the best movie scores of the century, a daily forum, and links to other Hollywood-related sites.

- *Images: A Journal of Film and Popular Culture* (www.imagesjournal.com). This site offers reviews, general information, critical essays, and articles about subjects related to movies and television. There's more in-depth research material than just prices and date information.

Unofficially...
In a recent auction of Marilyn Monroe memorabilia, single items that would normally be considered "boring" sold for hundreds of thousands of dollars.

- Movie Posters (www.blarg.net/dr_z/Movie/Posters/). This dealer offers photos and prices of posters from all over the world. The photos help the researcher and the prices he offers can give you a start on pricing your own movie collectibles.

- Hollywood.com (www.hollywood.com). This site tends to concentrate on current movies and celebrities, but it does offer a shop and articles on the business. It's a good place to go if you have something recent that you can't identify, but it won't give you any prices.

- Hollywood Toy and Poster Co. (www.hollywoodposter.com). This massive online store sells posters, photos, books, toys, scripts, and all other types of movie memorabilia. In addition, they offer 2,800 titles in their searchable database. The only negative about this site is that there aren't enough photos of the items being sold.

- Christie's(www.christies.com/departments/pac/overview. html). Here you'll find an article written by Christie's specialists that focuses on the film industry and the collectibles it has produced. Christie's also offers a film auction and does appraisals of movie-related memorabilia, as well as online auctions

Music

Another huge area of collectibles, this category can be broken down by instrument, type of music, musician, singer, and so on. We've suggested some general resources, but, again, be as specific as possible when doing your search for further information.

- Last Vestige Music Shop (www.lastvestige.com). This online and storefront shop specializes in music collectibles. They offer thousands of CDs and vinyl.

- *Alternative Records Price Guide* (Goldmine's). This guide includes prices and photographs of over 12,000 items.

- *Sheet Music: A Price Guide* by Debbie Dillon. This guide features over 5,000 entries, covering music from the early 1800s to the late 1900s. All are accompanied by their approximate value.

- Vintage Instruments (www.vintageinstruments. com). Though not an exceptionally fancy site, this company gives lots of information about the instruments they have to offer and even includes sound bites with some. In addition, their specific descriptions are incredibly detailed and should help with research.

- Fiske Museum (www.cuc.claremont.edu/fiske/ welcome.htm). Located at Claremont College, this museum of musical instruments houses over 1,400 examples of instruments from around the world. It also links to other sites that might be of interest to the researcher, such as the American Musical Instrument Society.

- Rock and Roll USA (www.rocknroll.com). This online store links to sites for the artists themselves, as well as radio sites, links to concert tickets, and specific information about broadcasts in the industry.

- The Music Mart, Inc. (www.musicmart.com). Though this site specializes in print music,

Unofficially...
More than 60 percent of sites that sell musical items also feature free downloadable songs or sound bites, the perfect way to "test" the music to see whether anything on the site is of interest to you.

collectors will be happy to note that there are
categories for all different kinds of music, and
the site has an internal search engine that
enables the user to look for a particular style of
music, instrument, or songwriter.

- Internet Music Hound (www.bandstand.com).
  This site searches for particular music sources
  on the World Wide Web and links to a number
  of sites specific to certain kinds of music. Some
  of the sites might be helpful for research.

Photographs and photographic equipment

- *Cameras, Antique and Classic* by McKeown. The
  world's leading camera guide, this book
  includes thousands of photos and over 10,000
  listings of all types of cameras made all over
  the world.

- *Collecting Photographica: The Images and
  Equipment of the First 100 Years of Photography* by
  George Gilbert. Originally published in 1976,
  this book contains information and photos
  of various equipment, as well as types of
  photographs.

- *Photographica, A Guide to the Value of Historic
  Cameras and Images* by Charles Klamkin.
  Loaded with photographic plates, this book
  gives lots of details and valuable historical
  information about cameras and assists the
  collector in identifying certain types.

- Photographica (www.photographica.com). At
  this site, dealers and collectors can search for
  different kinds of cameras and photographs.
  Here you can buy, sell, or research any type of
  photographica, as well as make connections with
  people who can help you identify your items.

- George Eastman House International Museum of Photography and Film (www.eastman.org). This museum, located in Rochester, New York, houses all kinds of cameras and photography. It also acts as a conduit for the education of people interested in researching the topic, offering information about the different development processes, as well as programs and services for various age groups and school levels.

Pottery, glass, porcelain

If you know the particular company that made the piece you're trying to research, we suggest you first search for the company name. These other sources are general ones you might use if you're not quite sure who made your piece of pottery, glassware, or porcelain, or when it was produced.

- *The Encyclopaedia of British Pottery and Porcelain Marks* by Geoffrey A. Godden. This book is a valuable resource tool for collectors who need to identify marks made on British pottery and porcelain. Each company, as well as its years of production, is identified.

- *Imperial Glass Encyclopedia, Volumes I & II* by James Measell. This two-volume set includes information about thousands of items made by the Imperial Glass company, photographs, identifying features, and a comprehensive index of the different types of glassware available.

- *Kovels' Bottles Price List* by Ralph and Terry Kovel. Over 12,000 prices and 350 photos are included in this volume, designed to help the novice to the advanced collector in identifying collectible glass bottles.

Timesaver
Discerning the correct maker's mark (the color of the mark, wording, number) on a piece of pottery or porcelain can save both time and money for a buyer and/or seller.

- *Flow Blue, a Collector's Guide to Patterns* by Jeffrey Snyder. Hundreds of color photographs and an easily referenced index accompany this book about one of the most popular types of chinaware collected today. Values and ages of most pieces are given to help collectors identify patterns and their history.

- *The Collector's Encyclopedia of Limoges Porcelain* by Mary Frank Gaston. This book is filled with color photos and easily identified pieces of this French porcelain. The company is still in existence, so this volume helps collectors discover the different phases that the Limoges Company has undergone through the years.

- *Kovels' American Art Pottery* by Ralph and Terry Kovel. Hundreds of plates, marks, and companies are identified in this concise volume, which also contains over 700 photos.

- Graylings' Antiques (www.staffordshire-figures.com/). Specialists in Staffordshire figures, this antiques shop is both online and storefront. They offer a search feature for finding items they might not necessarily have for sale.

- Ohio Pottery (www.ohiopottery.com). Pottery collectors who visit this site can get information about such famous pottery-making companies as Shawnee, Hull, McCoy, Watt, and Weller. In addition, the site links to other pottery sites, resource books, online auctions, and pottery collectors' events.

- Clarice Cliff Collectors' Club (www.claricecliff.com/). Made during the 1920s and '30s, this Art Deco pottery has attracted a large enough following to warrant its own Web site. This

United Kingdom site offers information about the artist, the patterns of pottery she produced, and free advice to the collector.

- Westmoreland Glass (www.jcwiese.com/). The J. & C. Wiese Collectibles shop not only offers all types of glass made by Westmoreland, but also links to the Westmoreland site, as well as to sites offering more books on glassware collecting.

- Early American Pattern Glass Society (www.eapgs. org/). Formed in 1994, this society offers information about American pattern glass and all of the companies who produced it. They produce a newsletter called *The News Journal* and hold an annual convention for collectors of pattern glass.

- Noritake (www.noritake.com). This official company Web site offers historical information about this popular porcelain, as well as connections to its home page in Japan. The site also gives information about retailers in your area.

Sports/recreation

Because each sport has specialized collecting groups and hundreds of items that collectors might like identified, this category is broad and unwieldy. We suggest that you do specific searches for your item within the larger resources we've provided here. Search by sport, team, athlete, or type of item.

- Professional Sports Authenticator (http:// psacard.com). This Web site is devoted to identifying and selling sports cards of all kinds. They offer an appraisal service, as well as auctions.

- Collectors Universe (www.card-universe.com/). Devoted to all types of collectibles, this site has good information about sports cards. Prices

Bright Idea
Always ask about an item's condition. If the item is breakable, you want to know if it has a hairline crack. What might not be bad in the photo can turn out to be a real problem when the piece is being shipped.

and evaluation services are included, as well as articles.

- Sports Collectors Universe (collectors.com/ sports/gallery). This site is divided into the various sports and includes information about collectibles in each one (baseball, basketball, football, hockey, and miscellaneous). Autographs, cards, and miscellaneous collectibles are included.

- NFL History and Card Collecting (www.angelfire. com/tn/pkholling/). This site provides historical information about the football leagues, and includes a section devoted to collectible cards and other links. It provides Super Bowl histories, links to NFL sites, and a wealth of information for the collector.

- SAM, Inc., Sports, Accessories and Memorabilia, Inc., Bobbing Head Dolls and Figurines (www.bobbing.com/). This site is the place for all information about bobbing head dolls and sports figures of all types. They have built an archive, as well as information about dealers of these figures.

- Turn4Racing (www.turn4racing.com/). Designed for race car enthusiasts, this site devotes itself to buying and selling items. It is categorized by driver and sells diecast models.

- *1999 Sports Collectors Almanac* by the editors of *Sports Collectors Digest*. This book offers information on all types of sports collectibles, identifying features, and pricing.

- *Coykendall's Complete Guide to Sporting Collectibles* by Ralf W. Coykendall. This book offers information about football, baseball, fishing, hunting, and other sports collectibles.

Stamps

- The American Philatelic Society (www.west.net/
  ~stamps1/aps.html). This Web site includes
  information about the society, membership, its
  affiliates, and dealers. It also offers searchable
  listings and verification.

- St. Rowlands Stamp Collecting Guide
  (collectstamps.about.com/hobbies/
  collectstamps/library/blguide.htm?iam=ma).
  This site includes many links to stamp collecting sites, information from experts, articles,
  newsletter connections, and news about the
  latest stamps on the market.

- *Linn's Stamp News* (www.linns.com/). The
  largest stamp newsletter on the Net, this
  weekly e-zine provides collectors with the latest
  news about the stamp collecting industry, as
  well as links to a stamp market index, a basic
  glossary of terms, a postal history, and collecting basics.

- *Top Dollar Paid: The Complete Guide to Selling
  Your Stamps* by Stephen R. Datz. This book is a
  mere 167 pages, but collectors we've talked to
  say it's a good source.

- *The Official 1999 Blackbook Price Guide of United
  States Postage Stamps (21st ed.)* by Marc and Tom
  Hudgeons. Collectors say this book is comprehensive, informative, easy-to-read, and invaluable. It deals with stamps from 1947 to 1997,
  with indexes and photos.

- Smithsonian National Postal Museum (www.
  si.edu/organiza/museums/postal). When all
  else fails, ask the Smithsonian! They have a
  library, online exhibits, collections, and education services.

Watch Out!
The words "rare"
and "collectible"
are not synony-
mous. Before you
buy something
you believe to be
one-of-a-kind, do
some research!
Too many people
have been burned
thinking they
have found the
only copy of the
Declaration of
Independence.

Toys

This is another huge category that houses many smaller categories. Search for your particular toy first. If you can't find the toy, search for the company. If that fails, try the general category or some of the following resources.

- AntiqueToys.com (antiquetoys.com/collecting. html). This site, run by Santa Barbara Antique Toys, offers information about toys, links to toy collecting sites, appraisals, a history of toy collecting, and help in getting started.

- *Star Wars* Toy Resource Page (pages.map.com/ starwars/). One of the many movies that has spawned numerous toys, *Star Wars* fans generated many Web pages full of information (this is only one). This resource is included here to show you how much you can find out about a company or type of toy by doing a simple search.

Watch Out!
If you are selling a toy, don't discard the box it came in, no matter how torn or tattered. An item in its original box is always more valuable than one without.

- Toy Soldier and Model (www.toy-soldier.com). Designed for toy soldier and military figure collectors, this Web site offers a bookstore, magazine, information about the newest figures and where to get the toys, and a classified section where buyers/sellers can advertise their wares.

- Toy Collecting (toycollecting.about.com/ hobbies/toycollecting/mbody.htm?iam=ma). Packed with links about all kinds of toys from Barbie dolls to Pokémon, antique to modern and anywhere in between, this site also offers links to magazines and newspapers, a chat room, a forum where collectors can ask questions, and sources for where you can shop for toys.

- Hakes Americana (www.hakes.com/index.asp). Hakes has written about antiques and collectibles for years and has specialized in toy auctions in the past. Now he's got a Web site where he's holding auctions and offering information about toys (as well as other objects). He even has a free online catalog of items that are currently for sale.

- The Wengel's Disneyana (pluto.njcc.com/~wengel/index.htm). The Wengels are well-known Disney collectors who have written articles for many publications and whose collection has been featured by many. They offer items for sale or trade and are currently writing a book, so one would imagine they might do appraisals for a fee.

- Delaware Toy and Miniature Museum (www. thomes.net/toys/). Featuring dollhouses, dolls, toys, boats, and miniatures, this museum also offers some connections to toy makers, a reference library, and a museum shop at the museum itself.

Just the facts

- Avoid bidding on items when you feel you don't have all the facts you need to make an educated decision.

- Don't bid in increments—simply place your bid for the most you'll pay for the item.

- Conduct thorough research to find out information about the items you'll be bidding on so you'll be aware of both bargains and fakes.

Bright Idea
If you really want to purchase certain collectibles or products you can't find at your local store, and you don't have the time to do hours of online shopping, consider using a "personal shopper." A fairly new wrinkle in the online auction business, personal shoppers will search for items (even while you sleep) and e-mail you when they've found them.

Selling at Auction

GET THE SCOOP ON...
What it takes to begin selling ▪ How to price
items ▪ When to get an appraisal ▪ When to use
a reserve ▪ When should your auction end?

The Right Way to Sell

You're all registered, you've discovered the thrill of bidding on items up for auction, and now you're ready to take the plunge into selling. Whether you're marketing crafts you've made in your basement, photos you've taken of your kittens, computers you usually retail out of a shop, or vacation time at your chalet in the North Carolina mountains, just think about all the money you'll save in overhead and expenses by joining the virtual auction community. No longer do you have to worry about heating a building, running your items to flea markets or shows, or even making sure your clothes are pressed so you can be seen the public. Now you can use your computer to its best advantage, reach millions of possible customers, and never bother to get out of your pajamas unless absolutely necessary! Items no longer take up shelf space, because they sell more quickly. No longer do you have to wait all day for four or five people to wander through your shop. Now you have hundreds, possibly thousands, of buyers choosing to look at the ads for your goods.

161

Never has a seller had such a worldwide market as on online auctions.

Auctioning your items can be as simple as entering a few lines of description and attaching a JPEG (Joint Photographics Expert Group) or GIF (Graphics Interchange Format) file (the most common image formats). It's much easier to load a photo and sell an item than it was several years ago, and most people don't require any special skills beyond learning a few simple steps.

There are, however, many different ways to load your items for sale, and your choices of programs are as varied as your choices of which auctions might be best to market your items. It's best to take your time to learn the best selling techniques. We'll offer you all the secrets we know, and we're sure there are others that you'll learn along the way. If you have any tips to share, write to us so we can pass them along to others. We're hoping to have some precise information on our Web site in the future, so please check in with us at the address listed in the introduction of this book.

Now, let's get to the good stuff: making some money!

Are we making money yet?

There are many things to consider when you're getting ready to sell. The way you list an item is important, the words you use in describing it can determine whether it sells (and even influence the price), and the graphics you use to represent your item are usually the first thing a buyer will check out. If your description is snappy, if all the details are included, and if the photo images you use are clear, you will likely sell your items quickly.

Unofficially...
In 1999, Unity Marketing, a market research and consulting firm specializing in the collectibles business, stated that more than 50 percent of collectors have used the Internet to add to their collections or to gather information.

But those aren't the only things you need to consider. What if you don't know how much to charge for your item? How do you figure out what it's worth? Where do you place your items? Is one category better than another? Should you spend a little more listing the item and put it in a special category where more people might notice it? How long should your item remain on the auction site?

Baffled? Don't be. All options are made clear to you on the selling form each auction provides, but we're going to provide what they do not: an honest opinion on whether you should go with all the bells and whistles or use a streamlined ad for the minimum price. The answers to some of these questions might surprise you and will help you save valuable time. Instead of letting you swim around in unfamiliar waters, basically teaching yourself the ropes, we'll do the work for you!

To sell at auction, you must either give the auction house your credit card number or establish another sort of payment plan with them (for example, an escrow account). The easiest way to pay the fees for listing your items is to allow the auction house to charge your credit card after the auction ends. However, some people want to keep a closer rein on their spending. If that's the case with you, perhaps an escrow account is the best bet. That way you won't be able to list items for sale when your money runs out. You should already have decided which way to set up your account when you registered, but if you only registered as a bidder or haven't activated your seller status up to this point, now is the time to decide how you're going to handle your account.

66
I sold my sister's old poodle skirt for $47 and my *Star Trek* action figures for $212. Now I'm ransacking my closets for more items to sell!
—Amy Beth Fuller (*Woman's World*, 6/15/99)
99

The fees they'll charge you are determined by a number of factors: what you decide the opening bid will be, whether you chose to invoke a reserve (the lowest price you'll accept for an item), and what the final bidding price (the amount the piece sells for) is. So far, we've only found one Web site that doesn't charge sellers: Yahoo!

How do you get your items up for sale?

Although we talk in detail in Chapter 10, "Auction Management Programs," about the best programs for uploading your items, we'll explore them a little here, just to get your feet wet. There are more than 50 auctions that make the process extremely simple, offering bulk uploading capabilities that allow the seller to describe up to several hundred items offline and then, with a couple of clicks of the mouse, upload them all to the Web site. Others are more easily accessed with a program like Auction Assistant, which not only helps you design ads in a format acceptable to whatever auction you want to enter, but also helps you organize an automatic e-mail service to contact your buyers once the auction has ended.

All auctions have a form you must fill out to get your item listed. If you want to sell an item that doesn't necessarily have to be represented by a photograph, just fill in the information required and with a couple of clicks, your auction has begun. (See the following chapter for more information about how to write your description and the details you need to offer to possible bidders.) However, that's what we call a "plain Jane" ad, and we've discovered the hard way that ads without photographs don't get half the attention that those with graphics do. Let's face it, when you're buying something from an unknown source, it's best to see what you're buying, even if that item is something very familiar to you.

The information you'll need to properly complete the selling form includes:

- Registered identity (the name you're using for this auction)

- Password (either what you've chosen or what the auction has designated as yours)

- Location (most auctions ask for your country and/or state and zip code so that buyers can find items that can be easily shipped or picked up)

- Starting price (the amount of the lowest opening bid)

- Reserve price (the least you'll take for the item)

- Choices of payment (most auctions offer COD, money order, check, or credit card)

- Category (where your item belongs)

- Title (the first line the bidder will see)

- Shipping terms (paid by buyer or seller)

- Length of auction

- Image (do you have one, and if so, where is it located, or its URL)

- Description (the most important part of the form, it gives detailed information to the buyer)

"But I don't know some of the answers to these questions," you might say. Let's analyze the most important bits of information you need to include on your selling form and discuss where you might find the answers.

Timesaver
By simply hitting the Tab button on your keyboard, you can easily move from field to field whenever filling in a form anywhere online. Using this feature saves lots of time when listing your items for sale.

How do you price the items you're going to sell?

One of the most important aspects of selling your item is to know its fair market value. We don't know about you, but if we went to the store to buy a ream of paper for the printer and one store sold it at $3 per ream while another stated it was on sale for $7 per ream, we'd be pretty skeptical about the other items on sale. No one wants to pay more than they have to. That's why auctions are so popular; the chances of getting a bargain are excellent!

Determining how much you'll accept for your items can make or break your career as an online auctioneer. Once you get rolling, you'll discover that if you miscalculate an item's value and mark it too high, you'll be re-listing items on a regular basis. Or maybe the market just can't handle what you think the item is worth. Or maybe you're trying to sell something that was hot two weeks ago, but has now fallen out of favor (for example, Y2K-related items). On the other hand, you don't want to price your item so low that you don't make what you should from the sale.

We all want to find that attic full of van Gogh paintings or that stack of rare Batman comic books, but chances are you have something rather ordinary to sell, something that a lot of other people might also be selling. There are very few really rare items of any kind in this world, when you compare that figure to the billions of average pieces. Just because you have an old Batman comic book doesn't mean it's worth $200,000 (such as *Detective Comics #27*, released in May 1939 to introduce Batman himself). Don't be misled into thinking your grandmother's cobalt blue necklace might be just as valuable as the one worn by the lead female character in the movie *Titanic*.

The search for these rare items is what compels most buyers and sellers to continue the treasure hunt—and that is why you need to be careful to price the items you're going to sell as fairly as possible. Let the auction action sweep you away, but don't drown!

Sometimes pricing your item is as simple as opening the Sunday newspaper and finding a store's sale flier that lists other items like yours. Say your son has outgrown his bike and you want to sell it at auction. By checking to see what the local department stores are charging for bikes and deducting a fair percentage for age and use, you can get a ballpark figure of what you might get from a buyer online. Our advice is to give yourself a good 25 percent both below and above the prices you find (in other words, if you see the bike selling at one store for $150 and at another for $200, you can figure it might sell for as little as $100 up to as much as $250). Be honest with yourself. If the bike has seen better days, is five years old, and was ridden hard and long by a seven-year-old, you can be assured that you won't get anywhere near the price of a new bike. However, if your son rode the bike only occasionally, has had it for a mere six months, and the bike is one of the best on the market, you can guesstimate that you might get pretty close to its market value. On the other hand, if the bike is from the 1950s, has bright red fenders in mint shape and a gloriously intact leather seat, you can figure a collector will be willing to pay considerably more than what a new bike would cost.

How you price an item is also determined by how much you really want to sell it, how badly you

Moneysaver
If you're still unsure about how to price something and don't want to pay an appraiser, search the completed auctions for items similar to yours. You'll be able to get an idea of the average fair market value.

need the money, and the competition for items of that type. Consider also whether the piece is new or whether you'll lose money if the piece sells for less than a certain amount.

Naturally, you're not going to put a rare car up for sale at a starting bid of $1, and conversely, it doesn't make sense to hope that you'll get $1,000 for that bottle of cologne you bought from the Avon lady less than a month ago. In both cases, you'd be shooting yourself in the foot and would probably get no bids on either item. The reason for being in the auction business is to watch the bidding become more active as you draw closer to the end of the auction, and that will only happen if you create an auction the leaves room for some bidding.

Setting an opening bid

One of the ways to determine how much your opening bid should be is by searching the auction site where you're going to list your item. Check out similar items. What are they priced? Is your item in better condition than theirs? Is it newer? Older? Rare? Common? Are there any bids on those items at all?

Once you figure the average price of all the items similar to yours, you need to figure in the other variables. Condition means a lot to most people. *Anything* in mint condition (something still in the box or, in other words, in the same condition it would have been on the day it was manufactured or put up for sale) is worth twice as much as the same piece in poor condition. However, if a piece is one of a kind, it won't matter what condition it's in, because you have nothing to compare it to.

Our advice is to set the opening bid at about 10 percent of what you expect to receive for the item.

For example, if you have a Native American blanket that you've compared to others selling at $200, you'll set the opening bid at $20. If you cannot possibly sell that blanket for less than $200, your reserve will be set at $200. You'll hope that bidding goes past the $200 mark, but if it doesn't, you'll be happy to sell it at that amount.

Experience has shown us that the lower your opening bid, the better your chance of attracting bidders and ultimately selling the item. However, sometimes there aren't enough bids to get the price up to the point you'd be comfortable with, but that is the chance you take when you enter an auction.

Recently, we sold several of Dawn's books on Native American artists. We usually get a fair amount of bidding on these signed editions, but on this particular occasion, no one bid past the $1 opening bid mark. As a result, the shipping charges were higher than what the customers actually paid for the book. Though disappointed, we learned yet again that starting the auction at a more reasonable price ($3 to $5) would have netted us a little more in the long run. Did the loss of a couple of dollars ruin our week? No, but if we'd been selling one of the larger-ticket items and we'd made a comparable faux pas, we would have been in tears.

If you're a retailer and simply can't sell your items for less than what you usually do, you can start them at that price, but remember that bidders still like a little action, as well as a good deal. Because some of the auctions might bring a little more than you expected, while others might be right on the money, you should price your items a little low. If you're fair with both yourself and your customers, and price the items below what someone would pay

Bright Idea
If the item you're selling is one of hundreds like it, you're up against some tough competition. The best way to beat it is to start your bidding ridiculously low in order to lure in buyers looking for a bargain.

in a store, you'll discover that it all balances out in the long run.

Figure in your costs

There are certain costs that should be figured in to the pricing of an item, and one of the most important is your time. Never discount the amount of time it took you to fix that oak bureau or to restore the 1965 Mustang you're going to sell. Make sure you pay yourself first. If the refinishing on the bureau cost you $15 in materials and five hours of your time, figure out how much it would have cost you to pay someone else to do the job, and add that amount to the bottom dollar you'll accept for the piece.

Some costs you should figure in to your initial bidding price are:

▪ **Transportation.** If you travel to a flea market or go to a yard sale on the weekends, keep track of your mileage. You can deduct it from your income taxes, but you should also add it to the amount you need to recoup from the pieces you choose to sell at auction.

▪ **Repairs.** If a clock needs new hands or you've replaced the battery in a toy, keep track of what you've spent. Keep the receipts and add the costs to the price of the item.

▪ **Shipping materials.** Considering the way shipping companies (including the post office) handle our goods, you should buy the best materials available—and remember to add that cost to the price. We usually add a small percentage to our shipping and handling fee (approximately 50¢ to $2, depending on the size and fragility of the package).

- **Photography.** Film, developing, and scanning costs should be figured in to your opening bid. If you've spent all afternoon photographing items to upload to an auction site, figure the price of your time, the film, the developing, and the scanning, then divide that total by the number of items you photographed. Add that cost to what you need to recoup when you sell the item.

- **Listing fees and sales commissions.** Though there are several auctions that allow you to list items for free, none of the auction houses work without getting paid. Even if you don't pay a fee for listing the item (with eBay, the listing fee is determined by the opening bid, as well as by the reserve, if you choose to set one, and any other special listing fees, like bolding your title or listing your object in a special category), you'll still have to pay a commission of some sort. The initial listing fee starts at 25¢, but goes up depending on the opening bid. You still need to pay the auction service a percentage of the final sales price.

Though you don't know what the sales price will be when you begin, you do have some control over the listing fee, since you are the one who determines the opening bid, as well as any special listing procedures.

Reserve pricing

A reserve is the safety net some sellers use so that they won't lose the money they have invested in the piece that's up for auction. It's the minimum amount they'll accept in order to make the sale. Personally, we find it invaluable, especially when

Watch Out!
It's wise to keep listing costs low if you are selling items that aren't going to be big moneymakers.

we're acting as broker for other people's items. If we don't reach a certain price, we can't cover our own expenses, as well as pass on some earnings to the customer.

For example, we recently brokered a valuable piece of porcelain for one of our customers. We knew she had $400 in the piece, so that was *her* bottom dollar. In order for us to cover the expenses of photographing and listing the piece, as well as earning our commission for selling it, we needed to sell the porcelain for at least $500. After doing some research, we discovered that the item was highly collectible, but we couldn't nail down a value. Taking a chance, we put it on eBay, and watched as it reached a dismal $150. We re-listed it, and watched again as it failed to reach the reserve. In the meantime, we had expenses of almost $35—and we hadn't made a dime. Finally, we contacted some people who had bid on other porcelain pieces with us and sold it privately.

In another case, we failed to put a reserve on an advertising sign in which we'd invested over $100. Figuring the sign would garner the interest of collectors with whom we'd dealt successfully in the past, we felt confident in leaving off the reserve. Unfortunately, it didn't reach the $100 we had into it, and we lost money.

There have also been many cases that we've used the reserve feature and not only saved our investment but earned 20 to 150 percent *more* than what we had into the item.

Our advice? Think twice before putting a reserve on your item, because a lot of people won't bid on items unless they feel that they might be getting a bargain. In most auctions, the reserve price isn't displayed, so buyers feel a bit uneasy about whether what they've bid is close to the reserve. You have only a certain amount of time to get the bidder's interest. If someone really want the item, she might be willing to play the game of "testing the reserve" (entering bids until she reaches the reserve), but most buyers will just surf on to the next item.

If you simply can't lose the money invested in the piece, set a reserve and couple it with a fairly reasonable opening bid (something close to the price you've set as the reserve). That way, perhaps the first couple of bids will be enough to break the reserve and give your bidders the comfort of actively pursuing the item. Otherwise, leave the reserve off and let the item sell for whatever it will (and cross your fingers in the hopes that it'll be more than you planned!).

Should you bring in an appraiser?

If you don't know what that motorcycle part is worth or haven't a clue whether that commemorative is a $10 item or a $100 item, how do you find out? Do you ask your neighbor or check in with the chat-room folks at your auction? You can do that, but chances are good that you'll get a ballpark figure rather than a true value.

Instead of taking the chance and putting it up for auction with no protection (or a reserve price that is either too high or too low), it's better if you find out how much it's worth. That's when you start checking out appraisal services.

Appraisers will do the research on your piece or offer their years of experience to tell you the history of the item, how collectible it is, and what the fair market value is. They usually offer a printed version of their appraisal so that if a customer is going to insure a piece, they can offer the appraisal to the

Watch Out!
In July 1999, eBay sellers talked about a "bid shield" scam where one bidder would place a low bid, while the other would place a high bid. Right before the end of the auction, the high bidder would withdraw, allowing the low bidder to take the piece.

insurance company. That printed copy can also serve as a selling tool for you when you put the item up for auction. If a customer can get proof of an item's value, it makes him more comfortable in buying the item.

Professional appraisers must meet a certain level of criteria in order to be admitted into professional organizations. They offer their years of training, strict methods of evaluation, and professional report writing to such people as lawyers, accountants, investors, estate managers, and bankers. If an appraiser is a member of a professional organization, that organization's reputation is at stake if an individual appraiser makes an error, so appraisers go through a stringent education in "appraisal theory, principles, procedures, ethics, and law" (International Society of Appraisers). In other words, you can trust them.

There are several appraisal services that have begun doing business online, offering experts in a number of fields who will appraise one item or whole householdloads of items for a reasonable fee. Here are several options:

- Eppraisals.com (www.eppraisals.com) is a new online service headed by Leslie Hindman, a collectibles expert who's been part of auction houses and in the antiques business for many years. They offer appraisals for a straight $20 fee and have hired hundreds of experts (including us) in various fields to evaluate items and write up digital appraisals that are delivered to customers within three days. This site also includes an online magazine that is loaded with articles about specific items.

- The International Society of Appraisers (www.isa-appraisers.org) lists appraisers who specialize in many different categories, from real estate to jewelry to antiques. You can search their site for appraisers in your geographical area, as well as appraisers who are experts in the type of items you would like evaluated. They thoroughly educate and monitor their members, so you can be sure you're getting your money's worth and expertise that is invaluable when selling items with which you are not familiar.

- The American Society of Appraisers (www.appraisers.org) offers listings of their members by location, as well as specialty. They also have an Open Forum where you can post questions about your items in the hope that someone will offer some free information. When we surfed through the site, the Forum seemed more heavily weighted with questions about real estate appraisals than any others. Though there were questions about smaller items (like toys, pewter, and jewelry), it appeared that members discuss appraisal issues in the Forum rather than specific values—perhaps because they don't want to give away their expertise for free (and who can blame them!).

- The large auction houses (e.g., Sotheby's [www.sothebys.com], Christie's [www.christies.com], and Skinner's [www.skinnerinc.com]) often offer appraisal days when the general public can bring in their cherished collectibles and discover their true value for free (or for a nominal fee).

Timesaver
The American Society of Appraisers Web site (www.appraisers.org) offers a list of questions to ask potential appraisers so that you can determine whether they are reputable.

- *Antiques Roadshow* (www.antiquesroadshow. com), a PBS television show, travels all over the United States offering their professional services. Their list of professional appraisers includes experts in every area of antiques and collectibles, and they are all listed on the Web site.

- Auctions World Wide Association (www. auctionsww.com) offers a list of appraisers in a variety of categories, including land and homes, collectibles, industrial, antiques, jewelry, machinery, horses, automobiles, and businesses.

- Wines.com offers fine wine appraisals, as well as tips on the qualities considered when appraising fine wines. They also note that Christie's Wine Department offers free estimates to sellers "interested in offering $15,000 or more in fine wines at auction" and list the fax number at Christie's U.S. Wine Department (212-317-2470).

- Mackley & Company (www.mackley.com), estate jewelry specialists, offers online appraisals of fine jewelry, as well as a bulletin board where you can post questions about selling pieces of jewelry.

- A good resource for auto appraisals and auctions is found at sportscarmarket.com. Most of the appraisers listed state that they give free phone advice, and quite a few of them also have Web sites. Though most work only within an area they can easily travel to, some of them (like USAppraisal) are available nationwide.

- *Maloney's Antiques & Collectibles Resource Directory* (http://maloney.com) lists appraisers, dealers, experts, collectors, associations, and auction services. They have printed a book, available online, that includes all this information on an annual basis. For many years, Mr. Maloney has hosted the PBS television show *Collecting Across America*.

■ Dawson's Appraisals (www.dawsons.org), a member of the American Society of Appraisers, provides both traditional appraisals and "e-appraisals" over the Net. Formal appraisals are quoted at $75 an hour, while e-appraisals are quoted on request.

If you don't think your item is worth appraising, but you want to find out its value or history anyway, you can ask questions of the members of the chatroom that your auction hosts, or peruse some of the collectibles guides at your local library (check out Dawn's books on African American arts and collectibles, Native American items, and advertising while you're there!).

Knowing how much a piece is worth

The most likely mistakes that beginning auctioneers make are in listing items for more than they're worth. That not only sets you up for disappointment, it ruins your reputation as a seller.

Remember that some of the buyers to whom you're selling are people who are going to resell. Dealers, who are in the market to find some stock for their shops or for collectors for whom they buy, don't want to pay more than two-thirds of what a piece is worth. And everyone wants to believe they've gotten a bargain. After doing research and, possibly, paying for an appraisal, you will have a good idea what your item is worth, but you still need to consider what the market can handle.

Bright Idea
A quick way of finding your item's value is to do an image search on Alta Vista, then check the photo to see whether it's the same as yours. If it is, follow the link and you'll probably find its value.

Are you willing to take a gamble?

You've done your homework and are ready to put your piece up for auction. If you have a minimum amount of money in the piece (perhaps you bought a doll at the flea market for $1 and believe it might be worth a lot more), you might be willing to take a gamble. In that case, enter the item at a low opening bid and don't put a reserve on it. That way, you'll guarantee you will sell the item (if plans go awry and bids don't reach up past that $1 opening bid, you can always cancel the auction). If you're not the gambling type and would rather be sure your piece is going to bring in a minimum amount of money, simply raise the opening bid.

Again, putting a reserve on your listing might make some shy away, but you are the one who ultimately makes the decision about whether or not you're ready to let the "auction gods" sweep you into the excitement—or whether you want more control.

Which category do I put it in?

The category in which you list your item is almost as important as its description. We have often shuffled items from one category to another, especially when they don't seem to get any bids, and can guarantee that finding the right category is the key to selling successfully.

For example, we sell Dawn's book *Contemporary Native American Artists* (Alliance Publishers, 1995) at auction on a regular basis and have tried it in several different categories. Because it is a signed first edition, book collectors are often interested in it, but we've discovered that our best bet is to include the book in the Native American collectibles category since buyers/sellers use it as a reference guide.

We've had much better luck with it in that category than any other. We've also tried selling it at different online auctions, and discovered that only those with a specific Native American category are likely to garner us the highest bids. We recently sold two copies of the book in the book category of Amazon.com and were disappointed that they brought less than $5 each. During that same period, the books sold on eBay in the Native American category for approximately $20 apiece.

Because each auction we've researched has a different way of naming their categories, you should look at the complete auction index to be sure that you're not misplacing your item. Remember that the specialty auctions might be better for your item than the general ones, where you can get lost amidst thousands—perhaps millions—of items.

Your goal is to place your listing in the category where most interested buyers will be likely to see it. Because the larger auction houses might have thousands of categories, it's important to choose the right one. Some of the online auctions are now getting wise to the fact that placing an item in several categories simultaneously allows the seller more assurance that the item will be sold.

The benefits of the Gallery and "gift" icons

When eBay instituted icons such as photo alerts, gift alerts, and holiday symbols, sellers discovered they could add a bit more inexpensive advertising to their listings to make their items stand out from the crowd.

If you have a specialty item or something that is rather high-priced, you might want to list it in the Gallery (eBay's patent-pending term) or a featured auction. Buyers like to scroll through pictures of

Moneysaver
If you have multiples of an item and are unsure where to sell them, try listing singles in different categories and see which garners the most bids. That way you won't be pinning all your hopes on one category.

items without having to dredge through listings where they need to click on the listing description in order to see the photo. Does it helps sales? We think so. Will you get a higher price for the piece when you finally sell it? That's something that hasn't been proven—and you have to be prepared to spend the extra money to list the item in this special manner.

Some icons, like Amazon's special payment plan, offer bidders the ease of paying for their item in a more convenient way, while others simply alert customers that the item is new or that it is something seasonal (for example, Valentine's Day gift ideas might be accompanied by a blinking red heart, while Christmas items might be listed with a wrapped gift icon).

Icons make your listing stand out from the others, but they also cost more than the regular listing. Make sure you are willing to pay the price.

How long an auction?

The length of time your items are up for auction is determined by you when you list them. Most auctions give you the option of listing your item and if the item doesn't sell within that time period, you can re-list. Some (like Auction Addict) offer an automatic re-listing option so that your piece can be up for sale indefinitely, until it sells.

This is where you have to determine the amount of control you have over when your auction ends. Our experience has been that we want our auctions to end at a time when we can be there for the final closing minutes in order to answer any bidder's questions and to monitor the action during the height of the auction. To us, that's the most exciting time and it's always a thrill to see the bidding frenzy during the last moments. Because we don't stay up

66
This fall's Atlantique City show [an antiques show held yearly in Ocean City, New Jersey featuring approximately 1,600 dealers] was DEFINITELY down in attendance and exhibitors, probably due to the Internet, eBay, etc.
—Paul M. Rubin, *Ad Character News*
99

24 hours a day, we purposely schedule auctions to end during the daytime, and preferably, on a weekend. However, you need to determine the best time for you.

The amount of time you set your auctions for is also determined by when you need the money. It can also be determined by the season. You might have some Christmas ornaments to sell, and getting them on the auction block before Thanksgiving or during the first couple of weeks of December is important in order to get the attention of bidders who are in the holiday spirit.

When planning your auction, think ahead. Where will you be and what will you be doing when your auction closes? Are you going to be able to take care of questions and answer bidders' e-mails? Are you going to be around to get the checks that come in the mail and package the items for shipment? Might your item sell to people in other parts of the world? If so, consider their time zones. We regularly sell to Australian customers, and it's important that they are "in" on the end of an auction to bid.

You need to consider all these questions before choosing the duration of the auction. Your answers can determine whether your business thrives or flounders.

Seven days? Five? Three?

A seven-day auction is easy to figure out: It ends at the same time that it begins, only seven days later. If you're starting your auction on a Sunday afternoon, it will end the next week at the same time. Most sellers like to catch the weekend auction traffic when they schedule auctions, so timing a seven-day auction from Wednesday to Wednesday isn't the most conducive to selling. However, that same auction scheduled on a Saturday will get two weekends worth of auction traffic. If you're a night owl and start your auctions at 2 A.M., they will end at that time as well. Even though this might work for you, consider the fact that others might be asleep at that time.

Setting your auction for five or three days, you must take into consideration the time zone difference. Most experienced auctioneers set their auctions at a time when people on both the East Coast and West Coast are likely to be at their computers bidding.

Unofficially...
In 1999, Sotheby's budgeted $25 million to develop a Web site, while its competitor, Christie's, decided to stay out of the online auction business and concentrate on keeping its high-priced auctions in its showrooms.

We have discovered that most of action happens during the waning hours, so there are times when a three-day auction, scheduled over a weekend, works better for us than a seven-day, since we'll be reaching a vast number of bidders online. However, if we have a valuable item that we want to make sure bidders see, we might choose the longer period of time.

You should also check to see what time zone the auction runs in. For example, bid.com runs on Eastern time, so if you're on the West Coast, consider this when scheduling your auction.

The pros and cons of a quickie auction

Three days is the shortest period of time an auction can be held on eBay; however, there are a number of other auctions that are now promoting one-day auctions or "quickies."

Hagglezone.com has a one-day auction option, while ReverseAuction.com offers auctions where the declining price is posted and buyers can automatically purchase the items when they feel comfortable with the price.

A quickie auction enables you to sell your item with little hassle, to get the money from the customer, and to send the purchase within days. This is particularly valuable if you are in the process of moving and need to get rid of goods within a certain period of time, or if you know you'll be going out of town and won't be able to keep up with the details of an auction.

The cons of dealing this way include not being able to reach the maximum number of bidders, and possibly not receiving top dollar for your items.

It's all in the timing!

Whether your auctions are one-day, three-day, five-day, seven-day, or two-week auctions, it's important to remember timing when you plan them.

If you're uploading several hundred items, how will you manage the e-mails and shipping when all the auctions end simultaneously? It won't be easy, unless you have a staff to support you. Even if you are only uploading 10 auctions, the handling of items, questions, and customers at the end of an auction period can be overwhelming.

Our advice? Stagger your auctions so they end at least several hours apart until you get used to the ebb and flow of auction action.

Scheduling your auctions to end at "high time"

Though some experienced sellers always schedule their auctions to end on a weekend, others swear by ending on Mondays. Whatever you choose as your ending time, be aware that auctions have the heaviest traffic between 5 and 7 P.M. and on weekends.

Early mornings and late-late evenings are the slowest traffic times on auctions. Because bidders know that, some of them schedule their bidding time to catch the auctions that are ending at 3 A.M.,

Watch Out!
If you are planning a weekend away or a vacation, make sure your auction ends at least three days in advance and that you tell your buyers that you'll mail their items as soon as you return.

because they figure they'll get a deal. Most of the time, they're right.

If you want to catch the lion's share of the bidders, schedule your auction to end at a time when there's a good chance of catching quite a few bidders simultaneously online. This is especially true if you are selling items that are of interest to the majority of collectors/bidders. For example, if you are selling computers and computer parts, you might want to end your auctions during workday hours, since that's when most people shopping for computer parts are online. However, if you are selling adult goods (anything unsuitable for children), you might want to focus on mid-evening hours when people are more likely to be surfing for hobby-related items.

Think about what you're selling and the likelihood of buyers of that item being online during an auction's end. And remember that your buyers are adults, so don't figure in the "kiddie" factor.

The value of selling on weekends

No matter what anyone tells you, there is a definite advantage to having your auction spread over a weekend or end on a weekend day. Since for most people shopping at online auctions is a hobby rather than a career, and since the majority of people work a five-day week, they are 10 times more likely to be online during a weekend day.

Some sellers we know purposely start their auctions on a Saturday afternoon so they can take advantage of the Saturday and Sunday traffic for that weekend, and end on a Saturday afternoon the next weekend. By doing so, they give themselves two prime selling times, with a week of regular selling time in between.

Does this sales strategy work? Though friends of ours swear it does, we believe the only way you can possibly tell is to sell the identical item during two different time periods and involve the same people in both auctions. Is that possible? No, definitely not. But it *is* a fact that the lion's share of auctions end on a weekend, and if thousands of sellers swear by weekend sales, then you need to listen to them!

Just the facts

- If you're not sure what a piece is worth, get an appraisal before selling it.

- Begin your bidding price at a level where buyers will believe they'll get a bargain.

- The majority of online auctions now offer bulk uploading capabilities so you can enter multiple items simultaneously.

- Correct category placement can make a big difference in how many bidders will seek to buy your item.

- Some sellers swear that scheduling an auction over a weekend will guarantee it'll be seen by more potential buyers.

GET THE SCOOP ON...
Creating one-liners that sell your products
■ Honestly evaluating your items ■ Highlighting
the important details ■ Researching an item
that baffles you ■ Determining the
category for your item

What's Important to List in the Description?

In the advertising business, it's common knowledge that you only have a few seconds to interest a buyer in your product. If you don't nab that person, whet his appetite somehow, or give him enough info to make a decision, that potential buyer will be off to the next product. We hate to tell you this, folks, but those few seconds are down to even less time when people are coasting through auction listings. Surfers simply don't have the patience to hunt through millions of items. The listing that best describes the exact item they want (or at least entices them to look more closely) is the one they'll click on and explore.

If you haven't caught their eye in that split second, you've lost the game and might as well hang it up. Many tests have been done on the average surfer's attention span, and it's so minimal that sometimes they even scan over the most obvious eye-catchers. No patience means that the words you choose are the most important factor in selling online.

Why the right words are important

The hows and whys of choosing your words carefully in the online auction business can't be summed up in a couple of sentences, which is why we're devoting this whole chapter to the subject. Figure it this way: There are, at any given moment, millions of items for sale at the various auction sites we've mentioned. In order to be noticed, you must use the tools you have at your disposal. The most powerful tool any salesperson has is words (and, yes, you are now a salesperson!). The words you use in your ads will be the deciding factor in how well you do in this (or any other) business.

In this chapter, we'll not only give you some pointers in auction lingo, but a mini lesson in writing advertising copy as well. Why do we think this is important? It's not just because Dawn teaches English or has made a living writing books. It's because your words are the only way the bidders will know you. Your words represent you and your items. In order to put your best foot forward, you must first learn the basics, don't you agree?

In the first couple of months that Bobby started his business on eBay, I spent a lot of time trying to impress upon him the importance of the way he was writing the one-line listing descriptions, as well as the paragraph he was including with the item's photo. He was a little offended when I requested he use his computer's spell check feature and get rid of "empty descriptors" (words that really didn't say anything specific about the piece), but he changed his mind after furtively searching for an item one day. He requested my help, and I discovered the reason

Bright Idea
The first couple of words that describe an auction item can often make the difference between people surfing in to take a peek or not finding your object when they do a specific search for the item.

why he didn't come up with what he wanted: He was misspelling the important search words!

Once Bobby started using spell check, he noticed an increase in sales, and his listings started looking a bit more professional. In addition, there were fewer e-mails asking basic questions about the items he was selling. Customers are always satisfied when they know the little details (both good and bad) about the things they're purchasing. Thus, not only is it important to be concise and clear when you're describing something, but you also need to give the buyer sufficient information to make her decision about whether to bid on your piece or to surf on to the next possibility.

Let's put it this way: If you list your Chinese Export teapot as an "Oreintal teapot," the customers who are searching for Oriental items will not find the teapot. Do you want to lose all those potential bidders? We suspect you don't!

Use key words in the title

The first line of description that a potential buyer reads is what determines whether the person will pass on by or place a bid. If you include the info in the initial line that attracts that first bidder, chances are you'll attract a second and possibly a third. Maybe you'll even start a bidding war, and that is what you're aiming for, right? That's why we participate in online auctions! We want some of the excitement, the bidding wars, the possibility that your item is worth a little more than you expected, or that someone wants it badly. We're in this for the heart-pumping excitement at the end of an auction when that wooden horse remedies sign you expected to get around $25 for has been bid up to over $1,000! These are the moments we wait for, so remember that you are totally responsible for creating that type of excitement by the way you word your ad.

Watch Out!
Seller beware! The item descriptions are *very* important. If you want to make a sale, be specific!

Most online auction houses give you a specified number of characters you can use in the one-line description of your item that will show up in listings. eBay makes the cutoff point 45 characters. So, if you figure the average word contains at least five to seven letters, you have a total of approximately six words to make your point. You must concisely describe your item and its important characteristics in a way that will lure your buyer to look at your longer description.

How do you use every precious character of that line of description? We give you some suggestions in the following sections.

Omit all punctuation

Each piece of punctuation is a character. Use only punctuation that is absolutely necessary (such as the apostrophe or end quotes mark when you must indicate length in feet or inches). Leave out all the question marks, asterisks, and exclamation points. They are empty fillers that you could be using to give buyers a bit more of the important info they need.

For example, why use: "L@@@@@@K!!! FABULOUS doll with red hair," when you could have: "Redhead 1957 Bathing Suit Barbie Doll."

The second version attracts the attention of anyone who is looking for any kind of Barbie doll, plus those searching for 1957 Barbies, or Bathing Suit Barbies, or Redhead Barbies, or just any kind of doll. The point is, all those "@s" might attract attention, but they don't give your description any value. Give the customer some information instead of empty characters.

Consider the category

What are the key search words someone will enter when looking for an item like yours? If you want to sell a book on Martin Luther King, Jr. in the biographies section of the Book category, you'd definitely enter those words in your listing (Bio Martin Luther King, Jr.....).

Where you enter your item makes the difference in whether a collector will see it and bid on it or whether the item will sit there, lonely and unloved, and unsold at the end of the auction. Here are some general categories we've discovered exist in most online auctions listings. Each one breaks down into more specific subcategories, so you might find the exact place for your article. For example, you might have a movie poster of Elvis's last film. Though you could place the article in the general "movie collectibles" category, chances are the online auction you've entered has a "poster" category, or better yet, an "Elvis collectibles" category. Where do you think your item will best sell? My bet would be the Elvis category, but the article should be listed with as many specific key search words in the title as possible so that you'll also catch the regular movie collectibles search or the person who's searching for any kind of poster simply because he needs something to decorate his office.

The best way to decide where to list an item is to do a search for other items that are similar, then see which categories they are listed in. And if you *really* want to make sure everyone finds your article, place it in a specific category and then create several "hot" search words in your title.

Check the general listing categories for three of the top online auctions so that you can see where your item might fall. Before you pick a category, also check to see whether there are more specific subcategories.

Say I'm looking for a He-Man toy, I'll plug in "MOTU" because that stands for Masters of the Universe, which is what the figures are called. Or if I'm looking for Spawn figures, I'll enter Macfarlane, because that's the company that makes them...
—Bryan Cioffi, toy collector

Determine other important factors

When collectors are searching for their items, they normally search for something specific, so you need to study the category in which you're submitting the item. Make sure you use some of the stock phrases (for example, a book on Martin Luther King, Jr. might be listed as a Black Collectible).

Examples of the variety of words used in categorical information include:

- **Automobiles:** Type of car, model, make, manufacturer. When buyers are looking for a particular vehicle, they might search for it by name (e.g., Ford) or by model (e.g., Probe), or they might want a particular year (e.g., 1994).

- **Books:** Author, publisher, first edition, autographed. Book collectors might want only fiction written by Stephen King, or perhaps they like to collect first editions written by any author, or only autographed books.

- **Computers:** Model, component, speed, size, maker. Buyers searching for the latest in hardware might only be interested in Microsoft technology, or perhaps they want to buy a hard drive made after a particular date, or a laptop made by Dell rather than a desktop made by Hewlett-Packard.

- **Dolls:** Name of doll, name of manufacturer, year made, condition, color or hair or eyes, material. Though a collector might be perfectly happy with any Barbie made before 1974, her dream might be to own the 1957 brunette version with the maker's mark on the doll's lower back.

■ **Jewelry:** Type of stone, type of metal, age, style. Though diamonds are a girl's best friend, perhaps the buyer wants a tennis bracelet rather than a bangle, or maybe the shape of the stone is the highest priority, or the buyer wants an antique ring rather than a contemporary version.

■ **Music:** Instrument, band/singer, style of music, cassette/CD/album. Some collectors only want original LPs by Frank Sinatra, while others search for guitars made by Les Paul. Determining the type of music to collect might be important to some, but other collectors may be interested in any type of music produced in Japan after WWII.

■ **Toys:** Type of toy, manufacturer, artist, name brand, material, year made. Many factors determine what makes a toy valuable to a collector/ buyer. Who made the toy? When? Is it vinyl or celluloid? Aluminum or iron? Pre-1950 or post WWI? Still in its original package or well used?

As you can tell, there are many factors by which a buyer can search, and you must consider these when placing your item within particular categories. The examples we've given apply to only a few of the categories available to you when making the decision where to list your item. Make sure you use all possible key words.

Be specific

Include the most important fact about your article. Is the book a first edition copy? Is your poster signed and framed? Is the teddy bear from Germany? Does that car have special wheels?

Timesaver
Instead of running a spell check on every item as you write the description, set up your word processing program to check spelling and grammar as you type.

When we first started entering items on eBay and Amazon auctions, we made a few mistakes. Let's share a few with you so you don't make the same errors we did.

Here's an original one-line description:

L@@K! Martin Luther King Sr. book

Here's how we'd list it today:

SIGNED 1st ed. M.L. King Sr. book DADDY KING

Watch Out!
Remember that each character counts in your descriptions. Try not to use asterisks, percent signs, or otherwise "empty" words.

Notice we shortened "first" to "1st" and didn't spell out "edition." We kept "King" but shortened the first two names so that we could get the title on the line. Since the important selling points of this book are that it is signed by Martin Luther King, Sr., and is a first edition, those facts needed to be kept in the one-line description, but we certainly didn't need to waste space with "L@@K!"

Here's another original one-line description:

BEAUTIFUL Cinderella Doll in great shape

Here's how we'd list it today:

Effanbee Cinderella Doll 1978 w/orig dress

The word "beautiful" in the first description wasted nine characters that we would replace with the manufacturer's name (Effanbee) in the second description. Entering the year the doll was made and the fact that it is still in its original dress are important to appeal to doll collectors.

Our third example includes some common errors first-time sellers make:

This is a one-of-a-kind paintign by Whhitehorse

Here's how we'd list it today:

Native American oil painting by Whitehorse

What's wrong with the first example? Two misspellings, for one thing, and at least six words that don't tell the buyer anything about this painting. By adding Native American in the second example, we were assured that collectors of Native American art/artifacts would bring up our article when doing a search. By correcting the spelling of the artist's name, we knew that people who collected his art would find this item, and by adding oil painting to the description, we knew we'd find all of those collectors who check out all the artwork available for sale.

Tell the seller what makes your item different or unusual

Auction bidders like to know they're getting a treasure or a find. Some buyers are interested in only money, while others are looking for pieces to fill a particular space in their collection. Give them information that will enhance the piece you're selling.

Consider these examples of some words that succinctly show how unique your piece is:

- First edition
- Signed
- Trademarked
- Dated
- Limited edition
- Copyrighted
- Patented
- One-of-a-kind
- Uncirculated
- Rare

Try to include the exact size of your item

Sometimes it's hard to tell by a photograph how big that book is. If it's a normal-sized paperback, it'll be totally different than something that's considered coffee table–sized. A buyer who is specially looking for that paperback edition won't be interested in the coffee-table version. Is that an important piece of info to add to your description line? Yes, if you believe it's important to the piece.

Though it's preferable to give the exact dimensions (in inches or feet), sometimes a word will suffice. For instance, miniature items are sometimes more rare than regular-sized, but the opposite can be true. We collect Kachina dolls, and the smaller ones, as well as the extra-large ones, are more rare than the average foot-tall versions. The size of the items you are selling can be very important to a buyer. Think about the person who's looking for a room-sized Oriental rug. What size is the room? It could be 6' × 9' or 25' × 50'. Be specific! The 3" version of a particular stamp might be the one that was a mistake and thus quite rare, whereas the 1" version was made by the millions.

Tell about its condition

Be honest! If that book is frayed and the spine is broken, tell about it, but *not* in the one-line description. That's not the place to add the negatives. Instead, go into great detail about the piece's condition in the ad itself, where you can point out specifically where the piece is broken or what kind of wear it might have. Let the buyers decide at that point whether they still want the book. However, if that book is in absolutely mint condition, that will make the book more desirable, and that information should most definitely be included in the one-line description.

Here are some choice ways to describe condition:

- Fine
- Very fine
- Mint (MIB = mint in box; MIMB = mint in mint box; MOC = mint on card)
- NRFB = never removed from box
- COA = certificate of authenticity
- Pristine
- Rare
- Very rare
- Museum-quality
- Good
- Very good
- Usable
- Perfect
- Near perfect
- Flawless
- Well used
- Slightly used
- Well loved

Bright Idea
Including the condition of your item in a one-line description can determine whether a browser will click on the item to see more. Try to include condition whenever you think it'll make a difference to the customer.

Reveal the item's age

Some buyers would rather have the newest version of an object, while others would prefer to buy a vintage piece. It all depends on the collector. Though it doesn't matter with some items, it is important to note "brand new" or "ca. 1890s" in descriptions of items where the year it was produced was important. For example, the Martin Luther King, Sr., book was copyrighted in 1976—and that fact, plus its fabulous condition, makes this item more valuable than a fifth-edition copy of the same story, published in paperback in 1998. Check for date of manufacture or patent date, copyright date, or any indication of a certain period of style indicative of a particular era (e.g., the Art Deco style).

Some of the ways to describe when your piece was made are:

- The exact year (e.g., 1999, 1942) or better yet, the exact date

- The era (e.g., 1920s, 1880s, early 1960s)

- The style period, e.g.:

    Contemporary (within the last 10 or 20 years)

    Modern (since WWII)

    Post WWII (1950s)

    Art Deco (1920s–'30s)

    Art Nouveau (late 19th/early 20th century)

    Victorian (1837–1901)

    Edwardian (1841–1910)

    Baroque (1600–1750)

    Federal (mid- to late 1700s/America)

    Colonial (early 1700s/America)

    Post Colonial (late 1700s to early 1800s/ America)

    Restoration (late 1600s/England)

    Age of Enlightenment (late 18th century/ Europe)

    Queen Anne (early 18th century/England)

    Elizabethan (1558–1603)

Bright Idea
If you're not sure about an item's exact age, here are some words/ phrases that might be useful: antique, vintage, collectible, and unique.

There are many more style periods, depending on what kind of merchandise you're selling. For example, Asian art is determined by dynasties, such as the Ming Dynasty. Being well-versed in them is a definite plus when writing your descriptions.

Include the company name

If your item was produced by a certain company, there might be collectors who look for all the items made by that company. For example, the book was published by Maxwell Publishing (fictitious name), a company that specialized in classic books with fine leather bindings. All of their books are considered highly collectible since the company has been out of business for 10 years and only produced 1,500 copies of each of their titles. (See how we're building value into this book?)

Check for marks

If a piece is signed, it is often more valuable to a collector. Silver has its hallmarks (usually found on the back of a piece of silverware, on the inside of a piece of jewelry, or on the rim of larger items); porcelain is often signed somewhere around the bottom edge or rim; artists sign their canvases or sculptures with distinctive signatures (often depending on what time period the artist was "in" when the work was created); books might be autographed by their authors; and dolls are often marked on the back of their neck or buttocks. The maker's mark (whether the maker is a single artist creating unique works or a large corporation making millions of similar items) will tell a buyer of the piece's origin, and perhaps whether the item is of value.

If the mark on your particular item is not a name or letters that you recognize, include a photo of the mark in your ad, or describe the signature or mark as accurately as you can in the body of your ad.

Report color or style, if important

When color indicates age or might give a collector pertinent information, it should be mentioned in the one-liner. For example, if the bright orange lettering on this book cover indicates that it was a misprinted batch and extremely rare, it should be mentioned in the title.

Color is particularly important when an item's worth is determined by its hue. For example, a black diamond is far more rare and expensive than a clear one. Certain colors indicate the age as well as the region in which particular Native American rugs were made. In addition, if a color is worn on your item, it's important to mention that in your ad. Remember, too, that the computer imaging sometimes distorts color. A red piece may appear brown or pink on other computers, so make sure you mention the true color of the piece.

Point out the origin of the piece

The fact that the item you're selling was made in Greece might make a difference to someone who's really looking for the Russian version. A Japanese vase might not be of interest to someone who's looking for Austrian vases. If the Martin Luther King, Sr., book was printed in South Africa, it would make a difference to a collector looking for South African objects, or someone looking for a book that deals with a different perspective of the man's life.

Some items are made in America first, then copies are made in Japan. Collectors want to know whether they're getting the original item or a cheaper copy. And, believe it or not, some people would rather have the rip-off copy than the original. So, if you're aware of where the piece was made, include that detail in your description.

Be explicit!

Once you've decided what you need to include in your one-liner, you'll be ready to tackle the larger description. Basically, you should expand upon the

Unofficially...
Although eBay was unavailable for a few hours over the turn of the millennium, their stats the day before New Year's Day 2000 counted 2,527,533 items listed for sale.

details you've included in the one-liner. Include all the pertinent information about your article, as well as some selling points. For the most part, the online auctions let you set the length of your description (within reason), but keep in mind that the punchier and more informative the description, the more likely you are to sell your piece.

Always include the following information in every pertinent description you write for your online auctions:

1. Name of item
2. Manufacturer or maker information
3. Size, quality, and condition
4. Age
5. Signature/maker's marks
6. Color

This is where details are most important. If you call an item by an incorrect name or attribute it to a manufacturer who had nothing to do with the item's creation, or if you don't tell your audience that the piece was made in the Tuscan countryside, potential buyers might lose faith in you and your product. On the other hand, if you supply every piece of information buyers need to know, you will save them time and energy.

If a description is done well, the buyer shouldn't see the need to contact to seller to ask additional questions. It's time-consuming and frustrating when one has to wait for an answer before making a bid. We've seen bidders ask questions right down to the last seconds of the auction. If we hadn't been at the computer to field those questions quickly, the buyer would not have had the appropriate information with which to make an informed decision.

One of the things both buyers and sellers need to remember when bidding online is that each is asking the other for a bit of faith. Yes, the auctions are usually protected, but isn't it a lot easier to get the item you were expecting rather than one that wasn't represented correctly? Though most reputable dealers don't have a problem with goods being returned, it is time-consuming to have to repackage the item and mail it back, then wait for either a refund or another item. Whatever you can do to make the process smoother for your customers (and sellers), you should do. And the first step is to make your description as specific as possible. Better to have too much information than not enough.

Be honest about condition and age

Moneysaver
By being honest about your item's qualities, you will save yourself the possible loss of money if a dissatisfied customer returns the item—not to mention the extra postage costs and possible bank charges you'll incur!

It's very tempting to hide that age crack when you're photographing a vase to sell on eBay. We're often negligent of noting that the book we're selling on Amazon has some yellowing pages. And people often expect a certain amount of wear on Native American blankets. But, if you're going to make a decent business selling at auction, or even if you're just entering into the Yahoo! auction to get rid of an old collection of albums, you need to be as honest as possible about condition and age since those two factors are often of paramount importance with online auction buyers.

That minor ding in the metal sculpture done by your grandmother might not matter to you, but it will be the first thing a collector sees when unpacking it after receiving it from you. On the other hand, a major scratch might not bother the person who wants a new computer yet has no problem with the way the outside case looks as long as the internal parts are intact.

In addition to the condition of your item, you need to tell prospective buyers its age. If you're lucky, the piece is marked with a date. Books, newspapers, magazines, some advertising tins, prints, works of art, and many electronic devices are marked with their manufacture dates. However, you may have to rely on a reference to a particular era or decade to indicate date.

Why is the date an item was made of particular importance? Sometimes an item will be worth more because of the impressed date. For example, we just learned that a certain segment of U.S. state quarters that are currently being circulated were made incorrectly. Thus the quarters (we believe they were impressed with Connecticut on the back) are rare and likely worth more to the collector because there are fewer in circulation. Any quarters in the future will be made differently since the first ones printed were incorrect.

Spelling counts!

The first impression someone will get about you as a salesperson will be the words you use in your descriptions. If those words are misspelled or incorrectly punctuated, you are telling the reader something about yourself. If your ad is peppered with misspellings and grammatical errors, not only will it make the description difficult to read, the buyer might wonder if the seller is as lazy about the way she cares for and packs her items as she is about grammar and spelling.

The way you present yourself in your ads can determine not only how the buyer perceives you, but whether the buyer gets the correct information. For example, if the word "forth" is misspelled and reads "fourth," a buyer might be totally confused.

Timesaver
Instead of going to each auction site separately, you can save hours by doing an online bid search at a site such as BidFind. Com. Just enter the item you're looking for and the search engine will look through a number of auctions simultaneously.

In addition, if you misspell a word in the description of an item, the person to whom you really want to sell might not even see the item you're selling—specifically because you've misspelled the word. A search engine (whether one used within the auction site or one that searches the whole Net) will only find the exact word for which you're searching. If that word is misspelled, the search will not uncover it. Thus, if a buyer comes looking for "Hemingway's memoirs" and you've got a personalized journal written by Papa himself and have it listed as "Hemmingway's memoirs," your item will not appear when the buyer does a search.

Though it is truly sad that a good part of our population cannot spell correctly, there are ways to take care of this problem. Here are some suggestions:

- Create your descriptions in your word processing program, do a spell check on them, then cut and paste them into your description online.

- Use an auction program that includes a spell-check feature. Some of these include OpenSite Auction Software, Visual Auction Server 4.0, Auction Assistant (Blackthorne Software), and Mister Lister (available on eBay).

- Invest in a good dictionary and thesaurus (see the next section) and check them frequently as you're writing your descriptions.

- Proofread your work carefully, or ask someone you trust to proofread your online auction ads before you upload them to the auction site.

- Use an e-mail program that allows you to spell check your notes before you mail them to prospective customers.

You may think that all this spell checking might be unnecessary since you're only planning on selling a few items here and there. Why do this if you're not going to make a living at it, right? Look at it this way: If people surfing your site begin to feel bogged down because they can't understand what you're saying, they are not likely to spend the extra time and energy decoding your spelling or guess at what you're describing. You are competing against the very stringent test of time. You only have a second or two to get your buyer's attention. If you don't have it in the first couple of words, and if you don't keep it long enough to make a bid, you might not sell your item. Remember, you're up against millions of other items currently being sold on Web-based auctions. Give yourself the best odds of succeeding by paying attention to every last detail!

Attractive item descriptions—the value of a thesaurus

Most computer word processing programs include a thesaurus and a spell check feature; however, we have always believed that the thesauruses included with computer programs are not as thorough or extensive as some of the larger hardcover books. What a thesaurus will do is open up your description to more specific and image-oriented words rather than allowing yourself to rely on tried-and-true (and boring!) words that most readers skim over without really seeing (words like "very," "lovely," "beautiful," "truly," etc.).

By using your thesaurus on a regular basis, you'll be able to replace words like "black" with "ebony," "jet," and "raven." You'll be able to tell potential sellers that your porcelain platter is an exquisite shade

Timesaver
Bookmark a good thesaurus (like www.thesaurus. com) or buy the best book version you can afford and utilize it to find a quick substitute for the tired phrases you use to describe your items. Spending a moment or two spicing up your item descriptions will reap monetary benefits later!

of teal (instead of saying that it is a pretty blue). You can term that piece of material that goes over your bed a "coverlet," "quilt," or "counterpane," instead of plain old "bedspread."

Honesty in authentication and grading an item—don't guesstimate!

Most online auctioneers/sellers say that they try not to overrate an item's condition. Better to be safe than sorry seems to be the motto followed by most sellers. If you describe an item as being in excellent condition, you'd better be sure there are no nicks or worn spots, no cracks or chipped paint. If you tell a customer that the toy they are buying is mint-in-package, that package better be in absolutely perfect shape. However, don't err on the side of failure. If your item is fairly rare and in good shape, don't highlight its obvious show of age. As one of our antique dealer friends is fond of saying, "I'd have a wrinkle or two if I were a hundred years old!"

If you're fair with yourself and your customers, you'll watch your qualifying words (e.g., "might be," "maybe," "probably," "could be") when writing your description. If you think the toy might be a Tonka, but there's a possibility you're wrong and you can't find any maker's marks, then write: "Looks like a Tonka, but I can't find any marks." Don't misrepresent your items. Don't tell the buyer the painting looks like a Picasso if you're not a Picasso expert! You're safer saying "it's in the style of Picasso."

When determining the grade you'd give an item (such as A+, or "This one's a 10!" or "in great shape for its age"), be careful to slightly underestimate the grade. We have often seen items described as being in "good condition" that we deem to be far more valuable. Because of that reason, we feel like we're getting a bit of a bargain and might tend to pay a little more than usual for the item. That psychology works for most buyers. Why not leave them a little happier than they expected to be, rather than disappointed because you'd bragged about having an absolutely superb piece that they thought was pretty average?

Shipment and address info

Most online auctioneers include information about their shipping charges in the ad. Some auction programs include an automatic feature that adds shipping info to every ad you set up, but it's wise to also add this info to the body of your ad, especially when the item might be fragile. It never hurts to assure your customers that you will pack their item carefully.

Customers also want to know whether the shipping charges will be figured out for them ahead of time. By adding a line that says you charge $5.00 for shipping and handling, the buyer can automatically add that amount to the cost of the goods. If you need to figure out postage each time you sell an item, you're only slowing yourself down and leaving yourself open for problems.

Though we've always thought one set shipping and handling price is best (we lose money on some pieces and then gain it back on others), it does sometimes blow up in our faces. For example, until recently we didn't note in our auction ads any difference in shipping costs whether domestic or international. An item we'd estimated would cost approximately $4.00 to package and ship actually cost $17—when we discovered the buyer was in Australia! Now we make sure to add a line to our descriptions that states "The buyer picks up shipping costs of a certain amount for the United

"
You must do business on eBay. I've never seen so many boxes come through my booth as I do now that everyone's on eBay.
—Postal worker to a customer holding boxes
"

States. Internationally shipped packages are handled individually."

When mentioning shipping costs, you might also want to add the weight of the item to the description. For those who are bidding from another part of the world, the weight will help them determine whether it's worthwhile to have the piece shipped internationally.

If you intend to offer your buyers the option of insuring their packages (highly recommended; see Chapter 15, "Packaging for a Safe Journey"), mention that fact. Though most packages make it through the U.S. Postal System, United Parcel Service, or Federal Express just fine, there have been times when packages we've shipped have reached their destinations in pieces. One such item was made of iron and steel (an antique set of scales), and we were amazed when the customer contacted us, very upset that the scale that would have finished his set of Fairbanks scales was in jagged pieces. Mentioning that you offer the option of insuring your packages will instill a bit of faith in your business skills.

Bidders want all the information up front, so offer whatever you can to them regarding additional costs. Be as honest and personable as possible. Encourage them to bid or to ask any additional questions.

Know your products—research!

Though part of the glamour of an auction persists because people like a good story ("Hey, did you hear about the guy who found an old painting in his attic and when he took the frame apart, he found an original copy of the Declaration of Independence?"), you should not attempt to tell a story about an item unless you are certain your tale is correct.

If you're not sure whether the spoon you want to sell was actually owned by Paul Revere, don't state the possibility. If you have a bit of proof that the spoon really does have some provenance, then a bit of research is in order.

How do you find out?

When you are baffled regarding what to write about the items you're trying to sell, take a couple of moments to research the item. There are many ways to go about the discovery process; however, since you're probably online anyway, the first thing to do is an online search. But what if you don't have a clue about the words to use when searching for information about the item?

We believe there are three easy ways to do some quick research. There are plenty of other ways to find out what your item is and how much it might be worth, but try these avenues of research first:

1. Online search

2. Library search

3. Online auction chatrooms

The first thing you need to conduct your research is a good picture of your object (we suggest at least three photos, taken from different angles and possibly showing close up shots or details or any kinds of maker's marks). Then gather all the information you already know about the object, such as its size, weight, and color. Finally, try to determine who the experts are and how to contact them.

Can you trust your sources?

Some items are more easily identified than others. For example, you know that if you find something that looks like a coin, chances are you can find a coin dealer somewhere nearby who can tell you

Moneysaver
If you intend to get your item appraised before putting it up for auction, make sure you put a reserve on the item and build in your cost for getting the appraisal done so you don't lose the investment you've made.

where your coin is from and what it might be worth. But if you're not sure whether your item is a coin or something else, made of porcelain or pottery, or from the Ming or Ching Dynasty, it's time to ask an expert.

Certain specialists might give you the benefit of their years of expertise for free, but licensed appraisers ask a fee for their written appraisals. Naturally, if you pay someone for an appraisal, you have a right to expect the appraiser to be trustworthy. The new site that we're part of, eppraisals.com, makes sure their appraisers are well educated in their fields, so their nominal fees reassure you that the company will stand behind the people they've hired to do the appraisals. There are several sites like this online, and there are also local, national, and international societies of appraisers.

If you ask the local toy dealer to give you a general ballpark figure of what that 1964 Superman doll is worth, and she gives you a free guesstimate, then you can't complain—and you can pretty much believe that since the person makes her living selling these items, she should know what they're worth. However, if you ask a fellow buyer or collector to share some information, you are taking what we believe to be a 50/50 chance that the dates or other details will be accurate.

Doing a library search is often the safest bet. If there are books published on the subject you're researching, you can get an indication that someone checked to see whether the facts were correct. But in any book about any kind of collectible, we believe there is a certain amount of subjectivity, thus making it all just a matter of opinion.

Sites and books for instant info

There are a number of research sources, depending on what type of item you're selling. We could write a book on just the Internet and print sources you might use to find out the details about your items, but here are some appraisal and general research sources we've always found to be reputable and reliable:

- **eppraisals.com.** New to the online bidding community, this site offers appraisals of just about anything and has hired a host of experts in many different fields. Items are photographed and each expert is expected to perform a certain number of appraisals every week. The site owners offer a full staff of computer professionals to keep up with the traffic.

- **4antiques.com.** This site offers information on appraisers, chatrooms where you can find out about your items, links to other research sites, and other reference guides where you can learn how to appraise antiques and collectibles.

- **4anything.com.** This site offers information about collectibles, cars, hobbies, electronics, computers, jewelry, dolls, stamps, and much more. Whatever you are trying to research, you can take the first step in your research process here.

- **Books by Terry and Ralph Kovel.** This pair of antiques and collectibles experts has been publishing price guides for years. If you would rather flip through a book, the Kovels' guides are for you. The books are published by Crown and available in any bookstore. Special editions are also available about specific topics.

- **Books by Dawn Reno.** Yes, I have written specialized books on collecting African American items, Native American artwork and artifacts, country collectibles, advertising items, and romance novels.

- **Maloney's *Antiques and Collectibles Resource Directory*.** This is a listing of all the experts in many different collectible categories, such as those who buy or sell anything from agricultural items to automobiles, bicycles to bronzes, figurines to Girl Scout memorabilia, paper collectibles to tokens. If someone collects it, sells it, has formed an association, or started a magazine on the topic, Maloney lists him as an expert. Most are quite eager to share their knowledge (which is why they've consented to be listed). Some will charge for appraisals.

Just the facts

- The introductory line for selling your item can attract or repel your bidders. Every word counts!

- Remember to always include information about the size, age, and condition of the items you're selling.

- Honesty is always the best policy when offering evaluations of your items.

- The more details you can include about an item, the better.

- Getting appraisals of your items can offer you valuable information that you'll be able to share with your customers—and perhaps a better price for your goods.

GET THE SCOOP ON...
Taking professional photos ▪ Creating
digitized images ▪ Regular camera, digital camera, or video camcorder? ▪ Scanning images ▪
The best way to upload graphics

Should I Use Photos?

Chapter 9

When online auctions first started, you could get by without uploading a photo of your item in order to sell it, but nowadays, even the most mundane items are accompanied by a photo. Using digitized photo images, commonly called JPGs (pronounced "jay-peg;" stands for Joint Photographic Expert Group) or GIFs (pronounced "jiff;" stands for Graphics Interchange Format), in your ads allows your bidders to see what they're actually bidding on, and isn't that important? Listing items without photographs is like ordering something over the phone without seeing it first. Unless you know exactly what you're ordering (such as a subscription to a newspaper), you're not likely to buy without seeing the item first.

There are several choices of how to add an image to your listing—quite a difference from a couple of years ago, when the only type of picture you could see on a computer was a line drawing of some sort. Now you can not only include pictures, but moving images as well! We remember the days when the general public was amazed by *Star Trek*'s computers, but now those technological "marvels" seem like something from the dark ages.

Take heart in the fact that it doesn't take a photographic genius to create the types of images that will entice buyers to bid on your product.

People like to see what they're getting

Bright Idea
The better the picture, the more confident the buyer will be about making the purchase—and that's what it's all about.

Whether the item you're listing is a rare dime or a giant totem pole, bidders want to see the details. They might simply need to know what the piece looks like, or more importantly, whether it fits into their collection. A person interested in a certain type of dime will be inspecting your photo to see whether the dime has the correct markings, while a person interested in a totem pole that features a raven's head might look for that detail.

We are a visual society, lulled into laziness by constant hours watching a television or computer screen. Even menus in some restaurants have photos showing the various meals available. One of the reasons we've become so visual is that photos excite senses that words might not; however, another reason is that people are essentially in a hurry. A picture is worth a thousand words, isn't it? And you don't have space or time to cram a thousand words into your listing, so let the photo do the talking for you.

When considering whether to add photos to your listings, you should also think about how many photos to add and what type of shot would be best to represent your piece. Some items call for several different images, taken from various angles, in order to supply the bidder with details about size, quality of color, markings, and an idea of what kind of damage (if any) there is to the object.

A quick trip to several auction sites as we wrote this revealed the following:

- A rare silver dollar photographed only one time but in a very large format so that every detail of the front of the coin was highly visible. One of the comments in the list of e-mails about this item mentioned that the bidder would have liked to see the back of the coin.

- A 1964 Chevrolet Malibu in mint condition and photographed from the front, rear, and driver's side. The three photos were large and slow-loading, but revealed a car that looked as thought it had just come out of the showroom. The written description was simply one line: The car was purchased new by an elderly woman who'd kept it in her garage.

- A *Babylon 5*/Michael Garibaldi doll in its original package and photographed three times: in full view from the front, showing the foldout cover, and a close-up of the doll's face. Other items in the *Babylon 5* category did not include photos and appeared to have fewer bids than those accompanied by images.

- A signed Webb art nouveau cameo glass vase with lilies photographed seven times: from the top looking down, from the side (full view), a close-up of the signature, a view of the vase lying down and showing the signature, two more photos of the whole vase, and one showing the vase tilted toward the camera.

- A pair of Danecraft silver bracelets photographed four times: side by side on a purplish background, one of each bracelet, then the two bracelets together so that the bidder

Unofficially...
In the eBay chatroom, the conversation often turns to what makes a customer buy. Recently, eBay sellers stated that they find if they add more than one photo, the listing gets more attention from buyers.

can see the scrollwork and leaf detail on each bracelet.

■ A 19-piece set of dinnerware in the Weathervane pattern made by Blue Ridge China. Several full shots of the set itself, plus closeups of the pieces, as well as the markings on the bottoms of the plates. Figure 9.1 shows the listing so you can see how our friend and eBay auctioneer, Fred Elwell, has illustrated his product.

19 Piece Blue Ridge "Weathervane" Set, 4 chips. Set of dinnerware sold on eBay by dealer Collector123846.

As you can see, sellers are often using more than one image for items that are valued by collectors, are marked with a signature, or are large items (like the car) that must be seen from all angles.

A quick scan through a number of pages of listings tells us that the items without photographs have fewer bids than the ones with photos. Though some of them take a long time to load, it's worth it to the bidder/collector to see the item in detail. And because uploading photos is becoming easier every day, sellers are using several shots to offer bidders the opportunity to see everything they must in order to make a decision.

A professional's tips for taking great photos

We've all seen photos that look like they were taken in full sun (all bleached out and whiter than they should be) or in shadows that create defects where there aren't any. Or, even worse, double or triple images that make you want to rub your eyes in frustration.

Before we talk about how to transfer your photos into image files, let's discuss the best way to take clear shots of your items. Since Bobby (your co-author) has worked for the past 10 years as a professional photographer, he has some hints for you (both from personal experience with uploading photos and from mistakes he's made that you can learn from). Always remember: It's not the camera, it's the photographer behind it!

1. Make sure you have the proper lighting. This is the most important factor! If your item throws a shadow or you are throwing a shadow with your own body, it will ruin your photograph. Some photographers swear by natural lighting, but we like to use fill flashes to make sure that all details are lit and clear. A fill flash can be as simple as a piece of white paper angled to bounce off the light, or it can be a regular flash unit. A regular desk light (with a 100-watt bulb) pointed at the object from above will work like a spotlight, too, if you don't have one.

2. Use backgrounds that will contrast with the colors of the piece you're photographing. For example, a white item looks best against a blue

(not black) background. Black will blend in with the background if you scan your item.

3. The background should be larger than your item so that there is no clutter in the photograph. A plain colored sheet often works well as a background, but if it's wrinkled, each wrinkle will show in your photo. We use crepe or plain blue paper. If you're going to be taking a lot of photos, you might want to have several different backgrounds on hand. Photo shops have rolls of paper backdrops. The paper is seamless and you can pull new paper off the roll every time the piece you're using gets soiled or damaged.

4. Focus in tightly on the item. Depending on the type of camera you're using, you can zoom in or just take a close shot by moving closer to the item. You don't need background details of your wallpaper or the area behind the piece. Crop the photo closely so that your customers see only what they are buying.

5. Take more than one shot, showing the imperfections or highlights of the item (signatures, maker's marks, distinctive markings, country of origin, etc.). If your piece is decorated or marked, you should shoot it from both sides as well as from the top and bottom. This is especially important when you have a costly item or one that is recognizable from its trademark or maker's signature.

6. If you are photographing something covered by glass or with a highly reflective surface, be sure that your light is diffused. By that, we mean no bare bulbs. Sometimes a plain sheet

of white paper held in front of or over the light will help diffuse the bulb (don't hold it too close, however, or you'll have a fire!).

7. Make sure your film is advancing properly. Many a photographer has spent several hours carefully composing great photos only to realize at the last moment that the film never made it past the first frame.

8. Use good-quality film. We've always had luck with Kodak or Fuji. Check their Web sites (www.kodak.com; www.fujifilm.com) for additional tips and developing information.

We also recommend you get your pictures developed in disk or CD format whenever possible. It'll save you the time of scanning each photo, and the disk images usually are already in the JPG or GIF format that you need to add them to your listings. The only time you might want to break this rule is if you need your photos in a hurry (or if you have a tight budget; disk images and CDs are more expensive than photos). One-hour developing services only offer traditional photos; you must wait a week or longer for CD or disk versions of your images. For that very reason, a lot of online auctioneers are using digital cameras or video cameras these days to capture images and bring them online.

Cameras: Regular or digital? Or video?

The way you take photos and add them to your listings largely depends on how much you want to invest in your online auction business, as well as how graphically adept you are.

There are several different ways to take photos of your objects and digitize them for inclusion in your listings. You can go the traditional route of pulling out your Kodak or Nikon, taking photos, getting the film developed, and then scanning the shots. Or you can use a digital camera, which enables you to put the pictures directly on disk or to download them directly to your hard drive through an interface. Or you can use a video camera that will directly download.

You can download your images from a digital camera to your computer several different ways: through a serial or parallel port via the use of a cable that connects from the hard drive to the camera, or by using a flash or PCMCIA card (check your camera's instructions to see which is available to you). You can also connect through the "scuzzy" port (the SCSI port or "Small Computer System Interface"). However, we believe the easiest way to download digital images is to simply shoot the images onto disk and pop the disk into the computer.

The photographic options include regular cameras, and digital cameras that shoot both stills and video. Let's take a closer look at each.

Regular cameras

Though you can take photos with any kind of camera, one that has a zoom option is more desirable, because it allows you to get in closer to an item (especially important if you have a signature or maker's mark that you want buyers to be able to see). For example, Hummels are marked in many different ways (as well as different colors). In order for collectors to know when and where the Hummel was made, they need to be able to see the mark clearly. With a zoom lens, you can get in close and take a clear shot of the mark. By using this feature, you are offering your bidders the details they need in order to make the decision whether or not to buy.

Is one camera better than another? We like Nikon, although there are many on the market that offer just as many features without the big price tag. If you're looking for a good inexpensive camera, try the Pentax or Canon models that have automatic as well as manual features.

Naturally, you can buy just about any camera at online auctions, but there are also specialty shops online, such as:

- Access Discount Camera and Video (www.accesscamera.com)

- Capitol Camera (www.capitolcamera.com)

- Kodak (www.kodak.com)

- Pentax (www.pentax.com)

- Photographers Space (www.photospace.com)

- Wall Street Camera (www.wall-street-camera.com/)

Digital cameras

All the major camera companies now offer digital cameras. Depending on your budget and your needs, there are many from which to choose. Here are just a few that have been reviewed online:

- **Canon PowerShot Pro 70.** Although this camera has excellent images and is compact, light, easy to use, and expandable (you can add features to it), reviews state that it has a short zoom and is slow. On the other hand, the battery life is long and you can choose to use an 8MB card that holds 20 shots or an additional 80MB card that slips into a second slot that holds 215 shots. The sample photos we've seen are incredibly clear and detailed—just what online auctioneers need. The fold-out LCD screen gives a 2" preview of your photos. Users say it's easy to handle as well as to learn. Price: $700.

- **Kodak DC260.** Reviewers give this camera thumbs-up on its Digita controls and sharp images, but there are no automatic exposure options, which most amateur photogs rely upon. The LCD is also slow, so extreme close-ups are tough to manage. To download the images to a computer, you can connect via a cable that plugs directly into your computer, or you can store images on a card reader. This camera also gives you the option of numbering the images it loads consecutively, making it easy to drag or click on images and pull them into folders. That is a huge advantage for online auctioneers who might want to keep certain items in different categorized folders. Price: $899.

- **Nikon Coolpix 900.** This camera weighs an even pound and has the usual Nikon quality and heft that the company is well known for. As soon as you take a shot, it is shown on the LCD in a matter of seconds. The camera starts quickly and photos are clear and detailed. Reviewers state that the camera's controls are where you would expect them to be and easy to learn. It also has a battery-saving and metering option, and all menus are clearly displayed and accessible. The images load quickly, and time lapse between taking shots is approximately five to eight seconds. The automatic exposure is excellent. The Adobe PhotoDeluxe program is included with this camera so you can adjust images before saving them to your hard drive. Price: $799.

■ **Sony Mavica.** A large and clunky camera, this one definitely won't fit in your pocket. It's also heavier than the others, weighing in at two pounds. However, it's fast, easy to use, and has the only 14X zoom on the market. Because this camera is so large, the buttons and menus are accessible and easy to use. The zoom is the selling point on this camera, as well as the fact that you can see whole disk copies of the image in the camera itself. Reviewers say that the pics are better than some taken with a 500mm lens on a regular 35mm camera. Price: Over $1,000.

■ **HP C200 PhotoSmart Camera.** A small digital camera is one of the favorites of people who don't have much technical knowledge but need a digital camera. It stores 80 shots and has an easy "point and shoot" capability. However, the LCD tends to drain the battery, so users are warned to keep the LCD viewer off in order to make the batteries last longer. There is no zoom on this little camera, but for the money, it's worth a shot. Price: $299.

When shopping for a digital camera, remember that the higher the MB of storage, the more pics you'll be able to take and store before downloading. For example, 2MB of memory will save about 10 to 50 photos, depending on the resolution (the higher the resolution, the more space the image will take up in your memory).

Image quality depends on resolution, so the higher the resolution, the better the quality of the photo you're uploading to your listing. Low resolution (640 × 480 or less) is fine for the Web, but if you're trying to get fine details in your images, you're better off using a higher resolution. Remember, however, that it takes longer for photos with high resolution to load and you don't want your bidder to get tired of waiting.

Because digital cameras can be still (like the ones mentioned earlier) or video, online auction sellers need to decide which would be best for them. Still digital cameras take photos the same way traditional cameras do, but videocams "snap" an image from the continuous stream of video through the use of frame "grabbing" software. What this means is that while the video is on, you can save one or more still images from the moving images. Naturally, if your object isn't moving, you don't have to worry about camera shake—and that's the problem video cameras have.

If a video camcorder is attached to your computer, the resolution might be lower, meaning your images won't be as clear as a handheld digital camera.

For those of you who are working with WebTV, a movie camera or video camcorder is the only choice you have. Our brother, Bill, uses an RCA Autoshot 22x and is quite happy with the results. Another friend who's using WebTV has a Panasonic PVL 659 Palm Corder. (A comment here about WebTV: If you have the Classic version, you will need assistance in uploading your images—either a friend with a computer or access to a computer in a library or computer cafe. If you have WebTV Plus, you can do the image loading yourself. Check your instructions or the WebTV site [www.webtv.net].)

The best-selling and award-winning video add-on is Snappy. By plugging the Snappy hardware module into your PC or laptop parallel port and then adding your camcorder or still video camera to the port, you

Timesaver
Most of the cameras will work with either Windows or Macintosh programs, but check before you make the purchase!

simply watch the PC screen, then "snap" when you see the image you want to capture. The image is a high-resolution quality image that is then ready to be uploaded to your site. For more information, visit the Snappy site at http://cf.play.com/play/snappy/index.cfm.

One final comment: Most of the online auction sites offer information about cameras, including links to sites that review photographic equipment, often dependent on your particular needs. If you're going to make an investment, make sure it's in your budget, meets your needs, and is something you can easily use. Also make sure the camera will interface with the computer you're currently using.

Is it time for a scanner?

Scanners are used to scan photos or negatives you've taken with your regular camera. A scanner translates the colors and patterns in a photo or flat object into bits a computer will understand. Those little pieces of information are called pixels. The more pixels, the better (though it takes a long time for large amounts of pixels to load, they give the person viewing your image more digital bits of information; thus the image is clearer). The scanner, therefore, acts as the liaison between the photo and the computer. By translating those tiny dots of color and black and white into language the computer can understand, you can save that information in a JPG or GIF format and upload that image to your Web site or directly to the auction listing.

As we mentioned, scanners can be used when you take traditional photos of your items. However, remember that scanners can scan two-dimensional items, so you won't *need* to take photos of some of the products you'll be selling. This can save you lots of time and money. For example, if you are selling photos, postcards, comic books, books, or anything else that's flat, you can slip the item right onto the scanner's screen and scan away. No additional photos are necessary (as long as the item fits on the scanner screen).

A lot of sellers who've been doing online auctions for a while only use scanners, putting their noses in the air when others mention digital cameras. One of the reasons is that scanners not only create picture images, but can scan text as well.

Because you can buy a scanner relatively inexpensively these days (ours cost $59, after rebates), many people are able to add one to their computer. The average price falls between $100 and $300, and there are many options regarding how the computer and scanner will interface. Here are several that we (or someone we know) recommend:

- **Canon's CanoScan FB 620P** is cheap, scans in great color, and connects to a parallel port. At the time we were researching scanners, this one ran about $99. The scanner comes bundled with Adobe PhotoDeluxe, Xerox TextBridge Plus OCR, and Canon Creative Image software. The only complaint we've heard is that it is slow to scan.

- **Epson's Perfection 610** is fast and relatively inexpensive ($139). The scans are also rated as "crisp and sharp" by reviewers. The software is extremely easy and quick to install, and resolution is high. This scanner comes bundled with TWAIN software, PictureWorks HotShots (Mac/PC), NewSoft Presto! PageManager (Mac/PC), and Broderbund The PrintShop PressWriter (Mac/PC). It uses a USB interface.

- **HP's ScanJet 3200 C** has terrific gray scale scanning but is a little slow and less sharp when scanning color. The bundled software includes HP PrecisionScan LT w/Caere OCR and Adobe PhotoDeluxe. Some reviewers state that the software is inconsistent and most reported that they had uneven results with the color scanning and the amount of time it took to scan. The retail price is $89.

> **"**
> HP scanners seem best for non-Western fonts. Other than that, I like the EasyPhoto scanner I have in the lab, but it's awfully slow.
> —Sue Breeyear, Director of the University of Vermont Language Resource Center
> **"**

The upshot? It's worth it to shop around for a scanner that's fast and good with color photos, since time is of the essence and quality color images are important for online auctions. Pay attention to the maximum optical resolution settings on the scanners you research, as well as the price. If you can find something with high settings at a reasonable price and don't mind that it might be slow, check it out. Remember, however, that it's always a good idea to have some technical support if something goes wrong. Several of the scanners we checked out reportedly offered no technical support whatsoever. Before you buy, find out whether there is any support (check the box or the directions that come with the scanner for 800 numbers).

Make sure you have room on your hard drive!

One of the many things we've discovered the hard way is that images take up a lot of disk space. Before you even begin scanning or adding images, make sure you have enough room on your hard drive.

A quick check of some of the images saved on our hard drive shows that they average approximately 15 to 20 KB. When you are scanning a photo, figure on at least three times that much. Manipulating a photo on your desktop or through a photo program like Adobe PhotoShop means you need a lot of room to "work around it." Without getting too technical, figure that the larger the image (number of pixels), the slower it loads, and the more space you need to adjust it so that your bidders won't have to wait forever for it to load.

Remember that all computers are not created equal and some of the people bidding on your auction have older computers (or they might not be viewing the image in the same format that you used to upload it).

Once you scan a photo or object, you might need to adjust the image. There are many image editing programs available and some even come with the scanner itself. Ours came with Picture Mall, but that program doesn't really do everything we need. We have also used Microsoft's Photo Editor, and the new 2000 version does everything but bark.

Here are some other programs recommended by others for use in tweaking your photos (sizing, cropping, making thumbnails, brightening or darkening, sharpening focus, etc.):

- Adobe Photoshop (www.adobe.com)

- PaintShop Pro (www.jasc.com)

- Microsoft Picture It! (www.home-publishing.com/ HomePages/PIExpress_ProductInfo_Highlights. asp?RLD=256)

- QFX (www.qfx.com)

- GIF Construction Set Professional (Windows only) (www.mindworkshop.com/alchemy/ gifcon.html)

- Color It! (Macintosh only) (www.microfrontier. com/products/colorit40/index.html)

- Ulead PhotoImpact 5 (www.ulead.com)

Bright Idea
While pics in your item description are great, make sure you don't use too many— if they take too long to load, a prospective buyer may become impatient and "surf on."

You can download sample tutorials or the whole program at any of these sites. If you decide after trying a tutorial that you really don't like the program, you don't have to buy it. Some of these programs are also freeware/shareware, which means you need to put up with some ads when you use the program, but at least you don't have to pay for it!

If the program you want is not available for a free download, you can always search the online auctions to see whether there are any copies up for auction.

Uploading documents and photos

If the auction you're working with doesn't offer instant uploading services for your images, you need to upload your GIFs or JPGs to a Web page or Web hosting service, then make the link to your auction. This is a simple step, but one which frightens most "newbies" to the online auction scene.

Check to see whether your ISP offers free Web pages to its customers. Ours offered us 5MB of space, so we added a personal Web page (designed in Microsoft Word) and a simple link to our Web page in eBay. The Web page in our ISP's directory offered us the space we needed to store the images that were eventually included on our online listings (see Chapter 5, "The Importance of Making Yourself Known," for more information about creating your own Web page).

Make sure your ISP doesn't mind you doing a little side business on your Web page. Some have a problem acting as a host service for online auctions and might cancel your service if they find out what you're doing. Better that you do the research right up front.

Several of the larger search engines (Yahoo!, Netscape, Lycos) offer free Web pages to their members, as well as e-mail service. But, remember, you still need an ISP to get online!

Load those pics *fast*

There are also image hosting services online, such as Photo Assistant (www.photoassistant.com), Krickets Korner (www.kricketskorner.com), EyeNet Images (http://eyenetimages.com), and PayPal.com (www. paypal.com) that will act as a repository for your images.

These services make putting up your auction listings simple because they delete some of the steps you would normally take to upload images (such as using an FTP program). For example, Photo Assistant (used by lots of eBay customers) uploads a selected file straight from your computer to its server. You are given 5MB of space to store your graphics. Once you're finished with the auction, that graphic is erased, so you'll have room to put up your new files. It's fast, easy, and offers you the option of getting e-mails telling you how many visitors have viewed your images.

Of course, the quickest way to load your images is to find an auction where you just upload from your directory to theirs. Yahoo! offers this service, and quite a few of the newer auctions do as well.

And remember: Keep your image small (set your compression level at high) so it will load more quickly. Customers don't like to wait! If you can use thumbnails, your ads will load more quickly and if customers choose, they can view the larger image to see more detail.

Moneysaver
Always check the auctions first, rather than taking a trip to your local office supply or computer program store.

Just the facts

- JPGs and GIFs are digitally compressed images that are easily readable by all programs and commonly used in online auction listings.

- Both regular and digital cameras can be used to produce photos for your auctions, but there are definite advantages and disadvantages to both.

- Scanners can be used not only to copy your photos, but also to scan two-dimensional objects.

- A Web hosting service can make uploading your images to your online auction much simpler and faster.

- The larger your image, the longer it will take to load.

Auction Management Programs

Although you can get away without using a program for setting up your online auction listings and monitoring your sales, most professional sellers say that the programs not only help them upload their graphics files and manage their auctions, but they also help produce professional-looking ads.

For those who are going to sell more than a couple of items and perhaps make part of their living in the online auction business, an auction management program makes a lot of sense. It helps people create auction listings in a truly eye-catching manner, and saves sellers time by automating some of the standard entries one makes when putting items up for auction.

In this chapter, we'll discuss the different programs that are available and how they work. We'll give you the pros and cons, as well as a few tips for streamlining your work.

233

Should you make the investment?

Most of the auction management programs in use today were designed when eBay was still a pup. These programs worked directly with the eBay system, specifically designed to interface with eBay's format and guidelines. Sellers soon found out that the more attractive the ad, the more buyers who would drop in to bid. As a result, the programs became more popular.

Sellers started demanding more. They wanted programs that would help them communicate automatically with their buyers at the end of an auction. And they were developed. Then buyers wanted programs that would generate automatic bids at the last second on items they wanted (the term for those last-second bids is sniping). And they were developed. Ultimately, buyers wanted auction programs that took care of all the details. And they were developed.

Then auctions started doing all of that for the sellers. And the sellers said, "We still need our programs." But do we need to spend the money to get one or all of these programs?

The price of auction management software averages around $15 to $20, with some simpler programs starting below $10 and others topping out at around $60. Some are even free! (And free is good. Free is something any seller can handle!)

How do you figure out whether you need to spend the money on additional software? Simple: Determine whether you're going to be selling online on a regular basis, then figure out whether the items you're selling will be netting you a regular profit. If so, you can justify buying one or more of the programs we'll be discussing throughout the chapter. If you are using one of the auctions that allows you to upload directly to the site and you are just selling at auction as a hobby, you don't need to bother with a program.

However, if you're going to investigate putting together your own auction Web site, it would definitely be to your advantage to invest in some top-notch software to make your job easier. Because this software is being developed on a daily basis, your best bet is to check to see whether any of the programs we mention in this chapter have been updated.

Another consideration is whether you will be selling/buying in more than one auction. Keeping track of which items you're selling, which auctions are closing, and which items you're bidding on can get pretty confusing. In the past couple of years, metasearch sites have helped buyers seek items on many different auction sites simultaneously. Buyers need that "one-stop shopping" type of capability and many of them have decided to check out several of the programs available to see which one works best for them.

As we've stated, it's best to visit the chatrooms to see what the other pros are using. Ask questions. Don't be shy! All of the prominent sellers were at one time beginners, and most are willing to share their knowledge.

Which auction management programs are the best?

Some auctions (such as Yahoo!) offer the services we're about to explain, but others (such as eBay) don't offer all of the services the auction management programs do—and they'll advise sellers which programs work best with their auction. Because it gets mighty confusing, we've tried to wade through the products available and offer the information you need to make your decision about which is right for you.

Andalé (www.andale.com)

This auction management service works online and takes a short time to set up, actually organizing your sales right after you register. They offer you the option of deleting your records when *you* choose, rather than having the auction site itself delete your records automatically after 30 or more days.

The program manages closed ads, finances, images, customer data, live sales, and live bids on one or more auctions simultaneously. The beauty of this program is that you can load your auctions without the hassle of learning how to use HTML (which makes us quite happy since HTML often can be confusing).

Andalé currently supports information from Amazon, eBay, and Yahoo!, but it expects to add other auction houses in the near future. It offers 100MB of storage space for your inventory information and images (that's thousands of images). And its customer data function allows you to put together mailing lists and send target announcements to specific customers.

Price: 2.95 percent of the winning bid; minimum 10¢ (starting April 1, 2000)

Auction Aid/Auction Ad Pro (www.firstdesign.com)

This program is designed to take the confusion out of HTML. With Auction Ad Pro, you simply fill in the blanks with your description and the program inserts it into any of the forms used by eBay, Amazon, Aaands, AuctionUniverse, NuAuction,

Timesaver
Most auction sites offer advice on which auction management software they recommend. If you search the help site, you might find a program that fits all your needs and works well with the auction you like best.

Yahoo!, and many others. Its selling features include a small program download, the availability of six background formats, and the ability to link to other auctions or your home page.

On the downside, you can only add one or two photos.

The sister program to Virtual Auction Ad Pro is Auction Aid, which offers information on putting photos on eBay, getting free stuff for your home page, using a variety of different background graphics for your ads or Web site, and finding auction-related sites. It also offers info on shipping and tracking, pre-formatted ad templates, how to add music to your ads or sites, and how to manipulate photos, as well as links to many different useful sites.

Price: Virtual Auction Ad Pro w/Auction Aid, $15.99; Virtual Auction Ad Pro only, $12.49

AuctionAssistant or AuctionAssistant Pro (www.blackthornesw.com)

We use this program, and it is constantly being updated. It is sold by Blackthorne Software and can handle just about any detail of an auction that a seller deems necessary, including creating ads using Ad Studio HTML. You can design your own ads, using a variety of backgrounds, fonts, and standard designs. You can also use Ad Studio to create sounds and animations, frames, and other design factors. If you take advantage of all that Ad Studio has to offer, your listings will definitely catch any bidder's eye.

In addition to easily handling HTML, AuctionAssistant automates all the end-of-auction details, such as e-mailing customers, tracking payments and shipment, and feedback. Blackthorne has also teamed with Honesty.com to provide page counters that let you know how many hits the page has had.

Moneysaver
Use the auction management software program's free trial version, if they offer one. Make sure it's something that is easy and quick for you *before* you enter your credit card number and buy the program.

The downside? AuctionAssistant only interfaces with eBay and it does not offer an image hosting service. You must have your own Web site to use this program. And it doesn't offer a MAC program.

Price: $59.95

AuctionAssistant Pro, also created by Blackthorne, offers all of the same options as AuctionAssistant, but is augmented by additional services (such as the ability to list all your inventory, whether it's going to be sold in an online auction or over the counter). You can handle all different types of sales with this program, as well as keep track of consigned auctions, print out records for each consignor, keep track of multiple users of the AuctionAssistant Pro system, and upload batches of items rather than one at a time (they work hand in hand with Mister Lister, eBay's batch uploading system, which as of September 1999 wasn't accepting any new users). There are various other features, including correspondence handling and—one of Dawn's favorites—spell checking.

Price: AuctionAssistant Pro (for existing AA customers), $149; for non-AA customers, $199

Auction Helper (http://members.xoom.com/jsamuels/)

This program helps organize your auctions by printing customer address labels and return address labels. It also calculates profit for sales, runs reports for items not sold and payments not received, and keeps track of buyer, auction, shipping, and payment information.

The downside? It doesn't create ads or upload them for you.

Price: $29.95

AuctionManager (www.AuctionRover.com/sell/)

This program organizes and manages your inventory, bulk uploads and re-lists items, offers the ability to create enhanced listings, allows you to post your item to multiple sites (as we write this, the program offers interfacing with eBay, Yahoo! and Amazon, with more promised in the future), suggests scheduling options that allow you to stagger your auctions' beginning and ending times, keeps track of customer correspondence, sends automatic e-mails to bidders, leaves automatic feedback, works with iShip.com to give you competitive shipping prices, and offers extensive customer support.

The downside? There doesn't seem to be one—it's even free!

Price: Free!

AuctionMate (www.myauctionmate.com)

Another eBay-specific program, AuctionMate offers the unusual capability of retrieving and loading auctions that were posted to eBay prior to the purchase of AuctionMate. In other words, you can re-list items without retyping the information previously entered on eBay. This program truly manages the auction from beginning to end, using ad listing features, reports about auctions in-progress or completed, reminders to contact winners and send feedback, reports on sales history and profits or sales tax, and retrieval of winners' names at the end of auctions. It batch loads auctions, provides auction templates, generates winners' e-mails, and provides extensive online help. The best part of this program is the graph that shows you how much (or how little) you made on every item you sold on eBay.

On the downside, it works only with eBay and appears to have very little in the way of creative ad listings.

Price: $25 (or take your chances buying it at auction on eBay)

Moneysaver
It's better to try one of the free programs if you don't know how long you'll be in the auction business. Don't invest any money if you don't have to. Give the business a trial run first.

Auction Wizard (www.standingwavesoftware.com/aw/)

A fairly new program, this is used in conjunction with eBay's Mister Lister and was developed "by eBay sellers for eBay sellers." Auction Wizard offers an inventory control module, e-mail functions, an integrated ledger system, automatic creation of HTML for your listings and Web sites, a built-in image editor, automatic FTP transfer, templates for everything from e-mail to Web sites, and many other features.

On the downside, it only works with eBay.

Price: $100

ePoster2000 (www.auctionposter.com)

This program creates postings for both Amazon and eBay and takes away the hassle of learning how to do HTML in order to list your items. It has enhanced bulk loading capabilities that work with both Mister Lister (eBay) and Amazon's Auctions and eShops. It also offers free image hosting services and works with eBay's shipping options, as well as Amazon's 1-Click payment options. ePoster2000's templates and counters, as well as its offline listings feature, make it easier for people who don't know HTML to set up and control their auctions.

The downside? This is just a posting program without the additional features of auction management software like AuctionAssistant. And this program only works with eBay and Amazon.

Price: Approximately $29.95/year, depending on which programs you use

Lorena

Another software program that works strictly with eBay, Lorena takes care of the whole cycle of buying and selling on eBay: figuring which items need to be ordered, writing notes to the suppliers, listing items on eBay, closing ended auctions, sending e-mails to the high bidders (as well as notes to second-highest bidders), printing envelopes and/or labels for shipping, printing lists of checks and money orders to be deposited, giving feedback, re-listing items, and requesting Final Value Fee refunds for deadbeat bidders. The only thing Lorena doesn't do is create your auction listing ads for you. It does create Web pages where your bidders can see the items you have for sale, but the ads are not automatically loaded. It's a very complicated program that offers a lot that the others do not.

The downside? It doesn't create listings and only works in eBay.

Price: Purchase at auction on eBay

As you can see, there are many programs available for the seller that will help manage auctions; however, many of them are eBay-specific and won't help you submit items to other auctions. Of all the ones we've mentioned, AuctionAssistant, Andalé, and AuctionManager offer the most support and options, and also appear to be the most popular on all the online auctions we've visited.

But wait, there are more programs that offer other capabilities!

Tracking your auctions

If you've been buying and selling on several auctions or are simply losing track of what you're doing on the auction of your choice, you might want to try a program that will help you track where you're bidding or what bids you've been receiving on the items you're selling. These programs are primarily designed to save you time. Only you can decide whether it's worth spending money on a program to do so. With that in mind, here are your options.

Bright Idea
Check out the prices of auction management programs on eBay (or your favorite auction) and take your chances bidding on one there rather than paying full price.

AuctionTamer (www.envsoftware.com/auction/)

This is actually a customized browser that allows you to track certain auctions (e.g., eBay, Amazon, Yahoo!, uBid, and the FairMarket Network that includes Microsoft, Excite, Lycos, ZDNet, and others). The options include being able to switch from one auction to another with the click of a color-coded tab, a sound signal when the bids have changed on an auction you're watching, automatic ID and password entering, and a fully customized list that allows you to add columns whenever you wish.

The downside? It's just a browser. It doesn't do anything else.

Price: $19.95

Auction Ticker (www.blackthornesw.com)

Created by Blackthorne Software, the makers of AuctionAssistant, this program automatically tracks your auctions, tells you what the bids are on each, and who the bidder is. The tracking feature resembles a ticker tape (hence the name of the program) that tells you the date and time each auction ends, the eBay ID number, the high bidder's name, and the price that is bid. It also sets off an alarm when an auction is about to end, gives you information about items you are bidding on or selling, refreshes automatically up to four times a day, and allows you to set your own preferences.

The downside? A higher cost, and the fact that it only interfaces with eBay.

Price: $19.95

Auction Trakker (www.AuctionTrakker.com)

This auction tracking program works directly with eBay and supports AOL, Compuserve, and all other Internet Service Providers. It's easily interfaced, has a single screen that automatically updates all the auctions where you're buying or selling (set the time period yourself), downloads auction information straight from eBay, posts automatic feedback, sends e-mails, calculates shipment dates, automatically backs up your data, places unattended snipe bids, allows multiple user IDs, tracks purchases as well as sales, calculates sales tax, and maintains all information from auctions that don't sell.

The downside is it works only with eBay.

Price: $44.95 without a bid; $39.95 with a bid (on eBay)

OnScan (www.onscan.com/)

We found this free downloadable software on eBay and are wondering about something: Why would they have it up for auction if it's free? The auction started at 1¢, yet you can go to the Web site and download this software without charge. It tracks auctions on eBay, Yahoo!, and Amazon simultaneously, and also informs you about e-mail. You get immediate alerts on your pager, cell phone, or via e-mail. You can be alerted about a variety of things: bids on auctions, the release of certain items (e.g., books, CDs, videos), or whether you have e-mail in your inbox. You set the alerts yourself and customize the settings.

The downside? Haven't found one yet!

Price: Free!

The Oracle (www.the-oracle.com/main.html)

Designed to help buyers and sellers keep track of auctions on eBay, The Oracle lets you configure your own alarms and find out the current price, high bidder, and descriptions of your chosen items. It also tells you the time remaining in each auction, the

> " An auction management program has to pay for itself within the first week or so for it to be worthwhile to me—and it has to be easy to use!
> —Rita Dillard, Amazon seller "

ending time of each auction calibrated to *your* local time zone, and which items you have set the program to snipe (place your bids at the last minute).

The downside: There is no MAC version available, and this program works strictly with eBay.

Price: $19.95

Automated bidding programs

Some buyers/sellers have begun using automatic bidding programs because there is no way they can be at the computer 24 hours a day, 7 days a week. Though we think there is a word for this kind of necessity to bid on items at auction (it's called addiction!), there are many programs designed to automatically submit bids on items you might like to purchase. Sniping, or slamming in a bid at the last second before anyone else has a chance to react, is becoming more and more commonplace at auctions. For those who want that last-minute bargain, programs have been developed to automatically enter a bid right down to the last millisecond. Here are just a few.

Auction Express (www.auctiontools.com)

Another eBay-exclusive program, Auction Express's most prominent features are its "Auto-Snipe" and "Mega Search" features. It allows you to automatically search for the items you are most likely to place a bid on and then either automatically insert bids at the last second or choose to do your bidding the old-fashioned way.

The downside? Their Web site is quite difficult to read, with a black bar down the left side that obscures some of the information about their product. They also work specifically with eBay and offer limited capabilities.

Price: $9.99

BidSniper Pro (www.datavector.net/products/ bidsniper/index.htm)

Another eBay tool that works best in Windows, BidSniper enables buyers/sellers to automatically bid on certain items by entering the item and the price you want to pay. It also allows you to synchronize your system's clock with eBay's official time. You can manage your bids on the Bid Manager screen, and you don't have to be online for BidSniper to enter your bid. The program notifies your ISP and opens just at the right second to enter your bid.

The downside is that this program, like so many others, works only with eBay.

Price: $12.95

End-user auction management programs

Because some sellers like auctions so much that they want to start their own, we've included one Web site here that helps new business owners create their own auction sites. Creating your own auction might be useful if you are dealing in specialized items or if you know your customers and your product extremely well. Our warning to you is this: During the months we spent online researching new auctions for this book, we discovered many that were nearly empty—no bidders, few sellers—and wonder how many auction sites are begun by eager business people who do not have the customer base to support such a venture. If you decide you want to go into the auction business, make sure you have a mailing list of at least several thousand people you believe might be interested in your auction; otherwise, you might join the hundreds of others who have active sites with no business.

Moneysaver
If you download programs directly from the site, you can save on shipping fees.

Auction Broker Software (www.auctionbroker. com) helps those who want to create their own auction sites. In order to take their online tour, you must register, stating how much you'd like to invest, where you would like to host your site, how many customers you expect to serve, what database you're using, what operations system you intend to employ, and how many employees you expect to have. They deal with each client on a personal basis, which is kind of nice in this day of e-mails. Prices depend on how much they are going to support you.

Problems with the programs

Bright Idea
If you're not sure whether your computer will support the software's requirements, send a quick e-mail to the company before purchasing it.

No matter which program you use and what your purpose is for using it, you will likely encounter a problem or two while getting used to the program. Sometimes it's because it doesn't do exactly what you expect. Sometimes the program's writers didn't anticipate certain bugs or have not worked them out yet. Sometimes it's because you didn't read the directions.

Whatever the case, there are many ways to solve any problems that you have with the software you purchase or download. Exhaust all these possibilities first. Most of the time, the problems with computer software are not with the software itself, but with the human beings trying to use it.

Taking your time to do some research before buying software can circumvent some of your problems. Visit a chatroom, talk to fellow sellers, check the feedback on some of the programs, and find out if the company offers a money-back guarantee.

Read the directions

Even if you believe the best way to learn something is by simply jumping into the program and muddling your way through (and you're not alone—Dawn learns best this way, and also gets frustrated!), take the time to read the directions included with the software. One of the ways we decide whether a piece of software is user-friendly is by checking out the directions first. If we can't understand them or if they're not laid out in an easy-to-read format, chances are the program won't be easy either.

By taking 10 or 15 minutes to scroll through all of the directions before attempting to use the program, you can determine the exact steps you must take and what problems you might encounter along the way. There's an old saying that you won't learn something until hearing it or trying it at least three times, but we can assure you that you'll remember at least part of what you read.

How much time does it take to learn this?

Naturally, in this age of instant gratification, we want the programs to load and work immediately. And some of them do. But the chances of that happening are fairly slim.

Give yourself at least an hour or two with a new piece of software to learn its quirks and figure out exactly what steps you must take to make your job easier. Remember that if the software adds more hours to your day, it's definitely not worth it!

The caveat here is to give yourself some time to learn and to not expect yourself to be able to explore all of the program's options within just a few minutes. Often you don't need to use all the options in a piece of software, but if you discover that the program isn't doing everything you need, perhaps it's not the right one for you.

Timesaver
If the software you're interested in is selling on eBay, save yourself the time of learning all about it by asking the people who are using it rather than slogging through the problems all by yourself.

Make sure you get customer service

We all learn from our mistakes. Remember that bike you learned how to ride when you were five? How many times did you fall down? If you were a normal kid, you scraped your knees and elbows many times before you were speeding down the boulevard, wind in your hair. Why should learning a program be any different?

But what happens if you couldn't get up on that bike or if the pedals were on backwards? Your parents took the bike back to the store (or took the bike apart and put it back together again the right way!).

One of the problems we've encountered when using new programs is that the customer service isn't exactly as promised. There's nothing more irritating than being in the middle of listing items for auction and running into a snag, then e-mailing customer service and waiting and waiting for an answer. We've come to the conclusion that you not only need an e-mail address for customer service, but a phone number. When you need help right away and the e-mail you've sent hasn't been answered, it's good to have a phone number where you can reach a real live person who'll answer your questions quickly and efficiently.

Unofficially...
Yahoo! Auction's main page includes comments from buyers and sellers about the auctions, but they often give feedback about the products they've used to conduct their auctions, as well.

When scouting for a piece of software to make your life easier, check the comments on how other customers felt about the service they were given. If there aren't any comments or if the comments are lukewarm, you can presuppose that if you have a problem, you might not get a person who'll be able to help you solve it. You don't want that to happen when you're down to the wire during an auction. That's one of the reasons why word of mouth is the strongest type of advertising for products. If someone else in the auction business has used a product and will be honest with you about the way they were treated, you can trust that you won't be the one to get burned. Prompt and courteous customer service can make the difference between a great experience and a frustrating one.

Does it have a spell check?

Believe it or not, one of the first things we look for when employing new software is whether it has spell check capabilities, especially when you're loading new auction listings. No, really, we do.

One of the reasons some items don't get bids while others sell quite well is because the seller didn't take the time to check his or her spelling. If you have a program that does it for you automatically, you can rest assured that your auction listings are professional and that your customers will see you as a seller they can trust. But I must caution again: Don't rely entirely on a spell check program. It won't pick up every error. For example, a spell check won't tell you that you've incorrectly used "their" instead of "there." A good proofread is paramount if you want to build professional listings.

The same is true of your e-mail messages. If we receive a message from a buyer or seller and the message is barely readable, we instantly think one of two things: either the sender didn't think enough of their letter to check it for accuracy (and what does that say about what they're selling?) or that person isn't very intelligent.

With all the programs out there that will do the work of checking your spelling for you, why would you want to send out any messages or listings that are sloppy?

Loading time is important

In the online auction business, every second counts. The quicker an image loads, the less likely the customer is to surf to the next site. The quicker you can get in a last-minute bid, the more likely you are to win the item you want. And the quicker you can load items up to the auction site of your choice, the more time you'll have to spend with your family, preparing other auctions, or answering questions from customers.

Although there will be times when you have no control over loading time (perhaps your server is down or the auction site is offline making changes or refreshing their settings), you want to take advantage of every moment you can. Make sure that the program you're using is the most up-to-date version. Most software manufacturers issue new versions of their programs on a regular basis and offer free downloads of the upgraded ones to regular customers.

Check your software's home page from time to time to make sure you have the newest edition of your program. Bookmark the site so you'll be able to find it even if the company has moved. And if you visit the site and discover the company has gone under, start shopping around for another software program. Once the company goes out of business, you won't have the option of getting customer service, and chances are good that another customer program has been created that will do the job more quickly and easily than the one you own.

What about counters?

You need to know how many customers you've seen, and quite a few of the auction management programs we've discussed in this chapter offer free counters for your Web site and auction listings. What are the benefits of having counters on your page? You can see how many bidders have dropped by, and that should tell you whether your listings are getting the attention they deserve. If your numbers are low, you might be listing your items in the wrong categories, or perhaps you've misspelled something in your listing head. That means if someone is doing a search for, say, Elvis Presley items, it doesn't matter if you have a one-of-a-kind Elvis item. You won't get any bids on it if you've spelled his last name "Prelsey."

Counters can also be used to track the customers who visit your Web site, and some even capture customers' e-mail addresses so you can compile a mailing list. Some sellers use the mailing list to let their customers know when a new auction goes up, while others write newsletters to customers and use the list to send them out.

The benefits of using ads on your auctions

If you surf through a number of sites, you'll notice that buyers and sellers have clickable ads on both their ads and their Web sites. Why? Do you think they just like to promote other people's businesses? No, they add clickable links to their sites because they get a portion of the profits by doing so.

For example, on Dawn's list of published works, she has a clickable link to Amazon.com. By becoming an Amazon associate and linking to their site, she gets a small amount of money for everyone who goes from her site to theirs. Does it add up? She's not making millions, but at least the site is paying for itself.

Bright Idea
If your program doesn't offer free counters, check your server and the major search engines for free Web site counters.

Watch Out!
When you link to
a company's site,
see if they'll link
back to yours.
It's more prof-
itable that way.
Also, make sure
your links are
current and get
rid of the ones
that aren't.
Keep your site
up to date!

Check with the companies you do business with regularly. Can you share links with them? Do they have associate programs? By advertising them on your site, you can earn a little money. Why not take advantage of it? If you have an average of 50 auctions going and a link on each one and one person clicks that link each time an auction goes through, you could be making about $5 per auction. Multiply that by $50, and that adds up to a little more profit than you might have had otherwise. When an auction doesn't reap what you expected, maybe your links will make up for your losses.

Just the facts

- Auction management programs can help you keep track of sales, buyers, and details important to this business.

- Programs like Andalé and AuctionAssistant offer auction listing, as well as tracking services—sort of like one-stop shopping.

- Sellers who want to market their products on auctions other than eBay need to keep that in mind when searching for software, since a lot of programs are eBay-specific.

- Auction broker software helps entrepreneurs who want to build their own auction sites.

- Putting a counter on your listings and Web pages helps you monitor the action on your site.

- Linking to other businesses, such as Amazon.com, can help you earn extra money.

GET THE SCOOP ON...
Payment options • How to decide which is the
best option • The different types of payments
• What if you have a problem getting paid?

Chapter 11

And How Will You Be Paying for This?

One of the many decisions you must make when listing your item is what kind of payment you are willing to take from your buyers. Once you've decided that, you need to remember to add the options to each one of the listings you create. If you don't indicate that a buyer can pay by credit card, yet you have the resources for that option, you could be losing business. Ditto for the escrow account option.

In addition to deciding which payment options are most comfortable for you, you need to realize that some of your customers might not be located in the United States. What options will you offer to them? The translation of one currency into another is often a major deterrent to sales. Though there are many ways to deal with international currency, most e-commerce businesspeople claim that credit cards are the easiest. But, as you will discover later in the chapter, they come with fees.

What are your payment options?

The type of payment you offer to your clients largely
depends on the size of your online auction business.
You can always test the waters for about three months
to see what happens, determine your average
month's profits, then decide whether it would be
worth it to change your payment options.

All the auctions we've visited allow the seller to
determine what payment options he or she will
offer—and there are many:

- You can accept checks, and most auctioneers
  do. However, you should be very wary of buyers
  who have received negative feedback. Check
  the buyer's history before you approve payment by check. And once you get the check,
  no matter whose it is, hold it until it clears
  before you send out the merchandise.

- Money orders might make you feel a bit safer,
  especially if the item is a "large ticket item"
  (translation: expensive).

- You can ask for a cashier's check. This is like a
  money order, though it is most often used for
  large ticket items because money orders are
  usually only good for $500 or less.

- Credit cards are another option. If you have a
  storefront to begin with, you probably already
  have credit card services in place, so this is
  sometimes the easiest way for buyers to pay for
  your goods.

- COD (collect on delivery) offers customers a
  chance to monitor how much they spend, but
  it means you don't get paid until the item is
  picked up and paid for. The good thing is the
  item *won't* be released to the buyer until the

buyer pays for it with cash or a money order. The bad thing is that you have to wait for payment.

■ Escrow services are offered by most auction sites, but the process is a complicated one, requiring both the seller and buyer to interact through a third party. Often the payment to the seller can be held up for a month or more.

What do all of these choices mean for you and your customers? If you offer your buyers more flexibility regarding payment, you'll likely have more business. However, you may also have more expenses (especially when considering whether to add the credit card option). Each payment option also impacts the amount of time it'll take for buyers to get their items—as well as how quickly you'll actually have the money in your account.

Time-wise, let's look at the options and determine how quickly the funds will be deposited in your bank:

- Credit cards: 1 to 2 days
- Money order: Instantly
- Check: 7 to 10 days (depending on the bank)
- Escrow: A month or more

Now, let's talk about each option individually and explore the pros and cons.

Should you offer credit card service?

Because it's a fact that people will pay more for a piece when paying with a credit card than they would on the same item if paying by check or cash, a lot of auctioneers have started offering the customer the convenience of paying by credit. It's certainly an option to think about offering your customers in addition to other methods of payment.

Watch Out!
Remember that you need to make a profit somewhere down the line. Look closely at your expenses versus your profits before adding services for your customers.

This decision should be largely determined by your idea of where you belong in the auction world. If you tend to sell more than $500 a month, you could possibly increase sales substantially by offering credit card payment to your customers. Some sources say that customers who buy with a credit card are more likely to make instant decisions, and when they do, they are likely to spend more money than if they wrote a check or had to arrange a special trip to secure a money order.

You should also consider the fees that these credit card merchant accounts charge. A simple way of figuring out whether you can afford to add this service for your buyers is by following the next three steps:

1. Be honest with yourself about your earnings.

2. Figure out what your investment is in your saleable goods. Then decide what your expenses are. Include all your packaging materials, mailing expenses, and your time (how much are you worth an hour?).

3. Add your investment to your expenses, then add 50 percent (at least) for profit.

If you are making above your total expenses and investment costs, then you might start thinking about how much more business you could garner and whether the extra sales would cover the cost of maintaining a merchant account.

Questions to ask yourself about your online auction business:

■ Do you sell an occasional item, bid on a few things, and have fun with the process, or are you planning on making the auction part of your life?

Unofficially...
Since eBay made online auctions a household word, the number of side businesses related to auctions has boomed. Every day there are new online companies that assist auction-goers in establishing credit card accounts, managing finances, and handling and shipping.

- Are you expecting to have a regular supply of products that guarantee you a decent return on your investment?

- Will you be dealing with international clients who might find it easier to pay for their purchases with an internationally accepted credit card?

- Have your profits been averaging a rate that would cover the costs of offering credit card accessibility?

Questions like these should determine your next step: an investigation of the credit card services that offer merchant accounts.

In our research for some card services, we discovered the following information (all rates are subject to change:

- **1st American Card Service**
  (www.1stamericancardservice.com)
  Rate: 2.3 percent
  Application fee: None
  Monthly statement fee: $9
  Transaction fee: 30¢
  Monthly minimum fee: $20
  Purchase software: Virtual Web Terminal—$429
  Additional software/hardware necessary: None
  Installation time: Very short wait

- **Accept-It!/Universal Merchant Services**
  (http://accept-it.com)
  Rate: 2.39 percent
  Monthly statement fee: Approximately $29.95 per month
  Transaction fee: 20¢–30¢ per transaction

Bright Idea
If you install a merchant account system, give yourself three to six months to see whether you've increased your sales substantially. Do a "test" accounting, and if you're not making enough to cover the costs, cancel the service.

Application fee: $125 (fully refundable if declined)

Purchase software: $995, your choice

Additional software/hardware necessary: Yes, $35 per month

Installation time: 5–10 days

- **EZ Merchant Accounts/Authorize.net** (www. ezmerchantaccounts.com)

  Rate: 2.25–2.49 percent

  Setup fee (includes application fee): $395

  Monthly gateway fee (access to a secure server): $20

  Transaction fee: 25¢ per transaction

  Monthly minimum fee: $25

  Statement fee: $10

- **iCardacceptance.com** (www.cardacceptance.com)

  Rate: 2.39 percent

  Monthly statement fee: $15

  Monthly minimum fee: $25

  Transaction fee: 35¢ per transaction

  Application fee: Not stated

  Additional setup/application fees: $30 per month.

- **New Horizon Business Services** (http:// newhorizon.org)

  Rate: available upon receipt of application

  Setup fee: $275

  Application fee: AFTER you are approved, $195

  Purchase software: You can lease processing equipment with one payment down

  Setup time: Within 48 hours of approval

- **Merchant USA** (www.online2020.com)

  Rate: 1.75–2.25 percent (depending on type of program)

Monthly statement fee: $10

Transaction fee: 25¢–35¢ per transaction

Application fee: None, but a representative will contact you directly

Additional setup/application fees: None

- **Online Credit Corp.** (http://onlinecreditcorp. com)

  Setup fee: None

  Monthly statement fee: None

  Rate: Given to each customer by representative after customer has filled out a request form

  Installation time: Several days

- **Payflow Link** (www.ezmerchantaccounts.com/signio.htm)

  One-time setup fee: $345

  Monthly fee: $19.95

  Number of monthly transactions: Unlimited

- **VERZA Payment System** (http://verza.com)

  Rate: 3.9–6.9 percent

  Monthly statement fee:

  Transaction fee/checks (U.S. buyers only): All single items from $10–$500 = 3.9 percent

  Checks (U.S. buyers only): $10–$500

  Transaction fee (checks): 99¢ per transaction

  Transaction fee (credit cards): All single items from $10–$500 = 6.9 percent

  Transaction fee (credit cards) : $2.99 per transaction

  Application fee: Free

  Additional setup/application fees: Reserve and chargeback fees

Bright Idea

If you're the type of business where customers might buy more than one of your items after being introduced to you during the auction, consider adding a shopping cart feature to your Web site. Any of the companies that handle credit card services usually also offer this option.

The pros and cons of the cost

The charges you'll incur by offering a credit card payment option for your goods are definitely a consideration when setting up your auctions. Even though it's a proven fact that accepting credit cards can increase your sales, what good is it if your sales figures are so low that the monthly charges will cut your earnings substantially?

If you are just cleaning out your attic and have less than a hundred items to sell at auction, chances are you won't need the credit card option. However, if some of those items in the attic might be worth thousands, the credit card option would definitely protect your investment. By using this option, you could garner some bids from people who might not have the money sitting in their checking accounts but definitely have the credit, and you also protect yourself against having to wait for a check to clear— or worse, against the expenses you might incur should the check bounce!

If you have a retail business and you know you'll be including items at auction on a regular basis, it would probably be a wise business move for you to calculate the difference between your earnings and the expense of offering credit cards. If you deduct the expense from the earnings and find out you are still in the black, then open a merchant account pronto!

Will you gain customers?

Many studies have been done on impulse buying, and most say that if e-commerce sites offer a variety of payment options, they are more likely to get repeat hits from customers. Here are some of the claims made by merchant account sites that offer credit card accounts to businesses:

- Revenues can go up by 1500 percent (Universal Merchant Services).

66
Since Billpoint's launch in early April, eBay customers have told us they want as many secure, easy-to-use and attractively priced payment options as possible," said Janet S. Crane, Billpoint's chief executive officer. "Electronic Check means faster transactions with no bounced checks, no paperwork and no chargebacks." (June 6, 2000 press release from eBay)
99

- You have to be able to accept credit cards to survive on the Net (EZ Merchant Accounts).

- Businesses lose over 85 percent of impulse purchases by not offering credit cards as a payment option (iCardacceptance.com).

- You can increase sales by over 200 percent.

Is it true? We believe it is, but we also believe that online auctions are the place where a million "tiny" businesses can survive simultaneously—and side by side—with giants of the industry. What works for the giants or even for medium-sized e-commerce sites might not work for the person who is currently selling a doll collection on Yahoo!.

Our advice? Don't sign up for a merchant account until you've been online long enough to figure out the intricacies of this business. But do prepare yourself for doing the best business possible if you're a retail company that is hoping to make a living (either wholly or partially) by selling through auctions.

What about the paperwork?

So you're not an accountant or anything close to one. Neither are we. But we can assure you it won't make any difference to the IRS when it comes time to report your earnings, so you need to keep careful records.

For a long time, earnings made from selling items at auctions online could be basically hidden. None of the states can levy taxes on items being sold online unless they're sold to someone else within the state. Basically, no one knows how to put federal regulations on the Net because it's not just this country that they're dealing with, but we're sure they'll find out how to do it sooner or later—and when they do, all online auctioneers better be ready to 'fess up!

How do you keep the paperwork with credit card payments? Most service providers will send you a monthly statement with your balances, along with whatever is owed to you. However, we strongly suggest that you keep records regarding every transaction you make with a customer, as well as your own activity as a buyer. At first, we found ourselves swimming in a sea of paper and wondered how we got there—especially since we were doing all our business on a computer! But it was often necessary to print out sales information in order to keep our accounts straight with the people for whom we are selling (we sell our own items, as well as items for several close friends).

Now we have a three-ring binder separated by categories (in this case, each person's sales). As the sales are recorded, the e-mail we send and receive with the customer's mailing information and sales/payment information is recorded. We slide it into the book and simultaneously enter the sale in an accounting program we devised.

As we've said, most of the credit card service providers offer record-keeping devices. Some offer special processing software, while others offer the option of maintaining all your records and activity by logging in with your password on their Web site. The largest companies also offer customer support. When you do your research to figure out what company to use, make sure you keep all of these factors in mind.

In addition to the help you might get from online processing companies, consider keeping all your auction records and transactions on an

easy-to-use accounting program. Some of the programs that help you upload your auctions also have
record-keeping abilities. We use AuctionAssistant,
which comes with a tool that helps you keep track of
the auctions, customers, payments, and shipments.

Picking an accounting/bookkeeping program is
a personal choice. Luckily, there are many different
types available, some of them tailored to small businesses, others to mid-range or large corporations.

For small businesses:

- BS/1 Small Business
- Microsoft Money 2000 Business & Personal
- Quicken 2000

For mid-range accounting needs:

- Account Pro
- Champion
- Business Works
- Peachtree Software
- QuickBooks

For high-end:

- ACCPAC Plus Accounting
- Real World
- Red Wing Accounting Software

Each of these programs has its strengths and
weaknesses. While we would love to give you all the
details, we think it's better for sellers to decide
which one is right for them (especially since there
are so many to choose from, and you're really reading this book to know about online auctions, not
accounting programs, correct?). Suffice it to say
that with a little research, you'll be able to find just
the right one for you.

Bright Idea
Check the con-
sumer magazines
for suggestions
about the
accounting/book-
keeping software
on the market
and read the
reviews of the
latest available.

Getting payment from international customers

Although we believe the safest way to get international payment is through credit card services, you can also have the customer transfer monies through the postal system. (You can do the same if you're buying from someone outside your own country). The United States Postal Service offers international money orders and what are called International Reply Coupons (for postage), and banks will also wire funds or create a bank check that can be cashed in another country.

A quick call to your local bank will determine whether they can convert funds for you. In our small town, only two of the major banks are able to do so; the others didn't have any idea how to go about transferring funds, which surprised us.

The best options when making an international sale are:

1. Credit cards
2. Bank check
3. Escrow funds

You can opt to take a personal check, if you can find out what the exchange rate is and know that you'll be able to convert the international funds to American (or other currency); however, that can mean you'll lose out if the exchange rate changes between the time your customer sends the check and the time you receive it. When we've traveled to foreign countries, we've been amazed at how quickly the exchange rate changes—even on a daily basis—so keep that in mind.

The value of online escrow accounts

As we've stated in the previous section, online escrow accounts make a lot of sense when you're

Moneysaver
Save money and time by calling your local banks to determine who has the best exchange rates.

dealing with international sales. It's a safe way of being sure that you'll receive all of the monies due you. But the transfer of funds often takes a month or more. If you're like us, you don't have all that time to wait. However, there are definite pluses to the accounts besides assuring you of international payment.

Online escrow accounts protect you against the possibility of getting burned by a bad check. If you see that one of your customers has recently been "reinstated" as a bidder/seller, or that the person has not built a track record you are satisfied with, it's safer to have the payment made through the online escrow account.

Another reason for tapping into escrow is when you have a large ticket item and want to be sure everything will clear. Some of the items we've seen on eBay include million-dollar homes, luxury cars, vacations to exotic places, and valuable paintings— all of which were sold for six figures or more. Personally, I wouldn't be able to let that money out of my sight until I'd inspected whatever I was buying. Sometimes that's impossible during an online auction (especially if you want that villa in Tuscany but cannot travel there to see it…), so while your payment is on the way—or while you're waiting *to be* paid (and waiting for a payment that large would definitely give us the quivers), you have time to inspect the goods you've purchased. And you'll at least be satisfied that you will not get burned by the buyer.

Getting auction insurance

Most auction sites guarantee their auctions. That means both the bidder and seller are protected. If, for example, you buy something and it turns out to be completely different than what you expected, you should be able to return that item. And if you, as the seller, are burned by a buyer who never sends the payment—or, worse, who does pay but bounces the check—you will get your money back. Some auction houses cover the whole amount, while others have a cap on what they'll award the seller.

Do you need auction insurance? Yes, we believe you do, and we're going to take a stand here and suggest that if you are part of an auction that does not give you any guarantee (and some of the big ones definitely do not guarantee anything about their auctions), you might want to take your business elsewhere. Consider the fact that you are dealing with millions of people, some of whom might not be as honest as you and I are. Do you want to go into business with them, buying and selling items, with no reassurance that either the item you're buying or the money for the item you're selling will come?

Unofficially...
Lloyd's of London, the best-known insurance company in the world, offers auction insurance for many items sold through the major online auction sites.

Most online auctions offer some kind of insurance or guarantee to anyone who registers as either a buyer or seller, but some will ask you if you want to add it to the fees you're paying. Our suggestion is that you take it. We've already had to invoke the guarantee and it saved some heartache during one transaction. Take it from the pros: Don't bid or sell unless you have some kind of insurance!

Holding the check 'til it clears

Most banks hold checks (especially any over $1,000) for seven to 10 business days, even though the Federal Reserve makes the money available to them within 24 hours. Don't ask us why. We know the chances are minimal of a bank being burned by one of the checks you're cashing for online auction items—and it would have to be a pretty big check to make even a blip of difference on what banks earn from us every year.

Be prepared to hold the check you received for at least a week before sending out the items the customer bought. If you mention that you'll be doing so in your ads, your customers will know beforehand that they shouldn't expect their items to come until after their check clears.

Remember that if a customer's check bounces, you could end up incurring some charges in your own account. We've had cases when checks were held and our account dipped low enough to bounce other checks we had out for payment, so we learned our lesson quickly. It means our bookkeeping is a little slow, but better to be slow than overdrawn. It also might be a good idea to clarify with your bank the amount of time they hold checks, so that you'll know their policy.

In addition to holding checks until they clear, you might offer your customers the option to pay by electronic check. This is a safer way for you to collect funds (because the customer's balance is checked before the electronic check is forwarded to you), and a faster way for the customer to get the product.

There are many companies that offer this service, and some of them are companies already mentioned as offering credit card services:

- **eCheck.Net** (www.ezmerchantaccounts.com)
  Setup fee: $99
  Discount rate: 2 percent and 30¢ per transaction
  Monthly minimum: $10

Watch Out!
Should you have the misfortune to bounce a check, you not only have to pay the bank charges but may be fined by the seller—in addition to getting a negative feedback rating.

- **New Horizon Business Services** (http://
  newhorizon.org)
  Setup fee: $30
  Check charge: 99¢

Clear explanations to customers are a must!

As we've said, it's incredibly important to keep your relationship with your customer and any explanations of your shipping procedures, payment options, and other questions as simple and businesslike as possible.

During the past couple of years, we've heard certain buyers' life stories, and while some of those customers have turned into regulars (and some into friends), it's really better that you keep personal information out of your business dealings. When you start getting bogged down telling a buyer/seller what's going on in your life that caused the package/check to be late, then you are, essentially, wasting valuable time. Better to say, "I'll be sending payment out next week, due to unavoidable delays on my end," than to tell the seller/buyer all about Uncle Henry's emergency surgery and how you had to be in Tennessee for the past three weeks and that Uncle Henry is now home and doing well with a visiting nurse, but that you haven't quite caught up with the mail….

You should also be sure to clearly communicate any questions you have or concerns after a sale. Getting angry when something arrives broken or a check bounces really doesn't do anything other than to cause bad relations. Such unprofessional behavior may result in a negative feedback or a "black mark" on your record. Try to keep your emotions out of it and ask a few questions first. Make sure you understand the reasons why something happened before you start accusing the other side. In other words, keep it professional.

If the check bounces...

You have a problem when a check bounces, but most of the time, it can be resolved amicably.

The first thing you should do is to call your bank. Determine whether the bounced check is going to cause problems within your own account. If it is (and most people simply don't have the disposable income to cover a loss of any kind), you need to find a way to cover your account.

Next, get the seller's e-mail address and send a businesslike message that the check has bounced and you need to hear from the person immediately. Don't threaten or react in an angry manner. That kind of attitude won't solve the problem and might even reflect negatively on you. Take the proper steps toward resolving the conflict as amicably as possible.

Legally, most states allow the check writer up to seven days to make good on the amount. Online auctioneers are generally honest people, eager to please, and worried about keeping a good reputation. Most will work quickly to get the situation remedied. However, there are those who simply can't or won't make good on the check.

When a check isn't covered by the buyer, your next recourse can be with the auction itself (see the earlier section, "Getting auction insurance") or with small claims court. Laws regarding insufficient funds and other types of faulty checks vary from state to state, so check with your local Legal Aid advisors before moving into action.

Bright Idea
If you have the option of utilizing a "free trial" check insurance program, take it.

Naturally, you don't want any of your fellow buyers and sellers to get burned, so if someone bounces a check on you, make sure you remember that when it's time to enter your feedback. You'll be doing everyone in the community a favor if you tell them of your experience. However, if a buyer or seller makes an honest mistake and attempts to take care of it, remember that you might be in the same position one day—and everyone's allowed at least one mistake a lifetime, right?

Don't spend the money yet

You have the check, you've sent the item, and now the check has cleared. Do you spend it? You might think it's safe, but we have had the experience of believing that the coast was clear and—boom!—we get a phone call that the package we thought had arrived safe and sound was in pieces, and the buyer wanted his money back. Since it'd been so long since we'd sent the item, we naturally figured everything was right with the world and went our merry way. We learned the hard way that we need to hear from customers that everything has arrived safely. Though we eventually got reimbursed through the United States Post Office (they had wrecked the package), we still cut ourselves short when replacing the customer's expenses.

Some people wonder how you can cover yourself in case a buyer says he or she received an item broken when, in fact, it arrived in one piece. Here's the answer: The USPS and other delivery services (i.e., UPS) want to see the broken item before they make good on reimbursing the receiver.

Though we suggest putting a cap on the amount of time you'll wait before spending the money (our norm is about a week after the check clears), we believe you should also let your fellow auction-goers know your payment policy. Include some disclaimer in your regular ads simply stating that buyers have "x number" of days to resolve any issues after they get their item. After that time, they're on their own!

Just the facts

- When determining the payment options you'll give your customers, consider the added sales benefit of paying by credit card.

- There are dozens of companies that offer merchant accounts. Research them and find the one suited to your particular needs.

- Check verification services can save you time and money by clearing a customer's credit ahead of payment.

- Plan ahead and don't spend your earnings too soon!

During the Auction

PART V

Keeping Track of the Auction

Y ou've written your auction ad, included all the details about shipping and payment, made sure to cover yourself against bidders with negative feedback, taken the photos, and uploaded all of the above. Now you're ready to watch the action!

Your job is not done yet. In fact, it's really only just begun. Now you need to watch who's bidding, what their feedback is like, and monitor your e-mails so you can answer questions from bidders.

During the auction you'll be swept away in the action. Perhaps you'll check your e-mail only at a certain time twice or three times a day. Or maybe you're one of those people who are connected to the Net as if it were a lifeline. Whatever the case, the excitement of active bidding and the possibility that your item might bring more than you actually thought is what keeps people coming back to auctions.

And they're off!

Last-minute changes to your auction ad can only be made prior to the first bid. Once that first bid is entered, the item's description will remain the same. So, if you've made any errors, you'd best catch them before the bidding starts. Once the bidding begins, the only way you can let people know that you've made a mistake and that 18th-century English candlestick is actually a 20th-century reproduction is by e-mailing them, and that's something that is not only time-consuming but can often be misinterpreted by customers.

Watch Out!
Make sure you give your auction ad a close reading during the beginning moments of your auction. Then make any necessary changes quickly!

Sometimes we are too close to our own descriptions of our items to realize there is a mistake until it is too late. Most of the online auctions allow you to make changes (as long as that initial bidder hasn't started the auction). Making your ad as clear and detailed as possible is so important that we're going to emphasize it once again. For example, if you've misspelled an important word in your title or in the listing itself, you could be losing valuable bidders.

On eBay, you use the Revise option to change any mistakes you might have made. Most other auctions also offer this option, though the terminology is different for each.

For example:

- eBay's **Revise.** When your piece is listed, the initial page has a category called "Update Item" and notes to the seller that "if this item has received no bids, you may revise it." By clicking on that link, you go to another screen where you can update the information already listed. You can change the category or add information to the description, payment options, or shipping terms.

- Amazon's **View/Edit/Remove.** On the ad listing, there is a button called "Your Account." If you click on it, you are given the "View/Edit/Remove" option. When you click on that option, you can go to "Edit" and change or remove any information already up on your ad—but only if there hasn't been a bid on the item yet. If there has, you can add additional info, but you can't change what's already there.

- Yahoo!'s **Auction Manager.** Once your item is listed and before someone bids on it, you can click on "Auction Manager" to add information; however, you cannot make changes to or delete existing information from the listing. Interested bidders can pose a question by clicking on the "Questions" tab.

- LycoShop Auctions' **Edit a Listing.** As long as your listing is in "Upcoming Status," Lycos allows you to edit or change the listing, the auction duration, or the payment and shipping methods. Once the auction starts, you can add an image, but only the description can be edited.

- Haggle.com's **Adding information.** If you want to add something to an auction listing, you simply go to "Edit" and add the info. However, you cannot change existing information. You do have the choice to remove the listing entirely if you've made an error.

- Auctions.Excite.com's **Reviewing, Editing or Relisting.** You must search the listings first (by number or description). Once you have the listing, you have several options to select from. As with other auctions, major changes can only be made if there have been no bids on the

Bright Idea
If you are running auctions on more than one site, make sure you are completely familiar with each site's rules before you start. Rules do change from site to site, and you're better off knowing them before you get caught with your pants down!

item. By selecting "Edit This Listing," you can change the duration of the auction, any descriptions of the item, and payment/shipping methods. Once the auction is underway, the only thing you can do is add an image.

It's wise to make a final check of the items you've put up for auction before the bidding begins. If you've made any major errors (watch those prices and the reserves you put on your items), you still have time to catch them. But once the bidding begins, you'll be too busy fielding questions, watching the prices go up, and getting your next items ready to load for another auction to watch every listing. So, unless you have only a couple of items going on the block, make sure you do a final check right after you list the items and do any editing or re-listing before it's too late.

Then, sit back and enjoy the action!

Automatic updates

Bright Idea
Signing up for automatic updates or notifications can save you hours. If you're involved in more than one auction simultaneously, it's easier to follow them if all notices of change are sent via e-mail.

Most of the auction sites we've researched offer a form of automatic notification whenever there's a bid against you when you want to buy something, or *for* one of the items you're selling. Each online auction company used e-mail to notify bidders and sellers of action in the auctions in which they were participants. However, some auction houses have gone even further than the courtesy of an e-mail note.

In addition to updates on the items that you're bidding on or trying to sell, you can select a service that will automatically notify you when certain types of items are being auctioned. Here are only a few of the options:

- **Yahoo! Auctions:** Yahoo! employs a notification system that customers have some control over.

You can choose to be notified by e-mail, Yahoo! Messenger, or alphanumeric pager whenever a specific action occurs in any auction with which you are involved. You can find out if an auction's been canceled, closed, created, or resubmitted; if a bid has been received on one of your auctions; if you've been outbid on something you're interested in; or if a seller has canceled your bid. You can also find out if a question has been asked or answered, and you can be notified if you've received feedback. Yahoo! also employs Yahoo! Alert, in which you can turn on a ringing sound if you want to make sure you hear when an item has been added in your category.

■ **eBay:** eBay has added a new auction alert service called "eBay a-Go-Go." Instead of waiting for an e-mail, you can be alerted via pager when you've been outbid on an item, won an item, or sold an item. A system like this is perfect for the person who cannot remain in front of the computer screen to be updated.

■ **Bid.com:** Bid.com has a service called "Bid Buddy" that allows bids to be placed for you, even if you're not around to keep track of the auction. You indicate what you want to bid on, tell Bid.com what your maximum bid is, and it will increase the bid according to your minimum increment.

■ **Ezbid.com:** The Autobid feature on Ezbid's auction site lets the bidder set the maximum bid for certain items and the minimum next bid. The advantage? You'll never bid more than you want to for any item. The disadvantage?

You don't get the excitement of trying to get that bid in under the wire. Ezbid also automatically notifies bidders when they're knocked off the Highbidder List so they can decide whether or not to get back into the action.

- **Auctions.Lycos.com:** Lycos' Auction site notifies bidders and sellers by e-mail whenever a bid is increased or a buyer wins an item; however, they don't accept bids offline.

- **uBid.com:** Certain online auction houses, such as uBid.com, have created newsletters or bulletin services to notify prospective bidders. The uBid Daily Bulletin sends instant e-mails to buyers/sellers when certain items come up for sale. Their 24 categories cover every kind of item, from antiques to computers to vacations to real estate.

If you have quite a few items up for auction at the same time, it might get a little confusing to receive e-mails about every bid or notifications each time you receive feedback. You need to decide how much information is enough for you. Do you need to know about all the bids? On certain items, you might be curious to see where you stand. If it's imperative that Aunt Martha's teapot sell for its reserve, then you might want to watch the action closely. However, if it doesn't really matter how many people have bid on it, just set your preferences (if you can) that you'd like to know who the final bidder was and be notified only when auctions close.

In addition to having options for updates/notifications through the online auction house itself, you can set your auction uploading program to determine when you receive updates. For example,

Bright Idea
In addition to getting info about particular items, it's a good idea to ask the auctions you're interested in to send you their general newsletters so that you can keep up with the most recent innovations on their sites.

AuctionAssistant lets us automatically set up a system where an instant e-mail is sent to a bidder once he or she wins one of our auctions.

E-mail etiquette

When contacted by someone via e-mail, it's important to know that there are simple rules of etiquette that people use online. It's a dead giveaway that you're an amateur if you break any of the most basic Netiquette guidelines.

For example:

1. Never write in all caps. That's equivalent to yelling in someone's face.

2. Don't forward personal e-mail to others, especially members of a list serve. It's the ultimate in privacy invasion.

3. Be careful about how you use humor and sarcasm. Meanings are very easily misinterpreted when not accompanied by facial expressions, voice tone, or body language. Use emoticons (see the following definitions) whenever it's important for the reader to know exactly how to take what you've just written.

   - :-) Your basic smiley face. This smiley is used to inflect a sarcastic or joking statement since we can't hear voice inflection over e-mail.

   - ;-) Winky smiley face. User just made a flirtatious and/or sarcastic remark. More of a "don't hit me for what I just said" smiley.

   - :-(Frowning face. User did not like that last statement or is upset or depressed about something.

- :-I Indifferent smiley. Better than a :-(but not quite as good as a :-).

- :-> User just made a really biting sarcastic remark. Worse than a ;-).

- >:-> User just made a really devilish remark.

- >;-> Winky and devil combined. A very lewd remark was just made. (Author's note of caution: It's not a good idea to use lewd remarks in your business dealings.)

Unofficially...
The chatrooms frequented by online auction-eers are filled with the language of e-mail. In order to understand what is being said, the "chatters" use an abbreviated language now becoming known as "e-speak."

Other important things to remember when using e-mail to communicate is not to "flame." Flaming means your actions are being interpreted as abusive or meant to hurt someone's feelings. Such actions are controversial and can lead to a person's expulsion from online chat groups. They can also cause negative feedback for you if you're buying or selling in the auction community. Since feedback is so important in determining whether or not buyers and sellers will deal with you, most auction-goers are careful to treat each other with the same respect they'd like to be given.

Although acronyms are commonly used, messages filled with them can be confusing. However, some are easily recognized and are acceptable to use:

- IMHO (in my humble opinion)

- BTW (by the way)

- LOL (lots of luck or laughing out loud)

- OOTB (out of the box, brand new)

- OOP (out of print)

- NWT (new with tags)

- TIA (thanks in advance)

- TTYL (talk to you later)

For those of you still feeling your way around the Net, yes, it is a separate language and you need to understand it to do business. However, it's a world where just about everyone is ready to help you. If you can find the right place to ask your questions, you'll be surfin' with the best of them in no time at all and communicating with everyone in your life via e-mail.

Answer promptly and courteously—time is money!

When a buyer or seller stops long enough to send an e-mail to you during an auction, that person expects a prompt response. Remember that most auctions are not only selling your items but thousands (possibly millions) of others' as well. The fact that a person took the time to ask a question indicates that he or she is strongly interested in whatever you have to offer. Give that person the courtesy of a prompt response.

We've discovered that we could very easily sit at the computer all day long, fielding questions, adding more items to our auctions, doing research, and surfing. But life does need to be lived, so we can't chain ourselves to our desks. However, we do answer our e-mail on a regular basis so most correspondents don't have to wait more than six hours or so for a response.

However, when the auctions in which we're participating draw to a close, we monitor the sales fairly closely. It's imperative at that time to answer questions as quickly as possible. The sale might depend on how you answer a customer—and that customer has every right to expect an honest and complete answer from you. We've had moments at the end of an auction where I was fielding questions about a piece of porcelain right up until the last bidding seconds. The fact that I was there helped, and the sale was decided by the fact that the buyer could get answers to her concerns.

We're fairly sure that one of the major auction sites will soon find its way clear to adding instant messaging to their auctions so that buyers and sellers can have an open and instant line to each other during those final moments of the auction. And maybe, someday, even face-to-face auctions ... but we digress.

Honesty is the best policy

During the auction, bidders will have questions about your item. Perhaps they're looking for a specific mark on a piece of silver, or the exact RAM size of the computer you're offering. Maybe the comic book collector is searching for a particular rare issue of *The Green Hornet* and it looks like you might have it, but they want to be sure. Or perhaps the photo you took of that vacation chalet in the Alps doesn't do the place justice. Whatever the issue, buyers should be able to ask questions of the seller.

It is to the seller's advantage to answer any queries as quickly and honestly as possible. You might think the ironstone pottery piece you have is valuable even with the slight age crack, but another person might not. Still, you should not hide the crack or attempt to make an item better than it truly is. If your early Elvis album has a scratch on it, say so! Don't lie about an item's age, condition, or estimated value. On the other hand, if you don't know the answer to someone's question, it's better to say so rather than to fabricate something.

If customers/bidders feels you are being honest with them, they are more likely to offer a bid. If, however, they are dissuaded from bidding because

Timesaver
Get in the habit of checking your e-mail at the two busiest times of the day: the morning and middle evening. That way you'll get both the A.M. and P.M. folks and you won't find yourself online all day.

of your honesty, don't feel defeated. Those bidders will be more likely to look at other items of yours because you *have been* honest with them. Whichever way you look at it, being honest is the best way to go.

You might also want to "quote their message" (highlight the section of their original message to which you're responding), so that they will remember what it is that they've asked you and have a quick reference in case they want to return to your item and bid on it again. The easier you make it for your customers, the more active the bidding will be.

Keep your eye on the action

Now it's getting exciting. The messages about who is bidding and how much are piling up in your e-mail. The children's book you thought was worth a couple of dollars is now up past $50, and the costume jewelry you found at a local yard sale is way beyond what you paid for it.

What's the most effective way to keep your eye on the action?

Most auction sites have a place where all of the information about you and your account can be viewed. When the auctions in which you're involved are active, you can go to that page (e.g., my eBay, my Bid.com, "Your Account" page on Amazon) and stay there, reloading or refreshing the page every couple of minutes so you can get the latest bids.

You can click directly from "Your Account" page to whatever auction you need to bid on or to check out who's bidding on the items you're selling. For example, if one of the items we collect has gone past what we want to pay for it, we might silently watch the action until the final days of trading, then bid again. Depending on how much we want the item,

> ❝
> The secret of success in life is for a person to be ready for their opportunity when it comes.
> —Disraeli
> ❞

we might follow it through to its final stages and bid in the last moments of the auction. But other items will not garner that kind of interest, so we'll drop out of the bidding early.

On the other hand, if an item we're selling is having problems meeting the reserve, we might want to e-mail the top bidder during the auction to let that person know how close to (or far from) the reserve she is. The bidder won't always want to meet your reserve, but we've discovered that even if she doesn't, we can usually strike up some kind of business relationship—even if we just find out what the bidder is normally looking for and add her to our list of people to contact should we find those items. That is a selling technique we've used from the very first moment we started selling antiques. If someone comes in looking for something, we get her name, address, and phone number, then we make sure we notify her if something she might like comes in. We've carried the habit over into our cyberspace-based business and find it works just as well.

By watching the auction, you can also get a feel for whether a slightly disreputable bidder might be winning the item. You should keep yourself aware of the type of warnings each auction uses to let you know that a buyer/seller is new or has changed his or her identity in the last 30 or so days.

Checking on the bidders

As we've said, you really want to be sure that you know who is bidding on your items. Though some people have no problem with waiting until the end of the auction to see who won the items, we've always felt safer if we've been able to determine if there are any "shady characters" (i.e., someone who has negative feedback, a history of bounced checks, or is an established bidder hiding behind a new identity) we might need to deal with at the end of the auction.

Here are the various ways some of the major auctions let you know a bidder's history or control who is allowed to bid on the items being sold:

- Yahoo! allows sellers to add a "minimum bidder rating" to the ad site so that only bidders with good ratings are approved to bid. Yahoo! also allows you to blacklist a bidder and stop that bidder from trying to buy anything from you in the future. In addition, you can cancel bids on your auctions, if you so choose. In other words, if a bidder doesn't have the type of history with which you're comfortable, you can cancel his bid and he will not be allowed to place any future bids. Think carefully before you do this, because you might lose a customer who might, in addition, leave negative feedback in your account.

- eBay distinguishes new or changed identity buyers/sellers by adding a pair of sunglasses next to the auction-goer's user ID.

- Amazon shows that someone is new by placing a smiley-face sun with the words "I'm new" next to the buyer's identification. They also use a stars and numbers way of distinguishing a seller/buyer's rating. Five is the highest and one is the lowest on their rating system.

- AuctionAddict.com also uses a rating system (1 to 10, with 10 being the high end) to indicate a seller/buyer's standings in the auction community. The rating is added next to the bidder's ID.

Watch Out!
A word to the wise: Better to ask for a money order from someone with a questionable past than get stuck with a bounced check and nothing to show for it.

- Excite Auctions, a fairly new e-business, shows who's new with a "new!" logo. When we visited this site, almost everyone had that little logo next to their names.

- KeyBuy.com lists the bidders in their auction with their e-mail addresses and a number in parentheses that indicates how many feedback comments they have, but it doesn't appear that they have any indication that someone's new other than to show that they have no feedback (0).

Read the feedback

Once you have bids coming in on the items you're selling, you will begin to see who's bidding. If you've asked to be notified, you can check the bids whenever you get a moment. Otherwise, it's a smart idea to check in at regular times during the day, especially when your auction is coming to a close. When you check to see how high the bids have gone, you can also read the feedback on the bidders.

It's important to remember that a bidder with fewer than 25 feedback notes is just as likely to be as trustworthy as someone with 900 notes and some negatives. Someone in the online auction business long enough is going to have a problem at one point or another with a buyer or seller.

Read the feedback notes closely. Check the following:

- Does it sound like the buyer/seller regularly makes errors or is it an isolated case? If the bidder/seller has only one or two negatives, chances are he or she has had only minor problems. However, if both pieces of feedback mention similar incidences, you might want to check into the matter further. Sometimes a

Bright Idea
If you see someone bidding on your items and have an uneasy feeling about the person, send a friendly e-mail. This is equivalent to saying hello to someone as they walk in a store. It makes the bidder realize there's a person on the other end of the sale.

simple e-mail to the buyer asking what happened to cause the negative feedback will help clear up the matter for you and give you more confidence to let the bidder continue (or to buy from the seller).

- Does the feedback mention whether packing was a problem? There have been a lot of times during the past three or four years when the post office delivered a package to us (or to someone else from us) that was in less-than-perfect shape. Sometimes it's not clear to the person who's received the item that it might have been perfectly packed when it left the house. Unless you're planning on buying something extremely fragile, I would give the seller the benefit of the doubt.

- How about e-mail communication? People who have been noted as "hard to contact" might have had a computer crash or been out of town and unable to get to a computer to contact buyers/sellers. On the other hand, someone who is consistently noncommunicative will not be successful in this business.

How to make contact

Some of the auctions we've visited simply list the bidder's name and e-mail as a direct link so it's incredibly easy to contact them. Others, including eBay, require that you go through a couple of steps to get the bidder/buyer's e-mail address. Remember that this is for both your and the bidder's protection.

We are on both sides of the fence on this issue. Should you have easy access to the e-mail addresses of the people who are bidding on your items, as well as the sellers of the items you'd like to buy? We think it should be a fairly easy way of communicating, and that it's quite necessary for some transactions—and that it's an impediment to making sales if the buyer needs to stop and go through several steps to ask a simple question.

Some of the auctions we've visited have a chat-room type of feature that allows bidders to ask real-time questions of the seller. If you are involved in an auction like that, it's advantageous to spend some time at the computer during the last hours of your auction. You might be able to catch a buyer who's surfing through, just browsing.

On the other hand, if your e-mail address is available to everyone and no one even has to ask for it, you could end up the recipient of a lot of e-mail you don't want—or worse, on someone's e-mail list. When you get messages from undesirable sources, it's called spamming. Unfortunately, it's a common practice, and ultimately, we believe, one of the reasons why some of the bigger auctions insist that buyers/sellers have to request each other's e-mail address.

The important thing to remember is that when you e-mail someone, you should be putting your best foot forward. Try to remember that this is a business and be as honest as possible. Don't e-mail buyers and sellers just for the heck of it. Their time is just as valuable as yours. Keep your messages polite, to the point, and businesslike.

Unofficially...
According to CNET News.com, in November 1999 eBay blocked a company called AuctionWatch from allowing buyers to search for items listed "for sale on numerous auction sites."

Did you forget something important?

It's the last couple of hours of the auction and you realize you never mentioned that this particular book you're selling is a first edition. Would that make a difference in how much people bid? More than likely! You won't be able to catch the attention of people who are looking for that particular first edition, but you can take the time to e-mail those who have bid and let them know this detail. (Don't blame some of them if they doubt you, since that's an important piece of information that should have been mentioned in the listing, but do know that you might be doing someone else an incredible favor by telling them.)

What if that dainty piece of porcelain you had up for auction is now a pile of broken collectibles on your floor as a result of a freak earthquake? It's not fair to the people who are bidding on it if it's no longer available, so take the time to pass on an e-mail that the item has to be taken off the market. Make sure you apologize for the inconvenience and offer to give them a note of positive feedback for being a good sport. That will mean a lot to those who might otherwise be disappointed that the piece is not on the market any more.

The last minutes—going, going, gone!

The end of an auction is exciting. There's no doubt about it. As you sit in front of the computer screen, refreshing your screen every couple of moments, you realize that this is the reason everyone is having such a good time with online auctions.

Whether online or in person, auctions still have the power to give us that little rush. The end of an online auction is often akin to a horse race. During the last couple of moments, there are those auction-goers who sneak in, waiting breathlessly for the auction to end, then pumping in a bid to make it just under the wire. This is called sniping, and while we can guarantee it's fun, it's commonly the snipers who decide they really don't want the item they just won. Look at a sniper as an impulse buyer who's buying something at the last moment just to get in on the excitement, not necessarily because he or she really wants the item.

We're not saying you should be worried about the last couple of moments, but we do believe in being near the computer so that if anyone has a question, you can answer it right away. About a year ago, one of our auctions was ending and Bobby went to the store to run an errand. While he was gone, I got a question from one of the bidders that I couldn't answer—but he could! He came in the door only moments before the auction was ending. We got the woman her answer, she got in her bid, and she won the item. Without the answer to that question, she wouldn't have bought the item.

Just the facts

- You can make changes to your auction ad as long as no one has bid on it yet. Check your online auction's rules to see how to do it.

- Most auctions will automatically send you notices when sales end. Some will even notify you when items you'd like to bid on go on the block.

- Sending courteous and prompt e-mail messages is just one way to get and keep customers.

- Check out the bidders who are vying for your goods prior to the end of the auction. You want to be prepared in case you have a concern about their actions in the past.

- Try to be near your computer at the end of an auction. You never know what might come up that will need your immediate attention—and possibly garner you a sale!

After the Auction

PART VI

GET THE SCOOP ON...
How to re-list your items ▪ Whether to list your
unsold item elsewhere ▪ Deciding whether to
list the item in another category or a more
specialized auction ▪ What to do to make the
item listing more attractive

What If the Item Doesn't Sell?

Chapter 13

What's the worst-that-can-happen scenario? The auction is over, the dust has settled, and you're staring at the screen and the dreaded words: Bids: 0.

Before you get despondent and believe you won't ever make a living selling at online auctions, take heart. We all have an occasional auction that doesn't meet our expectations, and there are ways to deal with the issue. Anything (and we do mean *anything*) can sell at auction, but timing and placement are key. If you don't believe us, check out www.grrl.com/ebay.html to see some of the weird things that have sold on eBay.

There are many different reasons why an item might not sell. It could be as simple as the right buyer hasn't come along. Perhaps you listed it in the wrong category or in the wrong auction. Maybe your starting bid was too high or the reserve was more than those bidders were willing to pay. Could it be that the image(s) you included with your listing didn't show off the item in its best light? Or perhaps you mis-spelled a key word in your subject line? Maybe you were expecting a little more money than the market could handle, or the right buyer simply wasn't online when your auction was scheduled.

There are a variety of reasons why an auction goes bust, and the ones we've listed should be con-siderations before you take the next step: to re-list.

The pros and cons of re-listing

If your item doesn't sell, you have the option of re-listing it as is or putting it elsewhere (a new listing in another category, or perhaps even on a different auction site). If you believe the item didn't sell sim-ply because the auction ended at the wrong time, or if the item came close to selling and you believe it might if you change the price, correct the spelling, or add to the information included in the listing, you might choose to simply re-list.

Unofficially...
During the past couple of years, there have been kidneys, piles of marijuana, chil-dren, and other strange items listed on eBay and other auc-tions—and ultimately, taken off the list by the authorities in charge because the sale of these items is illegal.

Although many of the online auctions allow sell-ers to re-list items once or twice, the grandfather of them all, eBay, does charge a re-listing fee. However, the initial fee for listing is not charged if the item sells the second time around. In order to get that refund, three conditions must be met:

- The listed item must not have received any bids during the first regular auction.

- No bids met or exceeded your reserve price (if there was one).

- The item must be re-listed within 30 days of the closing date of the first auction.

Why re-list with eBay? Because if you didn't sell the item the first time, you still have to pay the list-ing fee, so why not re-list it for the same price and take your chances? The downside is that if the item doesn't sell the second time, you pay for *two* listings (the first and the re-list).

Other auctions handle re-listing differently. Here are some examples:

- **Yahoo!:** No charge if the item doesn't sell. You can resubmit automatically by choosing that preference when you create the original listing.

- **Amazon:** No charge if the item doesn't sell. Re-listing costs the same as any new listing.

- **AuctionAddict:** Listings continue 24 hours past closing time if there has been a bid. If there are no successful bids, the auction closes at the specified time. Auctions that don't meet the reserve are not charged, and there is no charge for re-listing unless the item meets the reserve.

- **Net4Sale:** Posting items for sale is free.

- **NuAuction.com:** No listing fee unless the item sells, which, to us, translates to no re-listing fee unless the item sells.

Should you lower the price?

One thing to consider when re-listing or changing your listing is whether the price is too high. But before you lower it, consider what you have into the piece. If you've spent $1 for something you believe is worth $100, is it really necessary to get the $100? Would it be acceptable to make 10 times what you paid for it ($10) and give someone else a bargain? The answer to that question depends on whether you feel the need to make an incredible profit or whether you simply want to sell it.

Most dealers I know are happy doubling their money on anything they sell. In fact, that's the rule of thumb. Anything above that amount is a gift.

> 66
> I utilize Amazon's re-listing feature to get all auctions that haven't sold re-listed that month. I also send out e-mail newsletters to my customers, giving them 10 percent off shipping if they buy from me.
> —Franziska Tinner, www.treasures.gifts.econgo.com
> 99

When considering re-listing an item that you've invested very little in, think about lowering the opening bid or the reserve to see whether it makes a difference in garnering bids. For example, if you put a fairly high opening bid or reserve on an item, you are telling bidders that you really don't want to sell it for less. However, if you find yourself with no bids at the end of the auction, you should consider whether that opening bid scared off potential buyers.

Since some auction houses will charge you if the item doesn't sell when you re-list it, you should adjust your opening bid or reserve accordingly. What's the sense of paying two fees for something that doesn't sell? And are you in this business to sell or are you willing to spend money for re-listing this item?

Sometimes an adjustment of just a couple of dollars makes a big difference in whether or not bidders will bite. Sometimes taking off the reserve encourages bidders who don't like being in the dark about whether their bid is going to be enough to put them in the running. And sometimes bidders simply like the excitement of participating in an auction where there are multiple bids and they can get in on the action.

After all, the whole idea behind an auction is to give people the opportunity to buy something at a price below regular retail market value. If you can't provide bidders with that deal, perhaps you should set up a retail site rather than offer your items for sale at auction.

Think about re-listing it elsewhere

There are times when your item will be listed in the wrong location or on the wrong auction. Perhaps you're not reaching the right audience or there are simply too many of the same item being offered for sale. Re-listing your piece elsewhere might make the difference between a sale item and a stale item.

Here are some suggestions for other places you might list your item:

- **List in another category.** If your Elvis postcard didn't sell in the postcard category, list it under Elvis memorabilia.

- **Try one of the specialized auctions.** If your Elvis postcard still doesn't sell, maybe you're not reaching the people who really want to buy it. Try an auction that specializes in postcards or celebrity memorabilia.

- **List in the gallery or specialized auctions' section of the original auction site.** This works best for items that are more expensive because it will cost a little more for the specialized listing, but sometimes it's worth it since many people just shop in the "gallery" or "special listings" category.

- **Re-list in a more general category.** Believe it or not, sometimes being in a category with more general items will cause a buyer who's just surfing through to make an impulse bid.

The benefits of specialized online auctions

Although the bulk of the sellers in this business are registered with one of the five or six major auctions and do most of their business with the big shots, there's something to be said for the smaller auctions that focus on specialty items.

Some of the benefits of visiting specialized auction sites include:

Moneysaver
If you re-list on another auction, consider listing on one that doesn't charge a listing fee. That way, if the item doesn't sell, you've saved money.

- Newsletters
- Links to other similar sites
- Online chatrooms
- Group bulletin boards to post desired items
- Trading message boards
- More diverse selection

By joining an auction where everyone is there for the same type of items you are, you can find out more about the hobby or item itself. Newsletters and message boards help you get the word out about the items you're looking for. Online chatrooms and bulletin boards get people together to share information they might have about the history of a piece. And you are likely to find a bargain!

We visited many specialized auctions while researching this book and discovered specialized auctions were a friendly place where community members were likely to help each other. We also discovered that prices were likely to be reasonable rather than off the scale. For example, at Beanie Nation (www.BeanieNation.com), both buyers and sellers are knowledgeable about Beanie Babies; thus, the bidding was stiff for the more rare examples, but the commonly found Babies were much more reasonably priced than on the larger auction sites. Why? Perhaps because the collectors knew more about the items for which they were bidding.

Another good example from specialized auctions was supplied after a trip to Bid4Vacations (www.Bid4Vacations.com). They have all their vacations separated into categories like adventure, beach, cruises, golf, and so on, which saved us a lot of time. In the larger online auctions, you visit the vacation or travel category and then must swim through a sea of poorly defined vacations to find the one that suits you. The vacation sites we visited were easy to navigate, the prices were good, and most vacations were guaranteed by either a travel agent or tour guide.

There are some online auctions that feature items simply not found elsewhere. At CyberHorse Auction (www.cyberhorseauction.com), you can bid on a gorgeous stallion or a mare ready to breed. Can't find too many of those on eBay, Amazon, or Yahoo!

Our advice? If you're selling a collectible, visit the auctions where dealers and sellers of that particular type gather. You have a captive audience for your item and don't have to swim through the millions of other items being sold at the same time yours is.

Timesaver
If you're looking for something specific in your field, it's easier to find it in a specialized auction where the items you want are separated into categories.

What about changing the category?

Often when we are about to list an item, we yell for each other and ask the question: "Where the heck should I put this? None of the categories are an exact match." Chances are good that the item we're questioning will have a poor showing if we put it in a category we're not sure about. Thankfully, you always have a second chance and can renegotiate the item's listing.

Although we've said that you should do a search for like items to see where they are listed before placing your own piece, there is always that one weird piece that just doesn't seem to fit. We have played with different categories for one or two items that we sell regularly and have discovered that it *does* make a difference where the item is placed.

Bright Idea
If all else fails, list your item in the "general" or "miscellaneous" category. Bidders who are looking for the odd or unusual item usually search there.

When you re-list an item that hasn't sold, changing the category often helps ensure the item will sell the second time around. For example, we sell my books at auction all the time. We've tried the book on Native American artists in the book category under art and discovered that it will sell, but usually the bids are fairly low. Since the book is always signed, we've also tried selling it in "rare books" or "first editions." We've also tried selling it in the "autograph" category. However, we've had the best luck with the Native American category—perhaps because most collectors of Native American items like to purchase guides to help them in their research.

Negotiating with the last bidder when the reserve isn't met

Sometimes you don't need to re-list, especially if you've had at least some bidding activity on your piece. For example, if your reserve hasn't been met but the last bidder is close, before you decide to re-list the item, try e-mailing the bidder. Explain the situation, telling the bidder that his or her bid was close to the reserve, then ask if he is still interested in the item. If he answers, you might be able to hammer out a deal. Remember to be honest with the bidder (treat him the way you'd want to be treated). The best you can expect is to split the difference between the reserve and the last bid the customer made. You might also want to reiterate the piece's description, because most bidders shop for more than one item and might forget yours if they don't win the auction.

If the bidder doesn't answer your initial e-mail, you are back to square one and can re-list the item. Simply go on with the show. Don't brood over the lack of response. Remember that most customers are members of the auction community because they love getting deals. They might have gone on to another item, found one like yours at a lower price, or decided they just didn't want it after all.

But it never hurts to try!

Better picture? More complete description?

If your item doesn't sell, it's time for you to give the listing a critical look. Two of the strongest reasons why a bidder makes a bid are the photos of the piece and the description.

Here are some factors about your photos and description to consider before re-listing:

- Is the photo clear? Are all the markings clearly visible? Is the size of the piece obvious? If not, take another shot or two.

- Do the images take a long time to load? Consider creating a thumbnail. Most photo programs offer the option of saving them as thumbnails or full photos. The smaller the image, the faster it will load. Customers get tired of waiting for a full-screen picture to come up—and frustrated if they have to slide back and forth to see its details. Keep the image small (12–20K).

- Does your description list all the important details, such as condition, age, size, color, and material? If you had any bidders ask questions throughout the auction, include the answers to those questions in your new listing.

- Are all the words in your description spelled correctly? Run a spell check on your description, then run a grammar check to see whether

66
I use a lot of background graphics and set an ad up to be appealing to the customer; however, sometimes this means the ad loads slowly, so I test and retest to make sure the listing is easy to read.
—Franziska Tinner,
www.treasures.gifts.econgo.com
99

your sentences are properly punctuated. Sometimes an incorrectly placed comma or period causes a misunderstanding. And make sure everything is accurate. If you're not sure of a date or size, now is the time to *make* sure. Don't guess!

One final suggestion: Ask someone else to look at your listing to see whether the photos and description are clear. It's often better to get a second opinion since you know the piece well and might not be able to tell whether you've missed something. Better to tell the bidder too much than not enough! But don't load the listing with too many photos (no more than three is best), since auction surfers are not known for their patience.

Maybe it's not the right time

If you've done everything we've suggested and the piece still isn't selling, it's time to think about whether you want to waste your time (and money) re-listing this item.

Watch Out! If your item doesn't sell because it's seasonal, make sure you don't pack it away where you can't find it! You'll want to be able to put it on the market again when the time is right.

Consider whether the item might be seasonal. Christmas items always sell better in October and November than in July (although there are plenty of Christmas collectors out there who shop year-round). Waiting to sell a seasonal item makes more sense than either taking a loss now or continually re-listing it.

There are also some items that simply don't sell because the item is no longer popular or hasn't caught on yet. For example, Michael Jackson items that were once hot don't move very well at auction these days. Perhaps there will be a day when Jackson will be hot again, but until then, you'd be better off packing those collectibles away.

Just the facts

- Re-listing fees are different for each auction. If you list the same item twice with eBay and it doesn't sell, you will be charged two insertion fees.

- Many of the major auctions offer automatic re-listing if your item doesn't sell, and they will not charge you a listing fee if there are no bids.

- Elements that contribute to an item's not selling include poor photos, unclear description, and slow-loading listings.

- If an item doesn't sell, it might be because it's seasonal or no longer popular.

GET THE SCOOP ON...
Getting help ▪ Dealing with financial difficulties
▪ The importance of feedback ▪ Other ways to
solve problems

Chapter 14

Dealing with Problem Buyers and Sellers

When you have a problem with someone in an online auction, you expect to get some customer support from the auction itself, but it doesn't always work that way. Some (like Yahoo!), saying that the auction is between the buyer and seller, don't assume any responsibility for problems.

But what about the customer support and service that *you*, as seller, should offer your buyers? You are responsible for answering questions and solving problems, and in most cases, you are the first person to deal with any misconceptions, disagreements, or grievances that others have with you or that you have with others. Before the problem goes to the customer support staff (if any) at your online auction, you must attempt to deal with the situation yourself.

Although this business is fun, it also comes with a certain amount of responsibility. Whether you're "playing the game" as a seller or buyer, you are entitled to (and should offer) a certain amount of customer support.

Hints from other sellers/buyers

Any business person will tell you that if you keep a customer happy, that person will continue to buy from you. If, however, you deceive your customers or neglect to meet their needs in any way, they will not only stop buying your product, they'll make sure everyone they meet knows about your poor business practices as well.

This train of thought is what prompted eBay and the other auction houses to implement a feedback policy. If you'll be dealing with people and businesses over the Internet, the only way to assure they will be fair in their business practices is to let them know that if they cheat you or send you a defective item, you will pass the word along to others.

So, how do you stop problems before they begin? You take the advice of sellers and buyers who have been part of the online auction business since its inception. After talking with dozens of auction pros, we've compiled the most important rules of conducting or participating in a successful auction, or what we call The Honest Auction Dozen:

1. **Follow the auction rules.** Be clear about the auction's procedures and make sure you follow them to the letter.

2. **Go slow and steady.** If you're not ready to sell, don't. If you're not sure about an item's history, check it out before you bid. Don't believe everything you read, and don't get carried away by the action of the auction. Better to be safe than sorry. (Are those enough clichés for you?)

Timesaver
To let your customers know you're offering them the best support they can get at an online auction, put a note on each auction assuring them that their satisfaction is guaranteed.

3. **Answer e-mails quickly.** Whether it's the close of an auction and you need to let the seller know you're mailing a check, or a bidder has asked you a question about the Ansel Adams photograph you're selling, be prompt! If a seller has e-mailed you asking about payment, answer as quickly as you would expect the seller to answer your e-mail asking about where your item is!

4. **Keep in contact.** Let the seller know you are selling a check or tell the buyer the item is on its way.

5. **Communicate clearly.** If you're going to charge someone a handling fee, make sure it's noted up front in your listing. If you're not going to ship internationally, note that as well. Conversely, if you, as the bidder, are unsure about something or need to let the seller know you're in Tasmania, do so!

6. **Represent items honestly.** When you have a damaged item, don't hide it. It's better to be honest with your bidders than to have them receive a misrepresented item and give you negative feedback. Flaws should not be hidden.

7. **Package and send items promptly.** You got the check yesterday, but you aren't going to send the package until Saturday—three days from now? You expect the money promptly, so show your buyer the same courtesy. And while you're at it, make sure the package is wrapped well.

8. **Keep accurate records.** Whether you keep paper invoices or store everything on your computer, make sure you note who won an auction, when the auction ended, and when you sent the package.

Bright Idea
Using an auction management program that automatically sends a note requesting (or providing) feedback frees you up to handle more important details—such as mailing out packages and checks!

9. **Use Web pages.** Some dealers send regular newsletters to former customers and some buyers do the same to inform people of their wants and needs. By keeping an up-to-date Web page, you'll be taking advantage of your greatest selling tool.

10. **Remember that buyers and sellers are human.** Extending a little courtesy to someone who needs extra time to send a check or an item creates good customer relations. By remembering that we all have other lives besides the online auction business, you create the compassion necessary to be a good customer or salesperson.

11. **Be accessible when an auction ends.** Nothing is worse for a buyer or a seller than wanting to find out some information and not being able to because the other person isn't around. It's also necessary to prepare goods for shipment or checks for payment right away. No one wants to wait.

12. **Leave feedback.** Don't wait for the buyer or seller to urge you to leave positive feedback. Make it a habit to leave it as soon as your transaction is concluded. However, think twice before leaving negative feedback. Remember that it can boomerang on you, so try to solve your problems before you rush to give someone a negative rating.

Finding a buyer's e-mail address and location

If you need to contact a buyer or seller and have forgotten or lost the information already provided to you at the end of an auction, how do you go about getting that information forwarded to you?

With most auctions, it's fairly simple to find a buyer or seller's e-mail address, and sometimes even his or her physical location. However, because most people want to keep that information private, there are several steps you must go through in order to find out.

First, you must be a registered buyer or seller on the auction in order to ask the question. Second, the information is usually e-mailed to your address shortly after you ask the question. Third, the member about whom you're requesting the info also receives an e-mail telling him you are requesting his e-mail or address information.

Another way you can find a person's e-mail address or retail location is to look at her Web page. In eBay, most members have created an "About Me" Web page that features their ongoing auctions, shows their feedback, and tells something about them. Often this page will contain links to the Web page that the bidder/seller maintains through her own ISP or on another server.

On Yahoo!'s auction site, you can view the closed auctions and find the winning bidder's ID and e-mail address, as well as the "Reserve Bidders List," if your auction had one. It's easier to get in touch with people this way, but the physical address is still kept private.

In addition, when you are viewing a listing, the seller sometimes has a link directly to his retail Web site, where you can often find his e-mail address, retail address, and perhaps a phone number.

Our advice when looking up another member's information is to use that service only when necessary. And *always* contact a member via e-mail before you resort to a personal phone call. Questions and problems should be communicated via e-mails first.

How long should you wait for an answer?

As you learned in Chapter 4, "Setting Up an Account—or Two," once the auction has ended, the bidder and seller have a specific amount of time to contact each other. After the initial contact, give yourself and the buyer/seller some time to respond. Because the Net has provided us with instant contact, we tend to be a bit antsy about getting immediate answers to questions, but remember sellers/buyers have real jobs and families. Give the other member several days to reply before you take the next step.

How long is long enough? Our rule of thumb is to wait a week for an answer after the auction has ended. Even if the buyer or seller has been on vacation or something has come up, they should get back to you within a week. After that point, you have a right to contact the next highest bidder if you are the seller or to leave the seller negative feedback if you are the bidder. We should add a caveat here that several times we've been ready to leave negative feedback and have decided to send the bidder/seller one more e-mail. More often than not, the person has responded.

An additional warning: Most people who frequently post negative feedback get nothing but negative feedback in return.

International sales problems

Quite a few of the online auctions we've researched cater to buyers/sellers from all over the world. Often it's obvious (the home page of the auction might indicate that it can be read in English and Japanese, for example), but sometimes it's not. If you're not willing to deal with people from another country, indicate that you won't ship internationally if you're a seller, and if you're a buyer, keep an eye out for the dealer's location before you bid.

Some of the problems that may come up include:

- Language issues (which we deal with in the next section).

- Shipping problems (it takes a lot longer to ship out of the country and special precautions should be taken when packing, which we'll discuss in Chapter 15, "Packaging for a Safe Journey").

- Currency conversion (there are software programs or online Web sites that handle this issue; see the next section).

Language and misunderstandings

If you indicate that you'll ship internationally, or if you are buying on a regular basis, sooner or later you might run into language problems. Thankfully, there are programs that deal with that, as well as money conversion issues.

Some of the ones we found include:

1. Language translation Web sites:

   - Global Language Translation and Consulting (www.gltac.com)

   - SYSTRAN Software Inc. (www.systransoft. com)

   - Transparent Language Enterprise Translation Server (www.transparentlanguage.com/ets)

2. Currency conversion Web sites:

   - Cloanto Euro Calculator (www.cloanto.com)

   - Xenon Currency Services (www.xe.net)

Bright Idea
If you plan on trading internationally, bookmark several language translation Web sites or get in touch with your local university's foreign language department.

- 1-Click Currency Conversion (www.currency. co.nz/). You can add this to your Web site to make it easier for your customers to figure out your prices.

Even though you may believe you've made yourself clear when dealing with a person from another country, he or she might misunderstand you. More than likely this will be because your words take on a slightly different connotation when translated.

To head off any misunderstandings, be doubly careful to be clear, concise, and grammatically correct. Above all, make sure you spell everything correctly. Run a spell check on your e-mails and any letters you include with your package.

In addition to watching your language, make sure you let your customer or dealer know the following:

- When your check or package was mailed.

- How it was mailed (ask the post office exactly how long the package will take to arrive at its destination).

- Whether it's insured and for how much (we *strongly* recommend you insure anything that's going internationally, whether a check or a package).

Also, it's a wise idea to ask your customer or dealer to send you an e-mail when she receives your package or check so you know it arrived safely.

When you're still not satisfied

If you've taken all the precautions we've suggested, given the buyer/seller the benefit of the doubt, and you still feel like you've gotten a raw deal, there are steps you can take to rectify the situation. But before you plunge wholeheartedly into either giving the buyer/seller negative feedback or taking some other step, consider the following:

1. **Did you read the ad carefully?** If you're buying an item and believe it was misrepresented, before you do anything, go back and read the ad for the item. Even if the listing has been taken off the active boards, you can usually find it in "closed auctions." That's one of the reasons we suggest you save the auction listing numbers of anything you buy. If you didn't save it, you can still go into your account and find the items you've bid on. Check to see if the item you've received is exactly the same as described. You might even ask someone else to read the listing to get another opinion.

   Sometimes you'll discover that the seller did indeed mention that the teapot you bought has a hairline crack on its spout, but in your zeal to own it, you skimmed over that part of the ad.

2. **Did you make a mistake in representing your own item?** Just as buyers are responsible for looking at the listing to see whether they totally understood it, so are dealers. Before you condemn someone for sending a nasty e-mail about the quality of your item, review your listing and see if you were as clear as glass in your description. Sometimes we think we said something specific and, come to find out, we didn't exactly spell out that crack on the spout of the teapot. People make mistakes, and you're as capable of making one as the next person. Before you send feedback, make sure you have something in writing to back yourself up—and make sure it's strong support for your argument!

Timesaver
When writing your listing, keep in mind that you need to note the five most important points: condition (and all the details), color (be specific), age, size, and markings. If you keep a post-it note above your computer noting these five points, you'll save time.

What if you get burned?

Okay, you've searched your soul and your e-mails, your listing and your checkbook, and you've decided you've been burned. You've tried to contact the buyer/seller and have had no luck. What do you do? We'll talk about feedback in a moment. First, let's talk about the steps you take in different situations and what your options are.

There are many different ways you can get burned in this business. We're not trying to scare you, only educate you. A buyer is usually just out the money paid and the product expected. A seller might have quite different and far-reaching problems, but a seller has a little more protection, especially since the law deals with some issues faster than the online auction protection service.

The best thing you can do for yourself is to keep copies of all transactions. Some people we've spoken to feel that the best way to do this is to keep paper copies, while others simply create files on their computers. The advantage to keeping computer files is that you don't have to manage piles of paper, and if you need to retrieve that info, you can easily print it out. However, computers have been known to crash, so we suggest you keep the files on both your hard drive and a backup disk. As you will see, you'll need that proof to argue your case if you get burned—either as a buyer or a seller.

Bounced checks and refused credit cards

A refused credit card is easy to deal with because the seller finds out up front from the credit card company that the customer's card is not accepted. If the auction has already ended, you simply send the customer a polite e-mail saying that the credit card company rejected the card, and ask if there's another way the customer would like to pay. Usually the customer has another card he can use, easily solving the problem. However, if there is no other payment choice, the buyer might have to forfeit the item. In that case, the seller might contact the second-highest bidder and take a small monetary loss. (You can ask the second bidder to pay the final price, but we suggest you sell the piece at the price the second bidder originally bid. It's good customer service, and you won't have to put the item up for auction again.) The other option is to re-list the item (as discussed in the previous chapter).

Bounced checks are a different story. If a customer's check is no good, again, be courteous and first e-mail the buyer, tell her the situation, and remember to find out how much your bank is going to charge you for the returned check fee. Ask the customer to make good on the check and charge her the fee your bank is charging you. After all, a bounced check puts a dent in your own bank account and you want to make sure you are reimbursed.

If the buyer is unavailable, has disappeared, or cannot make good on the check, first contact your local small claims court and ask what the steps are to make a claim, *then* contact the auction house and report the customer. Your final step is feedback. Why do we say that feedback is your final step? Because getting your money back is of utmost importance and should be taken care of first! Yes, you want to enter feedback on that customer, but first get your paperwork started to cover your bank account.

Unofficially... During the first couple of years that online auctions were popular, the Internet Fraud Watch warned consumers to "never give bank information to anyone unless you are authorizing a merchant to withdraw payment for products or services."

Fakes, reproductions, and counterfeits

The auction is over, you've received your goods, your check has been cashed, and a week or so later, a friend comes over to the house and in your excitement, you show her the item you've bought. To your surprise, the friend starts laughing, or worse, gasps. The item is a fake, she says, and you believe her because she is an expert in the field. Your heart sinks. You can't believe you've been duped. What do you do next?

Fakes, reproductions, and counterfeits have been on the market for years. Japanese vases, uncirculated coins, Impressionist paintings, iron banks, sterling silverware ... all have been faked, reproduced, and counterfeited, and some are so well made that it takes an expert to tell whether they are the real thing or a phony. Don't feel ignorant if you get caught with an item that isn't the real deal. Even the most knowledgeable experts get duped occasionally.

For your information, there is a difference between fakes and reproductions and counterfeits. A *fake* is something that is purported to be something else. For example, a fake coin isn't a coin at all (like a "plug nickel"). A *reproduction* is a later version of an item. For example, a reproduction Chippendale chair is one made to look like a Chippendale but produced at a different time. The original might have been made in the late 1700s, and the reproduction made in the 1900s. A repro isn't worth as much, but it can still be of good quality. However, most repros are advertised or labelled as such—no one is trying to pull the wool over your eyes. A *counterfeit,* on the other hand, is something that is created for the purpose of defrauding the buyer. For example, people who print a counterfeit dollar bill want to be able to use that bill the same way they would use a real one. What it all boils down to is that fakes are worthless, reproductions are good for people who want the real thing's "look" but are unable to afford the genuine article, and counterfeits are downright illegal.

So what do you do if you discover the priceless van Gogh you've bought isn't priceless at all? You take the same steps you would if the item was misrepresented. You contact the seller first. There's a good chance he might also have been duped. A good seller will automatically return your money and take the item back. If that doesn't happen, contact the auction. Some, like eBay, offer auction insurance and will refund a certain amount of your purchase price. Others, like Yahoo!, expect you to take care of the problem with the seller. Check your auction's rules and be prepared for this problem ahead of time.

If you've invested a great deal of money and cannot recoup it all either through a refund or auction insurance, it's time to contact a lawyer.

How to tell and what to do

How do you tell when you have a counterfeit? Research is the only way. Depending on the item, there are several tools used by professionals. For example, ultraviolet light is used to tell whether a dollar bill is counterfeit. It can also help discern whether a painting has been retouched or whether a piece of porcelain has been repaired.

When dealing with other items, you might want to employ such testing as carbon dating or something as simple as checking the signature on a piece. If you don't have any idea how to check your item for accuracy and have your doubts as to its veracity,

Watch Out!
If you can't find any information about the item you've bought, call or visit a local expert and bring the item with you to get it verified. Remember to look for some proof that this person is an expert!

contact an expert. The appraisal companies listed in Chapter 7, "The Right Way to Sell," can offer their assistance for a fee. If you don't want to pay someone else (for example, if your item isn't worth that much), check one of the books available on your subject. Collectibles and antiques are easily researched. Companies like Wallace-Homestead and Antiques Collector News have published books as well as magazines, newspapers, and newsletters to keep collectors up to date on easily recognizable fakes and counterfeits.

Another suggestion is to search the online auction where you buy for dealers who specialize in the item you've purchased. If you can find a knowledgeable dealer's e-mail address, you might be able to ask that person a few general questions about your item and get a quick answer to whether or not it's the real deal.

Damaged items

There are times when the seller is not at fault for damaged items. We've had several instances when a piece has been broken into smithereens by the shipping services we've used. (It's amazing what will break when sent via the U.S. Postal Service!)

If it's obvious that the package has been damaged en route, contact the seller first to see whether she insured the item. If the package was insured, the seller should have a receipt and can begin the process of getting the shipper to reimburse both of you for the price of the item and shipping. In this case, you would still be able to keep the damaged item, but you'd also get your money back. However, you will have to keep the packaging and the item itself to show the shipper that the item was indeed damaged in shipping.

On the other hand, if the package itself is in good shape but the item inside is damaged, first determine whether the piece was damaged *before* the package went into the mail (for example, hairline cracks are usually not caused by poor packaging or the bumps and shakes of regular shipping). If the piece was packaged well (using bubble wrap, foam, Styrofoam peanuts, or the like), it's probable that the item was damaged before it was shipped. In that case, go back to the listing and see if the seller stated the piece's faults.

If it's obvious that the item wasn't packed well and that it was damaged as a result, the fault lies with the seller and you should ask for your money back. If the seller performs good customer service, don't punish him by leaving negative feedback. But make sure the seller knows he's not packing his items very well and that you expect to be reimbursed for some or all of the original cost.

The importance of feedback

Every auction we've visited institutes some kind of feedback system and it usually works to show both the buyer and seller what kind of business they have done in the past. It's important that both buyer and seller provide feedback after the sale so that the next person in line knows what kind of experience it was. For the new customer, feedback provides the type of information that makes the buying experience more comfortable. Feedback can determine whether your business continues to improve or whether you're able to buy more items, so it's the "report card" of the auction business world.

For instance, you can provide (or obtain) information about:

- Whether a buyer/seller ships or pays promptly
- The quality of the items sold
- Whether a buyer/seller answers e-mails promptly
- Whether information provided about products is accurate and truthful
- Whether any problems were handled effectively
- Whether the buyer/seller has broken any rules or committed fraud or illegal acts
- How many transactions a seller/buyer has had (the number of transactions also indicates how much feedback has been positive, negative, or neutral)

Feedback builds auction-goers' reputations and can ultimately be the reason why a buyer deals (or does not deal) with a seller, or vice versa. If the auction-goer's feedback has been negative or lukewarm, a seller may choose not to let a buyer bid on an item.

How to give feedback and when

Depending on the auction with which you're associated, feedback is determined either by stars (eBay), ratings (Amazon and Yahoo!), or numbers (many other auctions). The stars (or any icon like them) are designed to encourage auction-goers to strive for a better rating. Naturally, the higher the rating, the better the business relations between buyers and sellers.

You are pretty much obligated to give feedback to a buyer or seller as soon as the transaction is closed. Some of the auction management programs we've discussed send feedback for you automatically, but if you're not using one of them, you are responsible for reminding yourself of that obligation.

To give feedback, you simply click on the user's name or nickname. You'll be taken to the user's home page or to the feedback page (depending on the auction) and given the option of leaving feedback.

Enter your comments in the box provided and be as specific as possible. For example, if the item was delivered within days of the check being received, say so. If the seller/buyer went out of her way to provide helpful comments, mention that. And if the item was something special that perfectly fit into your collection, mention what it was so that other buyers/sellers will know if this auction-goer has been selling/buying the same types of items on a regular basis. Remember that you are providing valuable information to other auction-goers who, like yourself, need all the details they can get to make a decision whether to buy or sell to this person.

If you've had a negative experience, be careful to word it in such a way that the problem you've had is clear—and try not to write the feedback while you're still steaming. As many auction-goers have mentioned in chatrooms we've visited, when you give negative feedback, you usually receive negative feedback. Be specific, calm, and remember that the feedback you give reflects on you as well as on the other person.

How to read feedback

To read feedback, simply click on the buyer/seller's name and you'll be taken to their feedback. Remember that you're looking for specific details rather than the repetitious "Great sale" or "Highly recommended."

Some of the details you are searching for might include:

Unofficially...
When Rosie O'Donnell began promoting eBay and selling unique items to support her 4allkids charity, some bidders began leaving messages for her even though they hadn't bought anything. Her feedback number is now private, but the last time we checked, she had a rating of over 2,200 feedbacks, mostly positive.

- How long does the buyer/seller take to complete a transaction?

- Does she pack the items well?

- Have payments been made by check, online escrow accounts, or credit card?

- How long has the buyer/seller been doing business online?

- What kinds of items has he sold in the past?

- Are former customers/buyers satisfied with the goods they've bought?

Keeping track of your own feedback

Because few auctions we've visited automatically e-mail customers when feedback has been posted, in order to keep track of your own feedback, you must regularly visit your online auction account page.

If you discover that someone has left feedback of a questionable nature (for example, if the person has left you a neutral feedback noting that you didn't reply to their e-mails, but the truth is that your computer went down or you were out of town) or if you would like them to add additional information, just click on the person's name. You'll either be taken to his feedback page where you can request his e-mail address, or you'll be taken directly to his e-mail address, where you can send him your request. You can also defend yourself if the feedback is inaccurate by going to the Customer Service people in the auction site.

Keeping track of your feedback is important because it's often the first place a new bidder/seller will go when they are ready to buy from you or if they have questions about selling to you. Maintaining a listing of helpful and effective

Watch Out!
If you receive a neutral or negative piece of feedback, you may be able to get the buyer/seller to add additional information so that your rating won't be affected, but you have to contact the person who gave it to you. (Note: eBay states that feedback cannot be retracted.) Handle this situation *very* carefully! Be kind and reasonable. You won't earn any brownie points by attacking the bidder/seller who left the less-than-positive feedback.

comments builds your business and credibility with customers. Consider it your calling card.

Beware of those sunglasses

There are times when auction-goers choose to "re-invent" themselves in order to re-enter the auction scene. It may be because they received negative feedback, or they may simply choose to use a different persona to have more than one way to enter bids.

eBay indicates that someone has changed his or her ID by adding a pair of sunglasses beside the user name. When you see a pair of sunglasses (or another indicator telling you a person's identity has been recently changed), you are being given a subtle warning that the user has chosen to use a different ID during the past 30 days. (Note, too, that brand-new buyers/sellers on eBay share this sunglasses designation, not just people who are hiding behind new identities.) Once that 30-day period is up, the sunglasses disappear.

Most users realize that a change of ID might indicate there have been problems in the past, but most auctions will give buyers/sellers a second chance to clean up their act. If they are caught doing something illegal or if they receive too many negative pieces of feedback, they are usually kicked off permanently. So, beware those sunglasses! They are there to warn you, and most auction-goers think twice before changing their ID so as to avoid the sunglasses icon and all it represents.

An "interesting" experience?

You may notice that some feedback is worded in a mysterious and confusing way. Remember that the word choice a buyer/seller uses when leaving feedback might seem pretty clear up front, but what exactly does an "interesting" experience mean? It can mean that the buyer/seller had some problems but eventually straightened them out, or it can mean that the transaction was such a successful one that the buyer and seller became friends.

If you're not clear on what a piece of feedback means, contact the buyer/seller who left it, tell him or her which item you're referring to, and ask if there are any other details you should know about dealing with this person before you finalize your transaction.

When in doubt, always ask!

Other recourses

If all else fails and you believe someone is committing an act of fraud, you can attempt to sue. We believe Americans are especially lawsuit-happy and that the act of taking someone to court should be your last recourse, but sometimes it's necessary. No matter how much protection an online auction offers, there are times when the losses sustained are so heavy that a buyer/seller has no other recourse but to retain a lawyer and take the guilty party to court. But before you take this serious step, make sure you have exhausted all your other resources. Suing someone over an online transaction is not easy to do, especially if you live in different states.

If you're considering taking this step, our advice is to do the following:

1. Contact one of the online legal services first and see if you can get advice from a lawyer or legal assistant.

2. If you discover through your initial research that you have a case, gather all your documents and make sure you lay a good paper trail,

Moneysaver
Instead of paying a lawyer up front, contact one of the services available online and ask a few simple questions. You will probably get free advice and save yourself both money and a major headache.

including dates of the auction, the address (both e-mail and residence) of the other party, copies of all e-mails and other correspondence, any bills of handling or shipping information, and all cancelled checks/money orders.

3. Contact a lawyer and ask about fees before you start a case.

4. Take a deep breath and remind yourself that this is a very unusual circumstance in the auction world!

Just the facts

- Make sure you can get support from the customer service department of your auction before you plunge in.

- To find e-mail and business addresses, click on the user's name and the info will be given to you automatically or e-mailed promptly by the auction house.

- Wait at least a couple of days after the suggested auction deadlines before giving up on the buyer/seller.

- Leave feedback for both buyers and sellers promptly after the transaction is completed— and use it to decide whether to deal with auction-goers.

- Use auction insurance whenever possible, but don't abuse the privilege.

- When you believe a buyer or seller is committing fraud and you've exhausted all other possibilities, contact your lawyer.

GET THE SCOOP ON...
How to guesstimate shipping costs ▪ Packing tips
for breakable and non-breakable items ▪ Where to
get the best shipping materials ▪ Which shippers
are reliable (and within budget) ▪ What kinds of
insurance to use ▪ What happens if an item is
damaged in shipping?

Packaging for a Safe Journey

Packing your items well and feeling fairly sure they'll get to their destinations safely is an important part of the online auction process. The buyer is expecting that special treasure to arrive in one piece. After all, that's what he or she paid for, correct? If the item doesn't arrive the way it was advertised, the buyer has several options: He can return the item and ask for a refund; return the item, get the refund, and leave you negative feedback; or simply leave you negative feedback. There are other options, however, and you should know what they are ahead of time. You should also be well aware of what it takes to pack something correctly and to keep the customer happy. After all, this is a business.

Remember that Samsonite commercial where the gorilla took a suitcase and jumped, punched, threw, stomped, and banged on it? Well, think of that gorilla's antics as equivalent to what your package will go through when it's traveling across the country. As much as you would like to think our postal system handles your boxes and envelopes as carefully as if they were babies, that's not the case. Packages are thrown from one place to another, envelopes are squeezed into mailboxes far too small for them, containers are packed under much heavier pieces, and all of the those factors can do major damage to your goods.

Take it from us, Murphy's Law presides over every delivery system: If the item can break, it will, and if it's not packed with every precaution considered, it doesn't have a snowball's chance. Even when it *is* packed correctly, there is still a chance of damage. So, know that up front.

Once you've started selling, you might as well consider yourself in business. Though there are ways to keep your expenses down, you would be quite wise not to try to cut too many corners when it comes to shipping—unless you don't intend to be in business very long.

Weigh items *before* the seller sends the check

In Chapter 12, "Keeping Track of the Auction," we talked about who pays for shipping. If you decided the buyer should, you need to figure out shipping costs as soon as you see who your buyer is and where she's from. If you mentioned in your auction ad that the shipping costs would be $5, but when the auction ends, you find that your buyer is from Australia (and this has happened to us!), it's *your* responsibility to pay the shipping fees above the $5—no matter how much they are!

That said, it should be obvious that the first step in packaging your item comes before you consider what size box you'll need. What you need to do up

Unofficially...
Approximately 7 percent of the items shipped in the United States are online auction products.

front is keep within the estimated shipping costs you gave buyers in your ad. Although you don't necessarily have to give a specific amount, you should have an idea what the costs for shipping the item will be before the auction ends, and let buyers know that they (or you) will assume the cost. Also, don't forget that unless you tell your buyers you are going to add on a little extra for handling fees (the cost of your packaging, boxes, bubble wrap, etc.), then you will shoulder the burden of that expense.

If you're just going to be selling one item every once in a while, we suggest you do a "mock pack up" when the end of the auction is in sight. That way, when your high bidder e-mails you about sending the item, you can already have an approximate price on the mailing costs. To do this, you must pack the item exactly as you would if you were shipping it that day, then take it to the post office. Some offices have scales where you can weigh the item and get the shipping costs. Write down all the prices: regular mail, priority, overnight, and parcel post. Usually your buyer will decide how she wants the piece shipped, and if you give her those options, she will feel like she is taking part in the decision.

You can also contact one of the online shipping services and give them the dimensions and weight of your package and obtain an estimate from them. One such place is iShip.com. They need to know where the package is going, its size, and its weight. Once you enter in those specifics, iShip.com will give you a table of shipping alternatives, from which you can choose the shipper you'll use.

The next step in the selling process would be to get your own set of scales. They're available in office stores in various sizes and types (the electronic ones are what

Bright Idea
If you can't get the package to the post office to weigh it, you can weigh it yourself at home. Step on your bathroom scale and weigh yourself alone. Then step back on with the package in your hands. The difference between the two weights is the approximate weight of your package.

the Power Sellers swear by). In addition, some of the online postage companies—such as Stamps.com—sell scales, and the U.S. post office also lets you order stamps and supplies online.

In addition to giving you an estimate on shipping costs, iShip.com offers you the option of providing your buyers with a link to iShip.com on your site, where they can find out the details about shipping the item on which they're bidding. They'll also offer you details on maximum dimensions and weights that the carriers will allow, as well as how to ship internationally and how to track items.

When you're weighing your item, remember that your packing materials will add to the total heft of the package. The reason bubble wrap and foam peanuts are so popular is because they don't weigh much, thus providing protection for items without adding much to the overall cost of shipping.

The right and wrong way to pack a box

There is very definitely a science to packing a box, carton, tube, or envelope. We have both moved a number of times, and we have packed and unpacked antiques for shows. Ninety-nine percent of the things we've packed have remained intact. Every once in a while, we get a teapot with a chipped lid or a frame with a cracked glass, but if that happens, it's usually because we were in a rush to get out of a show or to get the moving van loaded so we could get on the road, so the broken item or two is expected.

Here are some simple tips to remember when packing that precious china-face doll or that hundred-year-old bottle of wine:

1. Choose a sturdy box that is a little larger than your item. For example, if you're mailing a 6-inch-tall teapot, pick a box that's at least 10

inches tall. If you mail the teapot in a smaller box, there won't be enough padding between the teapot and the outside of the box.

2. Pad the bottom of the box with shredded paper or foam peanuts. Remember that your box will be traveling through a number of machines that aren't likely to be as kind as a human being would.

3. If your item is extremely fragile, pack it in a smaller box and nest that box within a larger one. Make sure the item is padded before you put it into the smaller box and then pad the larger box, as we suggest in the next several steps.

4. If the item is breakable, wrap it well. Then tape the wrapping and wrap it again—the opposite way. For example, if you've wrapped a bulbous piece from front to back, wrap the second layer from side to side.

5. Either separately wrap each removable piece of the object, or tape those pieces to the object so they won't rattle and chip or crack. One trick we've learned is to turn caps upside down so that the top is actually inside the piece, then we tape them closed. This works well with fragile pieces of pottery, porcelain, and glass.

6. When the item is in the box, make sure there's enough "breathing room" at the top of the box and fill that space with more shredded paper, foam peanuts, or bubble wrap.

7. Before taping the box, attach your address labels.

8. Use clear tape so that you can tape right over the labels and still read the address (this protects against moisture, heat, and machines that like to pull at loose corners).

Moneysaver
If you're packing more than one thing for a customer, see if you can use one item to buffer the other. For example, use a T-shirt to wrap up one of the wine glasses you're sending. Then put them both in a plastic supermarket bag before you wrap them in newspaper or bubble wrap.

9. Tape the box closed both by girth and length.

10. Make sure all exposed corners are securely sealed.

The right packing supplies and where to get them

We're all for saving money and being ecologically conscious, so we'll suggest the free ways you can get wrapping supplies first, then we'll talk about buying the more expensive (and professional-looking) packing supplies.

One of the things we've learned how to do through the years is recycle shipping materials. Here are some of the things you can save and use later when shipping items to your customers:

- Padded envelopes you receive from catalog companies and other shippers can be reused to send books, magazines, paper goods, and small toys. They can also be used as padding for small breakable items that are packed in boxes. Even if the envelope has been ripped, it can be reused as packing material.

- Plastic shopping bags can be used to wrap items that need to stay clean. In a pinch, they'll also do as padding, but you usually have to use quite a few to attain the level of padding offered by newspaper, shredded paper, or foam peanuts.

- Paper shopping bags are great for wrapping a book or flat object that then goes into a larger envelope or box.

- Any packing material (such as foam peanuts) from a package you receive can be recycled and thrown into the next box you are going to mail.

Timesaver
Wrap auction packages ahead of time so that when the checks come, you can pop the goods right into the mail. Your customers will love you for it!

- Used U.S. post office boxes (e.g., Priority boxes) can often be sliced down one seam, turned inside out, and retaped to be used again. Or, if the box is small enough, it can hold a small, fragile item that is then packed in a larger box.

- Catalogs and sale fliers are great as padding; however, they tend to weigh more than the shipping materials sold over the counter, so you might pay more for postage fees.

- Some food containers can be washed and reused as small packing boxes. For example, some ice cream containers offer the perfect size and weight to ship small toys or pieces of jewelry.

- When you can't find bubble wrap, baby diapers (not used ones!) are perfect for wrapping highly breakable objects, as they are thick and offer the same type of padding as bubble wrap, with another layer besides. If your neighbor's three-year-old just became potty-trained, she might be very happy to unload her unused diapers. (If you don't get them for free, you might want to invest in a box or two when they're on sale.)

- Save empty boxes, even if you don't know what you'll put in them yet. If your office tends to go through reams of paper, make friends with the janitor and tell him to save the boxes for you. Taking a pile home once a week can save you hundreds of dollars a year in shipping materials. And while you're there, ask the janitor how many bags of Styrofoam peanuts and other types of stuffing he disposes of on a weekly basis. Can it be saved? Not only do you cut corners in your budget, you help the environment by recycling materials.

- The United States Postal Service, FedEx, Airborne Express and other mailing services will deliver free shipping supplies to your door. The boxes are good for shipping by Priority or Overnight mail, but can also be used as packing materials. They will also give you free rolls of Priority Mail tape, as well as address labels.

- Local supermarkets are always happy to give away the boxes they empty on delivery days. The best packing boxes we've used for larger items are fruit and vegetable boxes. Banana boxes are great for storage, but their wide openings make them a bad choice for shipping.

- Plastic bottles and other containers make sturdy buffers for breakable items and are often malleable enough that you can cut them down or fold them over so that you can fit them within a box. A gallon milk jug can be sliced in half and used to ship a paperweight or valuable Christmas ornament.

- Newspapers and magazines are the most commonly saved items and are invaluable when you need filler (they're also a lot cheaper than bubble wrap or foam peanuts). One way to use them completely is to invest in a shredder. Shredded newspaper is lighter and cleaner than full sheets.

You'd be wise to bring all your shipping and handling supplies together so you can save time when there are a few boxes that need to be filled and sent. If you keep these tools in one place, you'll be more efficient later on.

Now, where do you get your supplies? You can go to the local department store and buy a box of

> **"**
> Whenever I want to stock up on packing supplies, I go to an auction site, do a search, then put in a couple of bids. Sometimes I get bubble wrap at about one-third of what I spend through office supply catalogs.
> —Janet Rich, eBay auctioneer
> **"**

bubble wrap, but chances are, the price is going to be higher than what you would pay at an office supply store. Even more surprising, the prices for packing supplies are even cheaper online. Those of you who are online bidding all the time will find that bubble wrap and mailing envelopes are available at auction, and sometimes you can get a real bargain. However, if you need your supplies right away and you'd like to develop a business relationship with a company that offers everything you need, here are some possibilities. We've also done a little price checking for you and have included sample prices with the company descriptions.

- **Office Depot** (www.officedepot.com):

  Fellowes corrugated $3^1/_2$" diskette mailer: $4.99

  Mail Away air bubble packing material, perforated roll, 12" × 175': $16.99

  Mail Away mailing and shipping tubes, 2" × 24", pack of four: $4.29

- **Bubble Wrap.com** (www.buybubblewrap.com):

  Variety pack includes two rolls 25' × 12" small bubble wrap; two rolls 10' × 12" large bubble wrap; two rolls 8' × 24" extra-wide bubble wrap: $17 (includes shipping)

  Two variety packs: $33; three variety packs: $49

  Single roll small bubble wrap, 12" × 250': $21

  Single roll large bubble wrap, 12" × 80': $15

- **3pak.com** (www.3pak.com/3paks.htm): This company offers prices including shipping from their office in New Jersey. To give you some idea of their shipping costs, all prices shown include shipping to Florida.

Three rolls small bubble wrap, 12" × 900':
$52.95

Three rolls large bubble wrap, 12" × 375':
$36.95

Moneysaver
Whenever possible, buy your supplies in bulk. You'll save money and won't be so likely to run out at a crucial moment—like when you have ten boxes to ship at the same time.

- **Fred King Office Supplies** (http://pw1. netcom.com/~frking/home.html):

  Clear bubble pouches, 8 × 11$\frac{1}{2}$": 34¢ each

  Clear shipping tape, 2" × 110 yds. (three rolls):
  $8.60

  Perforated bubble wrap, $\frac{1}{2}$" thick bubble, 12"
  wide, 85 ft.: $14 delivered

- **ShippingSupply.com** (www.shippingsupply.com):

  Styrofoam peanuts, 11 cubic ft. (weighs 30 lbs.):
  $19.50

  Book mailers (lot of 25), White Tuck-n-Fold
  (2" or 4" depths): $17.50

  Boxes, jewelry (lot of 25), 3" × 2$\frac{1}{4}$" × 1", filled
  with white cotton: $11

  Boxes, brown flat (lot of 25), 16" × 12" × 12": $30

  Bubble wrap, 5$\frac{1}{6}$" × 12" x 110', perforated
  every 12": $9.50

  Bubble wrap (variety pack), one roll $\frac{3}{6}$" × 12"
  × 50', one roll $\frac{1}{2}$" × 12" × 25', and one roll
  $\frac{1}{2}$" × 24" × 25': $11.50

- **OfficeMax** (www.officemax.com):

  Caremail bubble wrap, 16" × 9': $2.49

  Caremail bubble wrap, 12" × 175': $17.99

  Manco packing peanuts, 1 cubic foot: $4.49

- **Corrugated containers** (www.boxes.com): This
  company sells quantities of boxes at discount
  prices, but you need to buy at least 25 to 1,000.

- **L&R Shipping Supply, Inc.** (http://lnrshippingsupplies.com): A company specifically designed to meet the needs of e-commerce, L&R stocks bubble wrap, stretch wrap, boxes, scales, tape, envelopes, and more.

- **I.P.S. Packaging & Shipping Supplies** (www.ipspackaging.com): They have a complete line of shipping supplies and most orders are sent out within 24 hours; everything from tape to steel strapping.

  Packaging tape, Shurtape HP100 48mm × 100m (36 case): $0.95/roll (minimum 10 cases)

What do you need to keep on hand?

- A pair of good sharp scissors

- A utility knife or razor blade (a linoleum cutter does a great job and is safer than a straight razor)

- Several rolls of 1" (or wider) clear tape

- Marking pens or Magic Markers

- Labels (or white paper you can cut down to make labels—old envelopes work well too)

- Boxes (several different sizes)

- Envelopes (padded and manila)

- Padding, filler, and wrapping material (shredded newspaper, bubble wrap, shopping bags, foam peanuts, corrugated cardboard, air cushions, etc.)

For most online auctioneers, a good mix of recycled supplies and purchased shipping materials works best. However, if your item is one that needs special packing, don't skimp on it just to save a few pennies. What will ultimately happen is that the piece will not be delivered in the same condition in which it left your house, your customer will not be satisfied, and you might end up with bad feedback or, worse, a situation that will take forever to straighten out. Most of the time, online buyers are understanding and forgiving, but all you need is one person to complain about your business practices. That one bad rating or nightmarish shipping experience can sour the whole auction. Better to do the best packing job you possibly can rather than to risk damaging both the piece you're sending and your business reputation.

Building shipping costs into the price

Considering the makeup of an online auction, it's difficult to build shipping costs into the price of what you're selling. However, if you're up front with bidders and let them know it'll cost x amount of dollars for shipping and handling, you'll be sure that you won't be caught at the end of the auction saying, "Gee, I'm not sure what it's going to cost. Let me run to the post office and see."

Save yourself the time and energy of running around after the auction by figuring out a few things beforehand. For example:

- Make sure you have the right size box for the item you plan to ship.
- Consider what kinds of packing material you need, and how much.
- Weigh the item and packing.
- Calculate a fair cost for all of the above, then insert it in your ad when you put the item up for auction.

We emphasize these factors because we've discovered through what my father calls "the school of hard knocks" that we have lost money because items haven't sold for what we expected, then shipping costs were higher than what we'd planned. After all, you're not in this business to lose money, but to make money!

Don't skimp on packing!

When we first started doing auctions, we were in the process of moving from one house to another. As a result, we were pressed for time and also desperately trying to unload a lot of items. We put quite a few books up for auction on Amazon.com and were happy when they sold for more than we expected. Unfortunately, we were in such a rush to move that we used whatever envelopes we had to mail the books. We thought that it wouldn't be a problem to mail unbreakable items with little or no padding, so didn't think twice about sending a signed Frederick Forsythe novel in a heavy-duty envelope. Wrong! The book arrived at its destination with a little damage on the corners. Did the buyer e-mail to tell us about the problem or demand a refund? No, he didn't. He simply gave us negative feedback. Considering that we'd just started auctioning with Amazon, that negative feedback hurt. But we learned our lesson: Even when shipping unbreakable products, don't skimp on the packing!

Learn from our mistakes, and follow these tips:

- Don't use a regular envelope when a padded one will protect better.

- Use bubble wrap, clean diapers, or cloth padding instead of newsprint (newspapers leave black smudges that can damage cloth items or white porcelain, as well as other types of products).

Bright Idea
If you pack your items ahead of time and then weigh them, you'll be able to give customers the exact shipping price rather than just estimating. After you have the item wrapped, write the name of the product on the box, and when you've sold it, you can put the address label right over what you've written. Voila! Ready to go!

- Double-box fragile items.

- Pad, pad, then pad again.

- Use packing tape. Don't make do with Scotch tape.

- When you're finished, ask yourself if the package could withstand the Samsonite gorilla test!

Shipping large or extremely fragile items

Certain items that are too large, too fragile, or too expensive for standard shipping need special care. If you are selling an item that can't possibly be packed at home, you should consider other shipping methods.

There are restrictions for shipping within the United States. For example:

- USPS Parcel Post items cannot exceed 70 pounds or measure more than 130 inches in combined length and girth.

- USPS Regular mail cannot exceed 108 inches in combined length and girth.

- USPS Bound printed matter cannot exceed 15 pounds.

- United Parcel Service limits packages to 150 pounds and 130 inches total in length and girth.

- FedEx limits packages to 150 pounds and 165 inches in length and girth.

- Airborne's limits are 150 pounds and 56 inches in length.

For heavy items like furniture, you must use a freight system:

- Yellow Freight System (www.yellowfreight.com)

- Freight Quote (www.freightquote.com)

Bright Idea
Invest in a paper shredder and shred all your junk mail. Not only will you cut down on trash, but you'll create a free substitute for foam peanuts.

- Central Transportation Systems (www. centralsystems.com)

- ABF Freight System (www.abfs.com)

- Roadway Express, Inc. (www.roadway.com)

Most freight systems carry anything from a dining room set to combustible matter, but you must contact them separately and provide (in most cases) a bill of lading and specific information about your item. Charges depend on the size and weight of your item, as well as where it will be shipped.

If the items are extremely fragile (for example, a Tiffany lamp), the freight companies often pack them in crates for shipment. Naturally, they charge for the service, but isn't it safer to ship that way than to pack it yourself and possibly lose thousands of dollars?

Our suggestion? If you're selling something large, it might be wise to suggest in your ad that the customer pick up the item, if possible, or state his or her preference for delivery. When selling a car, dining room set, or other large item, the customer might choose to come pick it up or at least have control over shipping.

The benefits of a packing service

Sometimes people don't get the gist of how to pack or are frustrated by the details of having to keep supplies on hand. Perhaps you work at odd hours and have a hard time getting to the post office or UPS doesn't pick up in your area of the country. Maybe you just want the fun of the online action and none of the problems of packing breakable items for shipping. Or you simply don't have the time to crate everything up for its journey across the county, state, or world.

Moneysaver
AuctionSHIP.com is a national network of retail stores providing convenient shipping services at a discounted rate to Internet auction and classified customers.

Whatever the case, don't despair. There's help in nearly every city.

If auctioneering isn't your sole support and time is a major factor in your life, you might want to consider a packing service such as Mail Boxes Etc. They offer packing and crating services that are guaranteed. If your porcelain teapot doesn't make it to that buyer in Idaho in one piece, Mail Boxes Etc.'s insured. Since they use the United States Postal System, as well as UPS and other freight carriers, they can get several prices for you and offer you various options. They have offices all over the United States, so chances are you'll find one close to you.

If you decide to ship this way, all you have to do is to bring your item, as well as the name and address of the person to whom it'll be shipped, to the Mail Boxes Etc. office. They will pack it safely, using the best in bubble wrap, foam peanuts, crating, boxing—whatever your package needs—and send it on its way. If anything happens, they will take care of the problem for you. Lots of time and stress saved!

For more information about their services, look in the Yellow Pages under "Packaging" or check out their Web site (www.mbe.com).

Insuring your packages

Should you insure your packages? After all we've told you in this chapter, you should already know the answer: Yes!

If your item is damaged in shipping, the buyer will more than likely e-mail you immediately. Sometimes the process of making things right goes smoothly, sometimes it doesn't. But one thing is certain: If you insure your package, at least you'll be able to recover the monies lost if that precious

Moneysaver
Mail Boxes Etc. uses the United States Postal System, but they'll charge you more for shipping your item (since they need to make some money, too). If you are equidistance from both a Post Office and Mail Boxes Etc., it will be to your benefit to go directly to the Post Office.

painting arrives with a tear in it or that one-of-a-kind doll never reaches its destination at all.

All the shipping services we've mentioned offer insurance. For the most part, the cost of insurance is miniscule compared to what you'd lose. However, if your item is worth less than the cost of the insurance or you know that it's easily replaced, perhaps you want to take the chance of sending it uninsured. In that case, you might want to consider tracking the item in some manner. The USPS offers return receipts for merchandise for $1.40. With a return receipt, at least you know whether the package was received.

Insurance is available through the post office as well as through other shippers. The fees are determined by the coverage you want for your item. Starting at 85¢ (for items valued up to $50), the insurance goes up in increments for every hundred dollars' worth of value. It's a small price to pay to replace your items if they are damaged.

What if the item's damaged en route?

As we've said, the first thing you should do if your item arrives damaged is contact the seller. See if you can make arrangements for a refund or replacement. Perhaps the item you bought is one the seller has in quantity and he can instantly send you another.

Remember that it's often not the seller's fault if a piece arrives in shards. No matter how well an item is packed, it's very possible that the shipping service might damage it. Give the dealer the benefit of the doubt and wait for your answer before taking any other action.

Once you hear from the seller, the two of you need to work together to resolve the problem. Since you have the necessary documents in hand, you

Watch Out!
If you have to file a claim with the post office for damaged goods, make sure you have all your receipts with you before you head for the local office. Record the name of the person you speak with and the date. The postal system is huge and claims are often delayed for months, so it's important to keep a record.

should visit the shipper on your end. If the seller insured the item, he should visit the shipper on his end.

If you cannot resolve a dispute, remember that the feedback forums offered by all auctions are designed so that sellers who are not conducting business professionally are "checked." Do not give negative feedback until after you've explored all routes around fixing your problems. However, if you find you are getting nowhere, it's time to leave some negative feedback.

Contacting the shipper

All the shippers we've dealt with have toll-free numbers and Web sites where you can lodge complaints or get answers to your questions (see Appendix C, "Resource Directory"). If your package doesn't arrive or arrives damaged, go into action immediately. And remember to get everything in writing or to get the name of the person with whom you've spoken!

Make sure you have all documents in hand before you get on the phone or visit the shipper's office. It's frustrating to be kept on hold for half an hour then finally speak with a representative, only to discover you don't have the proper information to process a claim.

Remove the tag or label attached to the package (the one with the computer stamp on it) and keep it just in case you need to go to the post office, UPS, or FedEx to make a claim. If the box has an insurance tag or stamp on it, keep that, too.

Some shippers also want you to keep the package, as well as the item. Naturally, they're not going to believe an item has been destroyed without physically seeing the evidence.

Just the facts

- Your pieces have a better chance of arriving safely if you pack as though you expect the item to be mishandled during shipping.

- Many items you may have around the house (such as clean diapers, empty boxes, newspapers, and magazines) can be recycled into packing material.

- Invest in bubble wrap, foam peanuts, cardboard boxes, and strong packing tape.

- Shipping companies such as the USPS and UPS have restrictions on the size and weight of the packages they ship.

- Problems with shipping need to be taken care of promptly, both with the shipper and between the buyer and seller.

Taking Care
of Business

PART VII

GET THE SCOOP ON...
Keeping track of customers ▪ Using auction
management programs to keep earnings records
▪ What you can deduct ▪ Getting help at the
IRS information Web site

You Mean I Need to Keep Records?

Although you've probably figured out that it's almost impossible for the state and federal income tax people to figure out who is earning what on the online auction sites, remember that this is a business, and as such, you must report your earnings. It would be unfair for us to say you can simply slide by—and we certainly wouldn't suggest that!

Hopefully, if you've taken some of the suggestions we've made throughout this book, you'll be in pretty good shape once income tax time rolls around. Those of you who are dealing internationally should also keep your books in order to satisfy the taxman.

Some of the terminology you'll see in this chapter seems more likely to belong in an accounting book than in a book about online auctions, but it's only fair to give you the info you need so your records will be up-to-date and worthy of any scrutiny. You need to keep track not only of what you make but to whom you sell (and what), and what you spend. There are easy ways to do this, and some of

Chapter 16

351

your auction management programs already provide you with tools you can use. So, let's talk business.

Accumulating a list of clientele

One of the first tricks to running a successful business is to accumulate a list of clientele. The best way to do this is to simply keep track of everyone who buys from you or from whom you buy and add their addresses to your e-mail address book. But there are additional ways to get your name out to buyers/ sellers, as well as ways to identify the types of items the people on your list want to buy.

For example, when you enter a name into your e-mail address book, you can usually add some additional info quite easily. Our address books (we use approximately five of them between the two of us) allow us to enter such info as nicknames, addresses, telephone numbers, company names, and notes. If you add these pieces of additional information to your address book listings, you can create specialized mailing lists.

In addition to your own customers, you can also create mailing lists by joining list servers that are specifically designed for people interested in the same types of things you are. You can find groups of like collectors on AOL (check the bulletin boards), Yahoo! (check the chatrooms), and in the online auction chatrooms themselves. eBay provides community services, including general chatrooms, where both collectors and dealers can chat about general topics, and international chatrooms designed for eBay customers located in those countries (or others who want to attract customers in specific areas of the world). eBay also offers category-specific chatrooms where dealers/collectors can meet others and talk about items of interest. If you

Timesaver
When you complete a buying or selling transaction, transfer your e-mails to a file on your computer, and copy that file onto a disk so that you'll have your records even if your computer goes down. You'll also find it's easier to do your accounting at the end of the month.

find people in chatrooms or bulletin boards, you can add their e-mail addresses to your mailing lists. Just remember a general Netiquette rule: Don't spam! (Spamming is posting irrelevant or inappropriate messages to large groups of people.)

Discussion groups of all kinds are available on the Web. One of the easiest ways to get onto one of these mailing lists is by searching for your interest through a mailing list directory such as the following:

- www.topica.com

- www.onelist.com

- www.usenet.com

You can search many lists by checking out the search engine Liszt Search (www.liszt.com). This search engine prowls through almost 100,000 mailing lists to find the one most specific to your needs. Or you can look through the categories offered and find one that comes closest to the topic you're interested in.

Lists are not in chatroom format. Instead, you will be privy to e-mailed messages from the group to which you'll belong. You can choose to see the messages one at a time or in digest format. Usually when you join a list, you automatically get everyone's e-mail address. But you can send messages to everyone in the group simply by writing to the group at its address.

If all else fails, you can always create your own discussion group and invite others to join you in chatrooms or on bulletin boards. This practice expands your business world and allows you to share new information with others.

An address book

Your address book should be one that can be easily managed, since you might want to send out newsletters or notices to customers about items.

Moneysaver
Use your address book to send free notices about special sales to customers who might be interested. You can even notify others of changes to your Web site— and it won't cost you a dime of your advertising budget.

We separate our address books into folders, and since we're using four different computers, it sometimes gets confusing. We try to duplicate address books as often as possible so we have the most up-to-date lists on each computer. There's nothing more frustrating than being on the road and wanting to get in touch with someone, but not having that person's e-mail address on the laptop.

In Netscape (the program we use for checking our e-mail), creating a new list of specific people to whom you want to send messages is easy. Simply click on "Address Book," choose "File," then click on "New List." A box will pop up and you'll be asked to give the list a name. Our advice is to use a term that defines who's on the list or what the general preferences are of everyone you'll include. For example, if you sell iron toys, as well as paintings, you don't want both sets of customers on the same list. So create one called "iron toys" and one called "paintings" or "art." Every time you have a new item for these customers, all you need to do is send out one e-mail.

You can also combine all your lists whenever there is something of major importance you want to pass on. For example, if you've just made the score of your lifetime and want to let everyone know, you can e-mail all of your friends, family, and customers. But save that kind of e-mail for a very special occasion or for emergencies. Anyone who's in the online auction business gets plenty of daily e-mail, and an additional piece may get deleted or go unnoticed—especially if it's bulk mail.

What about reporting earnings?

We hate to tell you this, folks, but you have to report what you earn. Far too many people have been sliding by without telling the good ol' government what they've been making in online auctions. Sooner or later, those people will get caught, and then what? They'll be audited, and worse, fined. Better to keep track of your earnings now and be honest. Report what you've made, deduct all your expenses, and the IRS will be happy.

How do you keep track? If you have a good auction management program, you'll be able to retain your records right in that program. However, if your program doesn't hold records, you might want to save your e-mails. Any time you sell an item or buy one, file the e-mail in a folder. If you buy and sell 10 or fewer items a month, this will be an easy way to keep track of your expenditures.

However, if your business takes off and you're handling five or more sales a week, you'd be better off getting a program that will do the accounting for you. Your best bet is to get one that will keep track of your sales and sales tax, and also help you budget expenses.

Of the auction management programs we've checked out, the following have financial organization features that allow you to sort through data, use reports, and do automated bookkeeping. Some of these programs are free, while others can be bought at whatever online auction you choose to do business with.

- Andalé (www.andale.com)

- AuctionMate (for eBay) (www.myauctionmate.com)

- Auction Wizard (for eBay) (www. standingwavesoftware.com)

- Auction Trakker (www.auctiontrakker.com)

Bright Idea
If you're doing more than several thousand dollars' worth of business a month on eBay, you can apply to become a Power Seller, and by doing so, get around-the-clock help with accounting and customer service.

Accounting for everything

When you start doing some bookkeeping for your online auction business, you'll realize that there is a certain lingo in accounting, and you should know the basic language before you begin:

- **Gross profits:** Anything you make over what you've paid for an item.

- **Net profits:** Anything that's left over from the gross profits after you deduct expenditures.

- **Assets:** Everything you own and use to create your online auctions (computer, calculator, scanner, camera, etc.).

- **Revenue:** Everything that comes in as income; in other words, the sales you make during an auction.

- **Debits:** The deductions you make from your account for supplies, postage, accounting services, or to buy items to sell online.

- **Credits:** The money coming in.

Consider hiring an accountant or bookkeeper if your income is derived mainly from online auctions. Most accountants are paid by the hour, so if you can prepare your records before bringing them to the accountant, you'll save time and money. (This is where a good auction management program comes in handy.) A good accountant can show you where you're spending too much and how to manage what you're making, but don't expect your accountant to find money that isn't there.

Hiring a good accountant is just as important as finding a doctor who'll take care of a specific illness. Like doctors, accountants specialize, so ask a few general questions before you hand over your books: How long have they been in business? Do they handle any other customers who deal in online auctions? How often will they prepare taxes? (Most small businesses create quarterly returns.)

For more information on accounting, check out:

- **Quicken.com:** This company creates programs for small businesses, as well as personal financial programs. Their Web site offers free information for small businesses to help with taxes, setting up businesses, and even has a section just for auctions! There are a slew of books out about Quicken, and everyone we talk to agrees they are the premiere small office accounting program.

- **Microsoft Money 2000/Business and Personal:** This program offers info on the management of key business tasks such as tracking income and expenses, creating business reports, customer management with improved invoicing and contact management, and tax preparation with Schedule C planning features and tools. It also interprets Quicken files.

- **3SI Accounting and Inventory Management 1.0:** This program is designed for businesses that require inventory management and invoice/order entry features integrated with general-purpose accounting software.

If it's just a hobby or a part-time business, try one of the accounting books that will help you manage your inventory, as well as your income and expenses (see Appendix C, "Resource Directory").

Sales tax?

There's been an ongoing debate in the chatrooms of many online auctions about whether or not to charge sales tax. Most sellers feel that because the

Watch Out!
Make sure you purchase software or books that include the latest tax information. Even though the older ones might be a bargain, you'll have to double-check to see whether the tax information has changed.

auctions are going worldwide, there's no way the states can charge sales tax. We think they're all going to be in for a rude awakening. It's far too easy for the government to hire someone (or have someone in the office) to scan auctions and find the sellers/buyers in their states. In other words, if you have been audited or are called in, be prepared to be surprised with how much info they can dig up on you.

In a recent issue of *shift.com,* an article by Rick Overton titled "Watching the Detectives" quotes Mike Gerdes, the manager of the Corporate Information Security department at Xerox, as saying, "Computers are notorious for keeping records for long periods of time, and they're not your friends when it comes to trying to hide something you're doing. Even programmers sometimes forget that all the technology that lets them do their jobs also leaves their fingerprints behind." Gerdes headed the team that *Newsweek* called "the SWAT team on computer abuse" in a November 1999 article. The team exposed Xerox employees who "had been downloading porn … [D]ozens of people were canned."

"
To the greatest extent possible, the Internet should be free of taxes.
—Virginia Governor James Gilmore III
"

The reason we make this point is because we know that if the big corporations can tap into e-mails and files so easily, then so can the government. After all, it was the government who designed the Internet to begin with.

Should you be paranoid? No, but let us warn you that being careful and running a clean business is paramount. Keep track of your sales tax. If customers refuse to pay it, you'll be liable for it yourself. Better to pay the pennies you should be charging on the items you're selling than to be dragged into an audit by the IRS.

Keeping track of expenses

There's only one thing to say on the subject of expenses: Keep track of everything you spend to promote or sell your auction items! If you think you'll remember how many packages of bubble wrap you bought or how many rolls of stamps you used, you're wrong.

The best way to keep track of what you've spent is by using a credit card or check card that will automatically record your expenditures in categories. Divide expenses into specific categories. Include the following:

- Shipping expenses
- Packaging expenses
- Listing fees
- Credit card fees
- Money order/bank charges
- Telephone charges
- Home office expenses
- Auto expenses
- Computers and supplies
- Fees paid to accountants/bookkeepers
- Wages and employee fees
- Internet access charges

Remember that shipping will be one of your largest categories, and you want to make sure you get the best deal for shipping to your customers. Although most of you will add shipping charges to your customer's invoice and won't be able to take those expenses off your taxes, there will be times when you miscalculate what something costs to ship and you'll be responsible for it. Or you might need to return an item you've bought. Make certain you differentiate between the shipping you've actually paid for and what your customers have reimbursed you for. The IRS will ask that question, and you want to be ready.

When you use an online postal program, you are often charged a monthly usage fee, which you can take off your taxes. It's the same with credit card programs. Those fees are totally deductible. In addition, when you buy something with a money order or bank check keep track of the fee, even though it might seem miniscule at the time. Those fees add up and all are reasonable business expenses. Bank charges and monthly fees are also completely deductible.

Any time you use your car to deliver packages to the post office, keep track of your mileage. We record our mileage in a little notebook that we keep in the car. At the end of the year, those miles add up. In addition, keep track of what percentage of your time is spent in the car for business purposes (e.g., traveling to the local office supply store to get bubble wrap, or going to the bank to make a business deposit). If you're using the car mostly for business, start keeping track of gas, repairs, and car payments—all are partially or totally deductible.

Also remember to keep track of home expenses, especially if one room of your home is totally devoted to online auction work. We have two offices in our home, but only one is used strictly for business. The other one "masquerades" as a guest room. Although Bobby has all the auction info in that room and he does all his work from there, we cannot deduct it because that room is not used exclusively as an office. The IRS has gotten very strict about that in the past

Moneysaver
If you're using a check card to pay for expenses, make sure you keep track of the small usage fees you're charged for obtaining cash from ATMs other than your bank. They can add up!

few years. However, Dawn's office is totally business, so we can deduct one-sixth of our home expenses to run that office.

Of course, all charges associated with keeping your computer up and running are deductible. If you buy a new computer, it can be depreciated over three years. That new scanner and digital camera, plus all the supplies to run them, are also items you need to keep track of. And the charges your Internet Service Provider bills you for monthly usage are important, as is the extra line to hook that computer up, and any faxes you send, any printer ink you use, and so on. You get the point.

Hello, IRS?

Yes, folks, the IRS can audit you, and if they see anything unusual about your tax form, they will. Take it from us. It's happened three times, and we've gotten to the point where we keep track of absolutely *everything!*

Since the IRS mandates that all businesses must keep records, this means auction-goers and sellers need to pay attention. Though we're okay until 2001 regarding taxes on the Internet, all indications are that the freeze currently in place will be lifted and the government will figure out some way to tax all e-commerce transactions. Better to be safe than sorry. You don't want to be in trouble with the taxman!

Both federal and state taxes can be paid at the end of the year or quarterly. Check the IRS Web site (www.irs.ustreas.gov) for forms and your local state tax agency as well (state tax agencies Web site: www.tannedfeet.com/html/state_tax_agencies.htm).

On the bright side, the IRS does offer help for the small business owner. Who better to get the info

Unofficially...
The IRS can only audit you three years in a row. After that, it's considered harassment. But if you do get audited, you are responsible for answering to the IRS.

from than the IRS? Know the right way to do your accounting before you start rather than at the last minute. Simply go to their Web site and click on the small business info icon. They offer tips and helpful information for starting and operating a small business, providing employment plans, a listing of business-oriented publications, info on the IRS Corporate Partnership Program, and tax help.

Just the facts

- Most e-mail programs offer address book options that allow you to create mailing lists for specific clientele.

- It's easier to keep track of expenses during the year than to try to sort everything out before tax time.

- All expenses necessary to keep an online auction up and running are partially or totally deductible from your income taxes.

- Federal and state taxes must be reported and paid, no matter how small the business.

- The IRS Web site is the best place to go for answers to tax questions.

Online Listings

General Auctions
4AuctionDeals.com
Amazon.com (click on "Auctions" tab)
Auction.com
AuctionAddict.com
AuctionsOrlando.com (auction site hosted by the *Orlando Sentinel*)
Auctions.Yahoo.com
AuctionUniverse.com
Barter-n-Trade.com
Bidfarm.com
eBay.com
GalleryOfHistory.com (over 184,000 autographs and manuscripts)
Hagglezone.com
NuAuction.com
OhioAuction.com
Polar Auctions
Times Auctions (auctions.nytoday.com)

Art Auctions

Artnet.com

Biddingtons.com (contemporary paintings, sculpture, and prints)

HecklerAuction.com (antique glass and bottles, period decorative arts, singular art objects, and estates)

JustGlass.com (all kinds of glass—from marbles to barware to glass slippers!)

Pacific Glass (pacglass.com) (antique bottles)

PotteryAuction.com (features American art pottery)

TreadwayGallery.com

Auto Auctions

Classic-Car-Auction.com

Eqmoney.com/cars.htm (federal government car auctions)

IAAI.com (Insurance Auto Auctions sells wrecked vehicles on behalf of the insurer to salvage buyers)

Clothing Auctions

ClothingBids.com (wholesale clothing for professional buyers and sellers in the apparel and accessory industry)

FirstAuction.com (a general auction site that includes women's apparel)

VintageUSA.com/auction.htm (vintage clothing and collectible sneakers)

Collectibles Auctions

Popula.com (slightly funky site where you can get cool Hollywood memorabilia and various vintage items)

CollectorsAuction.com

Dolls and Toys

CollectingNation.com/dolls.shtml (dolls—including a large beanie baby collection)

PeddleIt.com (lots of collectibles—specializes in pedal-driven toys)

Theriaults.com (dolls)

Sports Memorabilia

Boekhout's Collectibles Mall (azww2.com/mall)

Sportsauction.com

SportsTrade.com

Stamps

Apfelbauminc.com (stamps)

Sandafayre.com (stamps)

Computer and Electronics Auctions

Auction-warehouse.com (electronics)

Bid.com (computer products)

Cyber-Swap (cyberswap.com/index.html) (computers and electronics)

Egghead.com (computers)

Haggle.com (mostly computers—both new and used)

Jewelry Auctions

Dickeranddicker.com

Gemtraders.com/auction (gems and jewelry)

Jewelnetauctions.com

Newageauction.com (gems, crystals, rocks, fossils)

Real Estate Auctions

AuctionAdvantage.net

Travel Auctions

Bidtripper.com

Goinggoinggone.com

ReverseAuction.com

Vacation Harbor (vharbor.com)

Glossary

"About Me" eBay's term for personal Web sites created by eBay auction-goers to tell their fellow eBay auction-goers about themselves.

acronyms A group of letters that stands for a phrase, particularly in e-mail language (e.g., IMHO = in my humble opinion, LOL = laughing out loud or lots of luck, BRB = be right back).

appraisal An expert evaluation of the worth of an item.

auction insurance A type of insurance that protects buyers and sellers during online auction transactions.

auction management program Programs that allow buyers and sellers to coordinate sales, listings, and other information more easily.

automatic billing When an auction deducts charges automatically from a bidder or seller's account.

bid shield A scam in which one bidder places a low bid, while another places a high bid. Right before the end of the auction, the high bidder withdraws, allowing the low bidder to take the piece.

bookmarks The addition or deletion of favorite sites to the list of often visited Web sites on a personal computer.

booleans Booleans are used to conduct a more effective online search. They are the type of expression with two possible values: "true" and "false." The most common Boolean functions are AND, OR, and NOT.

bulletin board Parts of a Web site where participants can leave messages or ask questions.

buttons Clickable graphics that create hyperlinks. *See* hyperlinks.

cafe Part of a Web site where participants might casually talk about business.

chatrooms Part of a Web site where participants can hold open discussions.

domain An area of jurisdiction on the Internet (e.g., .com, .net, .gov, .org).

Dutch auction An auction in which multiple numbers of a single item are sold.

e-mail Written messages sent via the Internet.

encryption The point where data (like credit card numbers) is scrambled into a secret code so that a person's privacy is protected.

escrow Money held by a third party until all conditions of the transaction are fulfilled.

e-speak Abbreviated language used by people who send and receive e-mail.

FAQ Frequently asked questions.

feedback Comments left by buyers or sellers regarding how the transaction has been handled.

flaming E-mailing someone in a manner that can be interpreted as abusive or meant to hurt someone's feelings.

fraud   The illegal deception or sale of an item.

FTP   File transfer protocol program. The program one uses to transfer information from a disk or hard drive to the Web.

GIF   Graphics Interchange Format file. A standard for digitized images compressed with the LZW algorithm, defined in 1987 by CompuServe (CIS).

graphics   Images, pictures, and text created to enhance Web pages.

help board   A place on a Web site akin to customer service where a participant can find help for problems or answers to questions.

home page   The starting point of a Web site.

HTML   Hypertext Markup Language. The code in which Web pages are written.

hyperlinks   Clickable links that will take you to various locations on the Web.

insertion fees   The charges an online auction imposes to put items up for auction.

Internet   A loose connection of thousands of networks and millions of computers throughout the world.

ISP   Internet Service Provider. Your connection to the Web.

JPEG   Joint Photographics Expert Group. A compressed image.

lurker   Someone who watches the action from the sidelines for a while, only coming "out" to say something in a chatroom (or via personal e-mail) when they feel the urge.

merchant account   An account that allows sellers to offer credit card payments to customers.

metasearch A search engine that searches multiple search engines simultaneously.

Netiquette The proper use of language and acronyms used in e-mail or chatroom discussions so that others are not offended.

1-Click The 1-Click option, offered by Amazon, allows buyers to pay in whatever manner they want, and Amazon forwards the money right into the seller's checking account.

online name The nickname an online auction buyer, seller, or chatroom participant uses instead of his or her real name.

parallel port A plug-in point on a computer that usually accommodates a printer, scanner, or other additional device.

password A code an online auctioneer uses to get into the site or access personal information.

pickers People who scout out particular items for collectors and dealers.

pixel Picture element. A single point in a graphic image. Thousands (or millions) of pixels, arranged in rows and columns, so close together that they appear connected, are what create the images on computer screens.

public relations The way news and business facts are released to interested parties in order to create positive public opinion of the business and its products.

Q&A Questions and answers.

rating The number a buyer or seller gives to another to determine how well or poorly a transaction was made.

re-listing   Putting an item up again for auction if it did not sell the first time.

reserve auction   An auction where the seller creates a minimum price for which the item can be sold. That price is not usually revealed to bidders.

SafeHarbor   eBay's patent-pending name for the way they protect buyers and sellers in online auction transactions.

scanner   A device that copies a document or photo and translates it into a graphics format acceptable by a computer (e.g., JPEG, GIF, Bitmap).

scroll   To quickly scan down a computer screen.

SCSI   "Scuzzy" port (the SCSI port or "Small Computer System Interface") where you plug a video cam or disk camera into the computer.

search engine   An Internet tool that searches for a subject or item within its parameters (also search metasearch).

serial port   A plug-in point on a computer that usually accommodates a printer, scanner, or other additional device.

shilling   When a seller hires someone he or she knows to up the bid on an item.

sniping   Getting a bid in at the very last moment of an auction.

spamming   Posting irrelevant or inappropriate messages to large groups of people.

surfing   Exploring the Web via the use of a browser. *See* Web browser.

thumbnail   A miniature image of a graphic that can be enlarged by clicking on it.

URL   The address of a Web site.

Web browser   Software (such as Internet Explorer or Netscape) needed to explore the World Wide Web.

Web hosting   Sites that allow others to maintain Web pages on their space.

Web page   An electronic document written for the World Wide Web in HTML (hypertext markup language).

Web page designers   Programs or people who create Web pages.

Web site   One or more related Web pages linked by hyperlinks so a person can jump from one to the other.

WWW (World Wide Web)   A system of links developed in 1990 by CERN, the European Laboratory for Particle Physics.

Yankee auction   An auction where multiples of a certain item are sold and the winners are the highest bidders.

Resource Directory

As in any business, there are resources that can help you become a better business person or that can help you expand on what you already know. We've included some of them here. Each of the professionals to whom we spoke had their favorites, and we're sure you will, too. But, for now, here's a selection of each.

Accounting programs

For small businesses:

- BS/1 Small Business
- Microsoft Money 2000 Business & Personal
- Quicken 2000

  For mid-range accounting needs:

- Account Pro
- Champion
- Business Works
- Peachtree Software
- QuickBooks

For high-end:

- ACCPAC Plus Accounting
- Real World
- Red Wing Accounting Software

Appraisers

- Eppraisals.com (www.eppraisals.com)
- The International Society of Appraisers (www.isa-appraisers.org)
- The American Society of Appraisers (www.appraisers.org)
- Sotheby's (www.sothebys.com)
- Christie's (www.christies.com)
- Skinner's (www.skinnerinc.com)
- *Antiques Roadshow* (www.antiquesroadshow.com)
- Auctions World Wide Association (www.auctionsww.com)
- Wines.com (www.wines.com)
- Mackley & Company (www.mackley.com)
- Sportscarmarket.com (www.sportscarmarket.com)
- Maloney's *Antiques & Collectibles Resource Directory* (http://maloney.com)
- Dawson's Appraisals (www.dawsons.org)

Auction lists and searches

- Internet Auction List (http://www.usaweb.com/auction.html)
- BidFind.Com (http://bidfind.com)

Auction management programs

- Andalé (www.andale.com)
- Auction Aid/Auction Ad Pro (www.firstdesign.com)
- AuctionAssistant or AuctionAssistant Pro (www.blackthornesw.com)
- Auction Helper (http://members.xoom.com/jsamuels)
- AuctionManager (www.AuctionRover.com/sell)
- AuctionMate (www.myauctionmate.com)
- Auction Wizard (www.standingwavesoftware.com/aw)
- ePoster2000 (www.auctionposter.com)

Auction tracking programs

- AuctionTamer (www.envsoftware.com/auction)
- Auction Ticker (www.blackthornesw.com)
- Auction Trakker (www.AuctionTrakker.com)
- OnScan (www.onscan.com)
- The Oracle (www.the-oracle.com/main.html)

Automated bidding programs

- Auction Express (www.auctiontools.com)
- BidSniper Pro (www.datavector.net/products/bidsniper/index.htm)

Auction news

- AuctionPatrol.com (www.auctionpatrol.com)
- Auction Watch (www.auctionwatch.com)

- *USAToday* (www.usatoday.com/marketpl/
  auctions.htm)

- Maine *Antiques Digest* (www.maineantiquedigest.
  com)

Camera dealers

- Access Discount Camera and Video
  (www.accesscamera.com)

- Capitol Camera (www.capitolcamera.com)

- Kodak (www.kodak.com)

- Pentax (www.pentax.com)

- Photographers Space (www.photospace.com)

- Wall Street Camera (www.wall-street-camera.
  com/)

Credit card providers/merchant account services

- 1st American Card Service (www.
  1stamericancardservice.com)

- Accept-It!/Universal Merchant Services
  (http://accept-it.com)

- EZ Merchant Accounts/Authorize.net
  (www.ezmerchantaccounts.com)

- iCardacceptance.com
  (www.cardacceptance.com)

- New Horizon Business Services (www.
  newhorizon.org)

- Merchant USA (www.online2020.com)

- Online Credit Corp. (http://onlinecreditcorp.
  com)

Currency conversion services

- Cloanto Euro Calculator (www.cloanto.com)
- Xenon Currency Services (www.xe.net)
- 1-Click Currency Conversion (www.currency. co.nz/)
- Payflow Link (www.ezmerchantaccounts.com/ signio.htm)
- VERZA Payment System (http://verza.com)

End-user auction management programs

- Auction Broker Software (www.allsingles.com)

Graphics programs

- Adobe Photoshop (www.adobe.com)
- PaintShop Pro (www.jasc.com)
- Microsoft Picture It! (www.home-publishing. com/pictureit
- QFX (www.qfx.com)
- GIF Construction Set Professional (only for Windows) (www.mindworkshop.com/alchemy/ gifcon.html)
- Color It! (only for Macs) (www.microfrontier.com/products/colorit40/ index.html)
- Ulead PhotoImpact 5 (www.ulead)

Image hosting services

- Photo Assistant (www.photoassistant.com)
- Krickets Korner (www.kricketskorner.com)
- EyeNet Images (http://eyenetimages.com)
- PayPal.com (www.paypal.com)

Insurance

- iCollector.com's iGuarantee (covers items up to $50,000)

- TradeSafe.com (acts as an intermediary between buyers and sellers during online transactions)

Language translation services

- Global Language Translation and Consulting (www.gltac.com)

- SYSTRAN Software Inc. (www.systransoft.com)

- Transparent Language Enterprise Translation Server (www.transparentlanguage.com/ets)

Metacrawler search engines

- Dogpile.com
- Mamma.com
- Altavista.com
- Google.com

Press releases

- Tips on how to write one: www.webpr.com/primer.htm

- Press-Release-Writing.com (http://www.press-release-writing.com/

Research sources (listed by item type)

Sometimes it's easier to have a book on hand that gives you quick and easy details about your items, as well as photos. Though it's great to do research online, you often have to wait for a photo to load or you simply can't find the specifics you want. Here are some sources where you can purchase research for your personal library.

Antiques

- Collectibles Books (www.collectorsbooks.com)
- Ruby Lane (www.rubylane.com)
- National Association of Dealers in Antiques, Inc. (www.nadaweb.com)
- *The Official Price Guide to Antiques and Collectibles,* by David Lindquist (chapters in the 9th–13th editions by Dawn Reno). (House of Collectibles Publishers.)

Art

- Artline (www.artline.com)
- Guild.com (www.guild.com)
- World Wide Arts Resources (wwar.com/java/index.html)

Automotive

- *2000 Edition Ultimate Collector Car Price Guide: 1900–1990.* (*Cars & Parts Magazine,* 2000.)
- *Car Memorabilia Price Guide* (Krause Publications, 1998; www.krause.com.)
- PL8S.com (www.pl8s.com)
- The Auto Channel.com (www.theautochannel.com)
- Corvette Club of America (www.corvetteclubofamerica.com)

Books

- Amazon.com (www.amazon.com)
- Barnes&Noble.com (www.barnesandnoble.com)
- Powell's Bookstore (www.powells.com)
- BooksAMillion (www.booksamillion.com)

- Borders (www.borders.com)
- FatBrain (www.fatbrain.com)
- WordsWorth (www.wordsworth.com)
- Huxford's *Old Book Value Guide 1999–2000.* (Huxford, 2000.)
- *Old Magazines Price Guide 1996–1997.* (L-W Publishing, 1996.)
- *Advanced Autograph Collecting,* by Mark Allen Baker. (Krause Publications, 2000.)
- Society for the History of Authorship, Reading and Publishing (www.indiana.edu:80/~sharp/intro.html)
- Antiquarian Booksellers Association (www.abaa.org)
- International Book Collectors Association (www.rarebooks.org)
- *Collecting Romance Novels,* by Dawn Reno and Jacque Tiegs. (Alliance Publishing, 1995.)

Clothing

- Victorian Elegance (www.gator.net/%7edesigns/links.html)
- Piece Unique (www.pieceunique.com)
- *Vintage Clothing 1880–1980: Identification and Value Guide.* (Costume Society of America, Publisher, 1995; www.costumesocietyofamerica. com.)

Coins

- Professional Coin Grading Service (www. pcgs.com)
- Numismatic Guaranty Corporation (www. ngccoin.com)

- *Coin Prices* (www.coinprices.com)
- Numismatists Online (www.numismatist.com)
- *Coin Connoisseur: The International Magazine for Investors and Collectors* (www.coinmag.com)

Collectibles

- Harry Rinker Enterprises (www.rinker.com)
- Ralph and Terry Kovel's site (www.kovel.com)
- The Price Guide Store (www.priceguidestore. com)
- CollectingChannel.com (www. collectingchanne l.com)
- Collectors.com (www.collectors.com)
- *Antiques and the Arts Weekly* (www.thebee.com/)
- Best Antiques and Collectibles Site on the Web (www.computrends.com/antiquering/)
- *Antique Trader Weekly* (www.collect.com/ antiquetrader)
- *Advertising Identification and Price Guide,* by Dawn E. Reno. (The Confident Collector/Avon Books, 1993.)

Comics

- Cyber Comic Store (pages.prodigy.com/ source/comics.htm)
- CollectiblesNet (www.collectiblesnet.com/ comics.htm)
- Collectors' Showcase (www.collectiblesnet. com/cshowcase.htm)
- 4comics.com (www.4comics.com)
- Comic book links (www.westol.com/ ~informer/links/comic.html)

- *Overstreet's Comic Book Price Guide,* by Bob Overstreet. (Harper Resources, 2000.)

Computers/electronics, hardware/software

- The Computer Museum of America (www. computer-museum.org/)
- The Computer Museum of Boston (www.mos. org/tcm/tcm.html)
- PriceGrabber.com (www.pricegrabber.com)
- Cyber Surfer Computer Resource Centre (www.cyber-surfer.com)

Dolls

- Dolls.com (www.dolls.com)
- Doll collecting (http://collectdolls.about.com)
- Barbie (www.barbie.com)
- Madame Alexander (www.madamealexander.com)
- Raggedy Ann and Andy (www.raggedyland.com)
- *Blue Book of Dolls and Values,* by Jan Foulke. (Hobby House Press, 1999.)
- *Modern Collectible Dolls Identification and Value Guide,* by Patsy Moyer. (Collector Books, 1998.)
- *200 Years of Dolls: Identification and Price Guide,* by Dawn T. Herlocher. (Antique Trader, 1996.)
- *Dolls Magazine* (www.dollsmagazine.com)
- United Federation of Doll Clubs, Inc. (www.ufdc.org)

Ethnic Art and Collectibles

- *The Official Identification and Price Guide to American Indian Collectibles,* by Dawn E. Reno. (House of Collectibles, Publisher, 1989.)

- *The Confident Collector: Native American Collectibles Identification and Price Guide,* by Dawn E. Reno. (Avon Books, 1994.)

- *The Encyclopedia of Black Collectibles: A Value and Identification Guide,* by Dawn E. Reno. (Chilton Books, 1996.)

- *Collecting Black Americana,* by Dawn E. Reno. (Crown Books, 1986.)

Home and garden

- AntiquesWorld.com (www.antiquesworld.com)

- *300 Years of Kitchen Collectibles,* by Linda C. Franklin. (Krause Publications, 1997.)

- *American Colonial Architecture, Its Origin and Development,* by Joseph Jackson. (Johnson Reprint Corporation.)

- *Collecting American Country: How to Select, Maintain, and Display Country Pieces,* by Mary Emmerling. (Clarkson Potter, 1983.)

- *American Country Collectibles,* by Dawn E. Reno. (House of Collectibles, 1990.)

- Architectural Antiques of Boston (www.archant.com/)

- Southern Accents Architectural Antiques (www.antiques-architectural.com)

- Doors of London (www.doorsoflondon.com)

- Home & Garden/About.com (www. homeandgarden.com)

- The Treasure Garden (www.treasuregardenantique.com/)

- Garden Park Antiques (www.gardenpark. com/antiques/)

Jewelry

- Gems.com (www.gems.com)
- Jewelcollect Auction (www.playle.com/jewels/)
- Costume jewelry (www.costumejewels.about.com/)
- 999fine.com (Native American jewelry) (www.999fine.com)
- Accredited Gemologists Association (aga. polygon.net/index.html)
- American Society of Appraisers (www.appraisals.com)
- *The Official Identification and Price Guide to Antique Jewelry,* by Arthur Guy Kaplan. (House of Collectibles, 1990.)
- *Collectible Costume Jewelry: Identification and Values,* by Cherri Simonds. (Collector Books, 1997.)

Movies

- *The Official Price Guide to Movie/TV Soundtracks and Original Cast Albums,* by Jerry Osborne. (House of Collectibles, 1997.)
- *Hollywood and Early Cinema Posters,* Bruce Hershenson, ed. (Bruce Hershenson, 1997.)
- *Lyle Price Guide: Film and Rock 'n Roll Collectibles,* by Anthony Curtis. (Perigree, 1996.)
- Film Collectors International (www.film-collectors-intl.com ScoreLogue.com)
- Images: A Journal of Film and Popular Culture (www.imagesjournal.com)
- Movie Posters (www.blarg.net/dr_z/Movie/Posters/)

- Hollywood.com (www.hollywood.com)
- Hollywood Toy and Poster Co. (www.hollywoodposter.com)
- Christie's (www.christies.com/)

Music

- Last Vestige Music Shop (www.lastvestige.com)
- *Goldmine's Alternative Records Price Guide.* (Krause Publications, 1996.)
- *Sheet Music: A Price Guide,* by Debbie Dillon. (LW Publishing, 1995.)
- Vintage Instruments (www.vintageinstruments.com)
- Fiske Museum (www.cuc.claremont.edu/fiske/welcome.htm)
- The Music Mart, Inc. (www.musicmart.com)
- Internet Music Hound (www.bandstand.com)

Photographs and photographic equipment

- *Cameras, Antique and Classic,* by Jim and Joan McKeown. (Watson-Guptill Publications, Inc., 1998.)
- *Collecting Photographica: The Images and Equipment of the First 100 Years of Photography,* by George Gilbert. (Hawthorne Books, 1976.)
- *Photographica: A Guide to the Value of Historic Cameras and Images,* by Charles Klamkin. (Funk & Wagnalls, 1978.)
- Photographica (www.photographica.com)
- George Eastman House International Museum of Photography and Film (www.eastman.org)

Pottery, Glass, and Porcelain

- *The Encyclopaedia of British Pottery and Porcelain Marks,* by Geoffrey A. Godden. (Barrie & Jenkins, 1991.)

- *Imperial Glass Encyclopedia, Volumes I–III,* by James Measell. (The Glass House, Inc., 1995, 1997, 1999.)

- *Kovels' Bottles Price List,* by Ralph and Terry Kovel. (Three Rivers Pr., 1999.)

- *Flow Blue: A Collector's Guide to Patterns, History, and Values,* by Jeffrey Snyder. (Schiffer Publishing, Ltd., 1999.)

- *The Collector's Encyclopedia of Limoges Porcelain,* by Mary Frank Gaston. (Collector Books, 2000.)

- *Kovels' American Art Pottery,* by Ralph and Terry Kovel. (Crown Pub., 1993.)

- Graylings' Antiques (www.staffordshire-figures. com)

- Ohio Pottery (www.ohiopottery.com)

- Clarice Cliff Collectors' Club (www.claricecliff. com)

- Westmoreland Glass (www.jcwiese.com/)

- Early American Pattern Glass Society (www. eapgs.org)

- Noritake (www.noritake.com)

Sports/Recreation

- Professional Sports Authenticator (http:// psacard.com)

- Collectors Universe (www.card-universe.com)

- Sports Collectors Universe (collectors.com/ sports/gallery)

- NFL History and Card Collecting
  (www.angelfire.com/tn/pkholling)
- SAM (Sports, Accessories and Memorabilia),
  Inc. (bobbing head dolls and figurines)
  (www.bobbing.com/)
- Turn4Racing (www.turn4racing)
- *1999 Sports Collectors Almanac,* by the editors of
  Sports Collectors Digest. (Krause Publications,
  1999.)
- *Coykendall's Complete Guide to Sporting Collectibles,*
  by Ralf W. Coykendall. (Wallace-Homestead
  Book Co., 1996.)

Stamps

- The American Philatelic Society (www.west.
  net/~stamps1/aps.html)
- *Top Dollar Paid: The Complete Guide to Selling
  Your Stamps,* by Stephen R. Datz. (General
  Trade Corp., 1997.)
- *The Official 2000 Blackbook Price Guide of United
  States,* by Marc and Tim Hudgeons. (House of
  Collectibles, 1999.)
- *The Official 2000 Blackbook Price Guide to United
  States Postage Stamps (22nd ed.),* by Marc and
  Tom Hudgeons. (House of Collectibles, 1999.)
- Smithsonian National Postal Museum
  (www.si.edu/organiza/museums/postal)

Toys

- AntiqueToys.com (antiquetoys.com/collecting.
  html)
- *Star Wars* Toy Resource Page (pages.map.
  com/starwars/)

- Toy Soldier and Model (www.toy-soldier.com)
- Toy Collecting (toycollecting.about.com/hobbies/
- Hakes Americana (www.hakes.com/index.asp)
- The Wengel's Disneyana (pluto.njcc.com/~wengel/index.htm)
- Delaware Toy and Miniature Museum (www.thomes.net/toys/)

Scanners

- Canon's CanoScan FB 620P
- Epson's Perfection
- HP's ScanJet

Shipping—big items

- Yellow Freight System (www.yellowfreight.com)
- Freight Quote (www.freightquote.com)
- Central Transportation Systems (www.centralsystems.com)
- ABF Freight System (www.abfs.com)
- Roadway Express, Inc. (www.roadway.com)

Shipping—smaller items

- United States Postal Service (www.usps.gov). This site will also do a search for the phone numbers and addresses of the post office closest to you (or the one from which your seller shipped a package).
- Roadway (www.roadway.com): 800-257-2837
- Yellow Freight (www.yellowfreight.com): 800-610-6500

- United Parcel Service (www.ups.com).
  Domestic services within the United States:
  800-PICK-UPS (800-742-5877), or e-mail:
  customer.service@ups.com

- International Export and Import Services:
  800-782-7892

- Federal Express (www.fedex.com). U.S. customer service: 800-Go-FedEx (800-463-3339);
  international customer service: 800-247-4747;
  in U.S., billing inquiries: 800-622-1147.

- Airborne (www.airborne.com). U.S customer
  service: 800-AIRBORNE (800-247-2676).
  Billing inquiries: 800-722-0081.

- Same Day Sky Courier Service: 800-336-3344.

- Airborne Logistics Services (ALS) (for customers using ALS services only): 800-637-5502.

- International Express Customer Service:
  800-ABX-INTL (800-229-4685).

Shipping and packing supplies

- Office Depot (www.officedepot.com)
- Bubble Wrap.com (www.buybubblewrap.com)
- 3pak.com (www.3pak.com/3paks.htm)
- Fred King Office Supplies (http://pw1.netcom.
  com/~frking/home.html)
- ShippingSupply.com
  (www.shippingsupply.com)
- OfficeMax (www.officemax.com)
- Corrugated Containers (www.boxs.com)
- L&R Shipping Supply, Inc. (lnrshippingsupplies.
  com)

- I.P.S. Packaging & Shipping Supplies
  (www.ipspackaging.com)

Web page programs

- Netscape Composer
- Yahoo!
- Global Cafe
- Microsoft FrontPage
- Dreamweaver
- Homepage

Web site space

- Freewebspace.net
- Yahoo! Geocities
- xoom.com
- Angelfire.com
- Tripod.com
- Crosswinds.com
- pBay.com
- AuctionWatch.com
- Spree.com
- internet-club.com
- Hypermart.net
- freeyellow.com
- AOL.com
- Prodigy.net
- Fortunecity.com

ABF Freight System, 343
"About Me" sites, on eBay, 32–33, 102, 311
Accept-It!/Universal Merchant Services, 257–58
Access Discount Camera and Video, 221
Account, setting up. *See* Setting up an account
Accounting, 356–57
Accounting programs, 262–63
Acronyms, 282–83
Address books, 71, 109, 352–54
Address information, 207–8
Adobe PhotoShop, 228
Advertising, 14, 101, 106–7, 111–12, 251–52
Age of item, in listing, 197–98, 202–3
Airborne Express, 336, 342
Amazon, 33–38, 251
    A-to-Z Guarantee, 35, 94, 95–96
    basics of using, 34–35
    buyer/seller protection, 94, 95–96
    chatrooms, 90
    fees, 82
    1-Click plan, 36, 37, 76
    other auction sites versus, 36–38
    pros and cons of, 35–36
    re-listing with, 297
    View/Edit/Remove, 277
American Musical Instrument Society, 149
American Philatelic Society, 155
American Society of Appraisers, 146, 175

Andalé, 236, 355
Antiquarian Booksellers Association of America (ABAA), 135–36
Antiques, 57, 132–33, 144
Antiques & Collectibles Resource Directory, 176–77, 212
Antiques Collector News, 320
Antique shops/malls, 22–23
AntiquesWorld, 144
AntiqueToys, 156
Apfelbauminc, 63
Appraisals, 14, 25–26, 132, 173–77, 209–11, 320
Art, 62, 133
Art Deco pottery, 152–53
Artline, 133
Artnet, 62
Atlantique City, 180
AuctionAddict, 82, 90–91, 287, 297
Auction Advantage, 66
Auction Aid/Auction Ad Pro, 236–37
Auction Assistant, 164, 237–38, 263
Auction Assistant Pro, 237–38
Auction Broker Software, 246
Auction Express, 244
Auction fever, 15–17, 123–29
    curbing, tips on, 16–17
AuctionFirst, 63, 82–83, 94
Auction Helper, 238
AuctionInsider, 46, 74, 129
Auction management programs, 233–52, 310, 355
    automated bidding programs, 244–45
    considerations for using, 234–35

Auction management
     programs *(cont.)*
  counters, 250–51
  end-user, 245–46
  price of, 234–35
  problems with, 246–50
  tracking your auctions,
     241–44
  types of, 235–41
AuctionManager, 238–39
AuctionMate, 239, 355
AuctionPatrol, 70
Auctionscape, 95
Auctions.com, 82, 85
AuctionSHIP, 343
Auction sites, 27–49
  accepted forms of payment
     for major, 80
  benefits of, 13–14
  categories and, 62–67
  choosing right one for you,
     62–67
  disadvantages of, 14–15
  established versus new,
     48–49
  fees and commissions,
     81–84
  guidelines for, 86–91
  in-person versus, 11–15
  major, 28–47
     Amazon, 33–38
     DealDeal, 42–44
     eBay, 27–33
     uBid, 44–46
     Yahoo! Auctions, 38–41
  new and specialized, 46–48,
     62–67
  online magazines rating,
     70–71
  payments, 76–77
  registration, 74–76
  rules for, 84–86
Auctions World Wide
     Association, 176
AuctionTamer, 242
Auction Ticker, 242
Auction tracking programs,
     241–44
Auction Trakker, 242–43, 355

Auction Universe, 62, 83, 94
Auction-Warehouse, 57, 65
Auction Watch, 35, 46, 70,
     116, 290
Auction Wizard, 240, 355
Authentication, of items, 206–7
Auto Channel, 134
Automatic updates, 278–81
Automotive, 47, 57, 62–63,
     133–34, 176, 192

Barbie dolls, 87, 142, 156
Barnes & Noble, 37, 147
Baseball cards, 66, 153–54
Beanie Nation, 300
Because Bid, 85–86
Best Antiques and Collectibles
     Site on the Web, 139
Bid4Assets, 66
Bid.com, 64, 279
Bidder history, 286–90
Bidding (bids), 13–14, 123–57
  on Amazon, 34
  automated programs,
     244–45
  "buyer beware," 124–30
  on DealDeal, 42–43
  on eBay, 29
  educating yourself before,
     129
  incremental, 131–32
  lurking online before,
     69–70, 130–31
  opening, setting an, 168–70
  putting in highest first,
     131–32
  research before, 68–71,
     132–57
  shill, 12
Biddington's, 66, 83, 86
BidFind, 61, 203
Bid4Vacations, 300–301
BidSafe Program, on Auction
     Universe, 94
BidSniper Pro, 245
BidTripper, 67
Billpoint, 260
Boekhout's Collectibles Mall,
     66

Bookkeeping. *See* Record keeping
Bookkeeping programs, 262–63
Bookmarking, 33, 58, 61, 140
Books, 23, 57, 134–36, 139, 192
BoxLots, 63
Browsing, 60–62, 68, 69–70. *See also* Lurking online
Budgets (budgeting), 128
Bulk uploading, 114, 164
Bulletin boards, 71, 89, 352–53
Business cards, 100–101
Business-to-business auctions, 87
Business-to-person auctions, 45, 87
"Buyer beware," 124–30
Buyer/seller protection, 93–94. *See also* Insurance plans
Buying (buyers), 55–62. *See also* Bidding
  browsing before, 60–62, 68, 69–70
  categories and, 57–60
  contacting, 289–90, 307–11
  ease of online, 13
  fees charged, 81
  finding e-mail address and location, 307–27
  problems. *See* Problem buyers and sellers
  questions to ask about items, 59–60
  researching before, 68–71, 132–57
  responding at end of auction, 93
  rights of, 92, 93
  testing the waters, 67–68

Cameras, 219–25
  digital, 221–24
  regular, 220–21
Canon CanoScan FB 620P, 226
Canon PowerShot Pro 70, 221–22
Carbon dating, 319–20
Cashier's checks, 254

Categories, 13, 57–60. *See also* *specific categories*
  by auction sites, 62–67
  changing, when not selling, 301–2
  list of, 57–58
  researching, 132–57
  titles and, 191–92
Central Missouri Internet Auction, 47
Central Transportation Systems, 343
Charges. *See* Commissions; Fees
Chatrooms, 71, 88–91, 282, 352–53
Checks. *See* Cashier's checks; Personal checks
Christie's, 148, 175, 176, 182
Clarice Cliff Collectors' Club, 152–53
Classifieds, 110
Clientele lists, 352–54
Cloanto Euro Calculator, 313
Clothing, 63, 136
  inspection of, 25–26
COD (collect on delivery), 254–55
CoinAuctions, 63, 83
Coins, 57, 63, 137
Collectibles, 47, 58, 63, 137–39
  newspapers and magazines dealing with, 70–71
Collectibles Books, 132
CollectiblesNet, 139
CollectingChannel, 138
CollectingNation, 64
Collectors Auction, 63
Collectors.com, 138
Collectors Universe, 153–54
Color It!, 228
Comics, 139–40
Commissions, 81–84. *See also* Fees
  opening bid and, 171
Community Help Board, on eBay, 89
Company name of item, in listing, 199

Comparison shopping, 129
Computer hard drive, 227–29
Computer Museum of
    America, 140
Computer Museum of Boston,
    140–41
Computers and accessories, 44,
    58, 63–64, 140–41, 192
Condition of item, in listing,
    196–97, 202–3
Contacting buyer, 289–90,
    307–11
Corrugated containers, 338
Corvette Club of America, 134
Costs, figuring in, 92, 93
Costume jewelry, 145–46
Costume Society of America,
    136
Counterfeits, 318–20
Counters, 250–51
Country items, 144, 212
Credit cards, 76, 77–80, 87,
    126, 254, 255–63
    Amazon and, 34
    automatic billing feature,
        81
    basics of using, 78–79
    eBay and, 29, 30
    pros and cons of, 78
    refused, 316–17
    uBid and, 45
Credit card services, 255–63
    increased customers with,
        260–61
    paperwork and, 261–63
    pros and cons of, 259–60
    questions to ask, 256–57
Currency conversion Web
    sites, 313–14
Customer service, 248–49,
    307–8
    for Amazon, 35, 36
    for DealDeal, 43–44
    for eBay, 30, 32–33
Cyber Comic Store, 139
CyberHorse Auction, 301
Cyber Surfer Computer
    Resource Centre, 141
Cyber-Swap, 65

Damaged items, 309, 320–21,
    345–46
D&M Internet Escrow
    Services, 80
Dawson's Appraisals, 177
Deadlines, 312
DealBucks, 42–43
DealDeal, 42–44
    basics of using, 42–43
    other auction sites versus,
        43–44
    pros and cons of, 43
Delaware Toy and Miniature
    Museum, 157
Descriptions, 14, 165, 187–212
    authentication and grading
        and, 206–7
    choosing right words, 188–89
    condition and age and,
        196–98, 202–3
    explicitness in, 200–202
    key search words in title,
        189–200
    research and, 208–12
    shipment and address info,
        207–8
    spelling and, 203–5
    thesaurus for, 205–6
    unclear, 303–4
Discussion groups, 353
Disk space, 227–29
Disney collectibles, 157
Documents, uploading, 164,
    229–30
Doll collecting, 141
Doll Nation, 64
Dolls, 58, 64, 141–43, 192–93
Dolls.com, 141
Doors of London, 144
Dutch auctions, 5–7
    bidding tips for, 6

eAppraisals, 25, 26, 174
Early American Pattern Glass
    Society, 153
Earnings, 354–58
eBay, 27–33, 62
    "About Me" sites, 32–33,
        102, 311

auction management
    programs, 234, 236–41
automatic updates, 279
basic rules, 84–85
basics of using, 29–31
bidder history, 287
bidding programs, 244–45
buyer/seller protection,
    93–94
chatrooms, 30, 49, 89–90,
    215
feedback, 30, 308, 325
fees, 31, 81, 82
    re-listing, 296
icons, 179–80
insurance plan, 84–85, 95
other auction sites versus,
    32–33
Power Seller, 355
pros and cons of, 31–32
re-listing with, 296–97
Revise option, 276
SafeHarbor program, 30,
    84–85, 95
tracking programs, 241–44
eBay Insider, 30
eBay Magazine, 28, 71, 234
eCheck.net, 267
Electronics, 42, 44, 65, 140–41
e-mail, 30, 74, 128, 204, 281–85
    address books, 71, 109, 352,
        353–54
    contacting buyer, 289–90,
        310–11
    etiquette, 281–83
    honesty in, 284–85
    responding promptly and
        courteously, 283–84, 309
Encryption, 74, 78
End of auction, 291–92
    responding at, 93
End-user auction manage-
    ment programs, 245–46
English auctions, 5, 7
ePoster2000, 240
Epson Perfection 610, 226
Escrow accounts, 77, 79–80,
    255, 264–65
Estate sales, 10, 21

Etiquette, 71, 281–85
Excite Auctions, 83, 277, 288
Excite's Classifieds 2000, 95
Expenses, 359–61
Explicitness, in descriptions,
    200–202
EyeNet Images, 230
Ezbid.com, 279–80
EZ Merchant Accounts/
    Authorize.net, 258

Fakes, 318–20
Family heirlooms, 24–25
Federal government car auc-
    tion, 62
FedEx, 336, 342
Feedback, 13, 310, 317, 321–26
    on eBay, 30, 308, 325
    how to give and when,
        322–23
    keeping track of your own,
        324–25
    negative, 93
    reading, 288–89, 323–24
    sunglasses and, 325
Fees, 80, 81–84
    for eBay, 31, 81, 82
    for registration, 68
Film Collectors International,
    147
1st American Card Service, 257
Fiske Museum, 149
Five-day auctions, 182
Flea markets, 21
4antiques.com, 211
4anything.com, 211
4comics.com, 140
Fragile items, 342–44
Fraud, 326–27
Fred King Office Supplies,
    338
Freight Quote, 342
FTP (file transfer protocol),
    118

Gallery, on eBay, 179–80
Gallery of History Simple &
    Direct, 47
Garden Park Antiques, 145

Gaston, Mary Frank, 152
GavelNet, 91
Gems.com, 145
Gemtraders, 65
George Eastman House
    International Museum of
    Photography and Film,
    151
GIF format, 213, 219, 225, 229
"Gift" icons, on eBay, 179–80
Glass.com, 66
Glassware. *See* Pottery and glass
Global Language Translation
    and Consulting, 313
GoingGoingGone, 67
Grading, of items, 206–7
Graylings' Antiques, 152
Guarantees. *See also* Buyer/
    seller protection;
    Insurance plans
    Amazon A-to-Z Guarantee,
    35, 94, 95–96
Guild.com, 133

Hackers, 74–75
Haggle, 64, 277
Hagglezone, 182
Hakes Americana, 157
Hard drive, of computer,
    227–29
Harry Rinker Enterprises, Inc.,
    138
Heirlooms, family, 24–25
Historical documents, 47
History of auctions, 3–4
Hobby Markets Online, 47
Hollywood.com, 148
Hollywood Toy and Poster
    Company, 148
Home and garden, 42, 143–45
Honest Auction Dozen,
    308–10
Honesty, 128, 167, 196,
    284–85, 309
    about condition and age,
    202–3
    in authentication and
    grading, 206–7
Hyperlinks, 251–52

iCardacceptance, 258
iCollector, 96
iEscrow, 30, 80
Image editing programs,
    228–29
Image hosting services, 230
Images. *See* Pictures
Impulse buying, 77, 260–61
Incremental bidding, 131–32
In-person auctions, online
    versus, 11–15
Inspection of items for sale,
    25–26
Insurance Auto Auctions, 47
Insurance plans, 95–96, 265–66
    for shipping, 208, 344–45
Internal Revenue Service
    (IRS), 361–62
International Book Collectors
    Association, 136
International Reply Coupons,
    264
International sales, 264
    problems with, 312–14
International Society of
    Appraisers, 175
InternetAuction, 66
Internet Clearing
    Corporation, 80
Internet Fraud Watch, 317
Internet Music Hound, 150
I. P. S. Packaging & Shipping
    Supplies, 339
iShip.com, 239, 331, 332
ISPs (Internet Service
    Providers), 113, 229
Items
    authentication of, 206–7
    categories for, 57–60, 178–80
    damaged, 309, 320–21,
    345–46
    descriptions of. *See*
    Descriptions
    fakes, reproductions, and
    counterfeits, 316–17
    grading of, 206–7
    inspection of, for sale, 25–26
    length of time up for
    auction, 180–83

listing. *See* Listing items
misrepresenting, 206, 315
multiples of, 6, 179. *See also* Dutch auctions
not selling. *See* Unsold items
questions to ask about, 59–60
setting pricing, 166–78
shipping. *See* Shipping
weighing, before the sale, 330–32
without pictures, 164–65

J. & C. Wiese Collectibles, 153
Jewelcollect Auction, 145
Jewelnet, 65
Jewelry, 58, 64–65, 145–46, 176, 193
JPG format, 213, 219, 225, 229

Keybuy Auction House, 83, 288
Key search words, 189–200
Kovel, Ralph and Terry, 138, 151, 152, 211
Krickets Korner, 230

L&R Shipping Supply, Inc., 339
Language issues, 313–14
Language translation Web sites, 313
Large items, 342–44
Last Vestige Music Shop, 149
Lighting, for photos, 217, 218–19
Limoges porcelain, 152
Lingo of auctions, 9, 12
Listing items, 162–65
    age of, 197–98, 202–3
    appraisers, 173–77
    categories for, 57–60, 178–80
    color of, 199–200
    company name of, 199
    condition of, 196–197, 202–203
    costs, 170–71
    descriptions of. *See* Descriptions
    dimensions of, 196
    knowing worth of item, 177

    length of time up for auction, 180–83
    marks on, 199
    origin of the piece, 200
    revising, 276–78
    setting price, 166–78
    size of, 196
    style of, 199–200
Liszt Search, 353
Lloyd's of London, 95, 266
Lorena, 240–41
Lurking online, 69–70, 130–31. *See also* Browsing
Lycos Auctions, 83, 277, 280

Magazines, online, 70–71
Mail auctions, 8
Mail Boxes Etc., 344
Mailing lists, 103–4, 352, 354
Maker's mark, 199
Management programs. See Auction management programs
Marks on item, in listing, 199
Merchant USA, 258–59
Message boards, 71
Microsoft Money 2000, 357
Microsoft Picture It!, 228
Mister Lister, 204, 238, 240
Money orders, 77, 254
Movie Posters, 148
Movies, 146–48
Music, 148–50, 193
Music Mart, Inc., 149–50
My Beanie, 47

National Association of Dealers in Antiques, Inc., 133
Native American items, 109, 146, 177, 178, 212
Netiquette, 71, 281–85
Net4Sale, 297
New Age Auction, 64–65
New Horizon Business Services, 258, 268
New sites, 46–48
    established auction sites versus, 48–49

Newsletters, 110–11, 137, 142
Newspapers, online, 46–47, 70–71
NFL History and Card Collecting, 154
999fine.com, 146
Noritake, 153
Notification updates, 278–81
NuAuction, 297
Numismatic Guaranty Corporation, 137
Numismatists Online, 137

Ohio Auction & Classifieds, 47
Ohio Pottery, 152
1-Click Currency Conversion, 314
Online auctions. *See* Auction sites; *and specific online auctions*
Online Credit Corp., 259
OnSale, 38, 64
OnScan, 243
Opening bids, 168–70
Oracle, the, 243–44

Pacific Glass, 66
Packing, 332–34. *See also* Shipping
  services, 343–44
  skimping on, 341–42
  supplies, 334–42
Padded envelopes, 334
PaintShop Pro, 228
Passwords, 74, 75–76
  tips for, 75–76
Payflow Link, 259
Payment, 14, 76–84, 253–71. *See also* Credit cards
  accepted forms, for major auction sites, 80
  escrow accounts, 77, 79–80, 264–65
  explanations to customers and, 268–69
  insurance plans, 265–66
  from international customers, 264

  options for, 254–55
  personal checks, 266–68, 269–70
PayPal, 230
PeddleIt, 64
Personal checks, 77, 254, 266–68, 270–71
  bounced, 267, 269–70, 316–17
Personal considerations, 8–9
Personal Web sites, 113–19, 229, 310
  information to include in, 116–17
  online auction versus creating your own, 113–16
  pictures for, 117–18
  text for, 118–19
Person-to-person auctions, 87
Pez dispensers, 14, 28
Phone auctions, 8
Photo Assistant, 230
Photographers Space, 221
Photographica, 150
Photographic Auction, 65
Photographs. *See* Pictures
Photographs and photographic equipment, 58, 65, 150–51
Picture Mall, 228
Pictures (images), 213–31
  cameras for, 219–25
  disk space and, 227–29
  opening bid and, 171
  for personal Web pages, 117–18
  poor, 303–4
  professional's tips for taking great, 217–19
  scanners, 225–27
  thumbnail, 34, 230, 303
  uploading, 164, 229–30
Piece Unique, 136
PL8S.com, 134
Popula, 63
Porcelain. *See* Pottery and glass
Postal Service, U. S., 264, 270, 336, 342, 344, 345

Pottery and glass, 58, 65–66, 151–53
Pottery Auction, 31, 65
Power Sellers, on eBay, 355
Press releases, 105, 110, 111–12
Price (pricing), 13
    appraisers for, 173–77
    commissions on, 82–83
    figuring in costs, 170–71
    knowing worth of item, 177
    lowering, when re-listing, 297–98
    opening bid, setting, 168–70
    reserve, 5, 7–8, 171–73
        negotiating with last bidder when not met, 302–3
    setting, for sale, 166–78
    shipping and, 207–8, 340–41
PriceGrabber, 141
Price guides. *See* Research
Price Guide Store, 138
Privacy concerns, 96–97. *See also* Passwords
Problem buyers and sellers, 307–27. *See also* Feedback
    bounced checks and refused credit cards, 316–17
    buyers not buying, 93–95
    damaged items, 320–21, 345–46
    fakes, reproductions, and counterfeits, 316–17
    finding a buyer's e-mail address and location, 307–27
    fraud, 326–27
    getting burned, 316
    Honest Auction Dozen and, 308–10
    international sales problems, 312–14
    not satisfied, 314–15
    sellers not selling, 93–95
    waiting for answers, 312
Professional Coin Grading Service, 137
Professional Sports Authenticator, 153

Proofreading, 118, 204, 249
Protective services. *See* Buyer/seller protection
Publicity, 101–2
    benefits of, 105–6
Public relations, 101–12

Quicken, 357
Quickie auctions, 182–83

Real estate, 58, 66
Reasons for auctions, 4–5
Record keeping, 309, 316, 351–62. *See also* Auction management programs
    clientele list, 352–54
    earnings, 354–58
    expenses, 359–61
    IRS, 361–62
Reference guides. *See* Research
Refused credit cards, 316–17
Registration, 67–68, 73–76
    for Amazon, 34
    basics of, 74–75
    for DealDeal, 42
    for eBay, 29, 74
    fees for, 68
    for uBid, 44–45
    for Yahoo!, 39
Re-listing, 166, 296–99
    auction management programs for, 238–39
    elsewhere, 298–99
    fees, 296, 297, 299
    lowering price when, 297–98
    pros and cons of, 296–97
Repairs, 170
Reproductions, 318–20
Research, 16, 68–71, 132–57
    descriptions and, 208–12
    online magazines rating auction sites, 70–71
    talking to fellow surfers, 71
Reserve pricing, 5, 7–8, 171–73
    negotiating with last bidder when not met, 302–3
Resolution, of digital cameras, 223–24

Retail value, 61
Returns, 15
ReverseAuction, 182
Revising listings, 276–78
Rights, 91–95
Roadway Express, Inc., 343
Rock and Roll USA, 149
Ruby Lane, 132
Rules, 7, 84–86, 308

SafeHarbor program, on eBay,
    30, 84–85, 95
Safe2Trade, 80
Safety concerns, 96–97. See
    also Passwords
St. Rowlands Stamp Collecting
    Guide, 155
Sales commissions. See
    Commissions
Sales taxes, 357–58
SAM, Inc., Sports, Accessories
    and Memorabilia, Inc.,
    Bobbing Head Dolls and
    Figurines, 154
Sandafayre, 63
Santa Barbara Antique Toys,
    156
Scales, 331–32
Scanners, 225–27
    disk space and, 227–29
Scheduling, 180–84
    end at "high time," 183–84
    for ending on weekends,
    184–85
ScoreLogue, 147
Sealed-bid auctions, 8
Search words, in title, 189–200
Seasonal items, 180, 304
Security, online, 74–76, 78
Selling (sellers), 17–23,
    161–85. See also
    Descriptions
    appraisers for, 173–77
    browsing before, 60–62
    categories for, 57–60, 178–80
    ease of, 13
    family heirlooms, parting
    with, 24–25
    fees charged, 81, 164

figuring in your costs, 170–71
form, 164–65
knowing worth of item, 177
length of time up for
    auction, 180–83
listing items, 162–65
list of items recently sold,
    18–19
places to look for things
    for, 20–23
problems. See Problem
    buyers and sellers
questions to ask about
    items, 59–60
reserve pricing, 171–73
responding at end of
    auction, 93
rights of, 92, 93
scheduling, to end at "high
    time," 183–84
setting pricing, 166–78
on weekends, 184–85
your interests and, 55–62
Setting up an account, 73–97.
    See also Registration
    payments, 76–77
Seven-day auctions, 181–82
Shill bidding, 12
Shipping, 15, 329–47
    charges, 170, 207–8
    damaged items and, 309,
    320–21, 345–46
    fragile items, 342–44
    insurance for, 208, 344–45
    large items, 342–44
    packing a box, 332–34
    packing supplies, 334–42
    pricing and, 207–8, 340–41
    weighing items before the
    sale, 330–32
ShippingSupply, 338
Silent auctions, 8
Silverware, 199
Smithsonian National Postal
    Museum, 155
Sniping, 291–92
Society for the History of
    Authorship, Reading
    and Publishing, 135

Sotheby's, 33, 62, 182
Southern Accents Architectural
    Antiques, 144
Specialized auction sites,
    47–48, 62–67
    benefits of, 299–301
Spell check, 188–89, 193,
    204–5, 303–4
Sports Auction, 66, 83
Sportscarmarket, 176
Sports Collectors Universe, 154
Sports memorabilia, 58, 66,
    153–54
Sports Trade, 66
SquareTrade, 30
Staffordshire figures, 152
Stampauctions, 63
Stamps, 57, 63, 155
Star Wars Toy Resource Page,
    156
Stein Auction, 47
Style periods, 198
Suing, 326–27
Sunglasses, on eBay, 325
Support Q&A Board (eBay), 89
SurplusAuction, 64

Target audience, 99–119. *See
    also* Personal Web sites
    best ways to reach, 107–12
    identifying your, 108–9
    public relations and, 101–12
    spreading the word to,
        100–101
Taxes, 361–62
    sales, 357–58
Theriault's, 64
Thesaurus, 205–6
Three-day auction, 182
3pak.com, 337–38
3SI Accounting and Inventory
    Management 1.0, 357
Thrift stores, 22
Thumbnail pictures, 34, 230,
    303
Times Auctions, 91
Titles, 165
    key search words in, 189–200
Toy Collecting, 156

Toys, 58, 64, 156–57, 193. *See
    also* Dolls
Toy Soldier and Model, 156
Tracking, 128, 275–92
    checking on bidders,
        286–90
    notification updates, 278–81
    programs for, 241–44
Transparent Language
    Enterprise Translation
    Server, 313
Travel, 58, 66–67
TravelBids, 57
Treadway Gallery, 65
Treasure Garden, 145
Turn4Racing, 154
Types of auctions, 5–8

uBid, 44–46, 280
    auction sites versus, 45–46
    basics of using, 44–45
    pros and cons of, 45
Ulead PhotoImpact 5, 228
United Federation of Doll
    Clubs, Inc., 143
United Parcel Service (UPS),
    342
Unity Marketing, 162
University of Michigan
    Auction Bot, 47
Unsold items, 32, 295–305.
    See also Re-listing
    better picture or more com-
        plete description, 303–4
    changing categories, 301–2
    moving to specialized
        online auctions, 299–301
    negotiating with last bidder
        when reserve not met,
        302–3
    wrong time to list, 304
Uploading, 164, 229–30, 250
    bulk, 114, 164
USCollector, 47

Vacation Harbor, 66–67
Variety, in online auctions, 13
VERZA Payment System, 259
Victorian Elegance, 136

Vintage Instruments, 149
VintageUSA, 63
Virtual Auction Ad Pro, 236–37
Vocabulary of auctions, 9, 12

Wallace-Homestead, 320
Wall Street Camera, 221
"Wanted posters," 110
Web hosting service, 230
WebTV, 224
Weighing items, 330–32
Wengel's Disneyana, 157
Westmoreland Glass, 153
Wine appraisals, 176
Wines.com, 176
World Wide Arts Resources, 133

Yahoo! Auctions, 38–41, 62,
    248, 311
  Auction Manager, 277
  automatic updates, 278–79
  basic rules, 85
  basics of using, 39–40
  bidder history, 287
  buyer/seller protection, 94
  chatrooms, 90
  fees, 82
  other auction sites versus, 41
  pros and cons of, 40–41
  re-listing with, 297
  weirdest items sold online,
    list of, 20
Yankee auctions, 5, 7
Yellow Freight System, 342

The Unofficial Guide to Picking Stocks
ISBN: 0-7645-6202-9

The Unofficial Guide to Starting a Business Online
ISBN: 0-02-863340-7

The Unofficial Guide to Starting a Home-Based Business
ISBN: 0-7645-6151-0

The Unofficial Guide to Starting a Small Business
ISBN: 0-02-862525-0

Home

The Unofficial Guide to Buying a Home
ISBN: 0-02-862461-0

The Unofficial Guide to Buying a Home Online
ISBN: 0-02-863751-8

Family and Relationships

The Unofficial Guide to Childcare
0-02-862457-2

The Unofficial Guide to Divorce
0-02-862455-6

The Unofficial Guide to Eldercare
0-02-862456-4

The Unofficial Guide to Online Genealogy
0-02-863867-0

The Unofficial Guide to Planning Your Wedding
0-02-862459-9

Hobbies and Recreation

The Unofficial Guide to Casino Gambling
ISBN: 0-02-862917-5

The Unofficial Guide to eBay® and Online Auctions
ISBN: 0-7645-5292-5

The Unofficial Guide to Finding Rare Antiques
0-02-862922-1

The Unofficial Guide to Selecting Wine
0-02-863668-6

All books in the *Unofficial Guide*™ series are available
at your local bookseller.